JOURNEY TO CORPORATE INDIA

Doing business in India successfully
utilizing innovative management
strategies and best practices

Dhirajlal C. Gami

Visit our Web Site www.journey2corporateindia.com
Published November 2009
ISBN:1-4392-4646-7
EAN13: 9781439246467

*Dedicated to my mother Kashiba and my wife Kokila
for their sacrifices & support without which I could not have
achieved what I could.*

Contents

Foreword

India began its journey towards rapid industrialization with the ambitious Second five year Plan. The central ingredient of the Second Plan was the development of heavy and basic industries like iron and steel, coal, heavy electrical, etc. This list also included fertilizes which were needed to enhance agricultural productivity. India, under the British rule, had experienced a declining trend in the production and productivity of its large agricultural sector during 1901 to 1945 and it was quite imperative to maintain sufficiently high rates of growth of agricultural production to avert recurring phases of acute food shortages. While the Government of India set up a few fertilizer units in the public sector by the end of second five year plan, the Government of Gujarat, after the creation of a separate State in May 1960, took a major initiative to set up India's largest fertilizer plant as a joint sector undertaking, the first of its kind in the country.

This led to the incorporation of Gujarat State Fertilizers & Chemicals Limited popularly known as GSFC. The State Government contributed 49% of the equity capital and the remaining amount was subscribed by the general public and the financial institutions. Around 25,000 farmers of Gujarat came forward to subscribe to the equity capital of this joint venture to the tune of Rs. 10 million prior to the public issue. This was indeed a significant event focusing on customers right from start. A second significant event was when the technical and management teams of the company completed the erection and commissioning of the complex and made it operational within a record time of 25 months. This was a significant milestone in the history of India's corporate sector and it was widely applauded by the commentators and the financial news papers in those days. The nascent industrial unit generated cash profit in the first year of its operation and could distribute dividend at the end of the third year, which is a commendable achievement for a core sector industry even by today's yardstick. This Book presents a detailed account and analysis of GSFC's business strategy and examines how Innovative Management practices played a crucial role in GSFC's continued success and sustained growth.

In those eventful years of the fifties and the sixties, while there was a lot enthusiasm all around about doing new things and thus contributing to the bright future of the resurgent and newly industrializing India, various challenges faced by the Top Management were enormous and formidable. There was a shortage of capital in general and of risk capital in particular and also a dearth of well trained managerial as well as technical personnel. Total dependence on foreign countries for technology and for plant and machinery was more or less inevitable and all encompassing. The silver line, however, was that some bright young men had began to go abroad in some well reputed universities in Europe and the USA for technical, managerial and science education. Shri D. C. Gami was one among such scholars. After B.Sc (Hons) in Chemistry, he went to the University of Michigan and obtained Masters Degree in chemical engineering and worked in USA on a research project involving cryogenic temperatures for a period of three years.

Before joining Gujarat State Fertilizers & Chemicals Limited, he had a stint at the Department of Atomic Energy for a period of 10 years where he worked on the design of the first nuclear reactor and planning for heavy water projects. He had the opportunity to be associated with the planning of the Rourkela fertilizer project and Trombay fertilizer project. After this he got involved in planning, execution and operation of fertilizers cum heavy water project at Nangal (Punjab) while he was in charge of heavy water project. The fertilizer project was commissioned in 1960 and the heavy water project was commissioned in 1962. He joined GSFC in November 1964. At that time hardly any progress was made on this important and unique project and, therefore, for all practical purposes, he came to be associated with the company from its very inception. This placed the author in a rare and unique position – his own professional growth ran more or less parallel with that of the company. The author's long association with GSFC and his passion for the organization are amply reflected in the book.

The management team of which Shri D.C. Gami was an important member introduced some very novel innovations and the company benefited immensely from each of those innovative ideas & actions. Dr. Jivraj Mehta, the then Chief Minister of the Government of Gujarat, did not want to make the proposed fertilizer complex either a Government company or a private company. It kept its share in the equity capital of the company limited to 49% leaving the remaining to be subscribed by the public. In those days, this was a major innovation in terms of the structure of the corporate ownership. This innovation later on came to be widely known as the Joint Sector.

The Government of Gujarat established State industrial corporations to help entrepreneurs by providing assistance in terms of finance as well technical support and also providing infrastructure to establish new industrial units in Joint / Associated sectors. Thousands of industrial units got established in Gujarat in this manner and later on in other States also. In later years, the Government of Gujarat established a number of profitable units in the joint sector to strengthen the industrial base of the State. The ownership and operating structure of GSFC can be viewed as an initial experiment that laid the foundation of what eventually came to be called the Public Private Partnership (PPP) structure in the nineties.

The technological innovations were brought about through selection and application of newly invented processes. Large scale operations were visualized for accelerated growth, which subsequently facilitated the growth of other related sectors. Innovations were introduced in many other corporate functional areas, such as project management, human relations, organizational structure and dynamics, marketing and strategy for growth and research, which enhanced the enterprise effectiveness. The author has discussed all these managerial and technical innovations along with the associated problems faced in the process of their implementation. This aspect makes reading of the book interesting as well as rewarding.

While Human Resource Management was not much talked about in the context of Indian Corporate Sector in sixties & early seventies, HRM received a great deal of attention at GSFC. The trainees in various branches were selected from different Universities and Colleges from the final year students after a rigorous selection process by the HR team of GSFC, and they were placed in the company's in-house training centre, where they were trained with the help of the process simulator on the operations and maintenance of plants. GSFC was the first company in India to introduce this practice. The newly recruited graduates were then trained in the fertilizer plants in South India and also at the sites of construction and commissioning of GSFC's ten plants. All officers and managers and some selected technicians were also sent for special training in Japan in the suppliers' plants. This added substantial value to their degree of professional competence and also inculcated in them the much needed quality of loyalty to the company. These HR initiatives also helped majority of the technicians, officers and managers to realize their full potential and eventually enabled them to rise to the coveted positions up to general managers and executive directors. For the first twenty years since the inception of GSFC, it was not necessary to recruit trained personnel from outside even for setting up new projects. Moreover, there was hardly any attrition at middle and senior management levels.

Criteria for selection of new products required that existing and new plants can be techno-economically integrated and that new products should have very good potential for growth for at least 20 years. Thus correct selection of new products and further derivatives of the existing and new products made the Company more profitable and allowed its customers to grow faster, which succeeded in keeping the competition subdued. Practically speaking there was no competition for three of GSFC's major industrial products even after 25 years of the launch of these products in Indian markets. That GSFC could help established other industrial units like GNFC is an ample testimony of the high level of the technical and managerial competence attained and the surplus funds generated by it. The challenge of the new product development and their marketing was met by the creation of 'Application Development Centre' as well as by promoting the culture of research in the organization.

Engineering research developed the indigenous technology and helped in manufacturing sophisticated and expensive spares and components at very low costs, which would have been imported otherwise by spending scarce foreign exchange resources of the country. It could also fabricate, in its own workshop, several equipments required for various new projects, thus averting the need for importing them. While the foreign equipment suppliers advised the company to import two very large equipments, which were damaged in different years during operations and each resulting in shut down of a major plant, the company could repair them efficiently with the help of in-house workshop facilities, resulting in substantial saving of 2 years in time and Rs. 400 million of funds. This is a telling example of genuine and effective import substitution driven almost entirely by indigenous technology that helped the company not only to save foreign exchange without sacrificing quality of the product manufactured with the help of in-house engineering facility but also provide confidence to the young technical personnel associated with it. Had this not been achieved, it could have meant colossal loss of production exceeding Rs. 400 million, which might have wiped out substantial part of the company's net worth and threatened its existence.

The company was also conscious of its social obligations. It undertook experiments in thousands of fields owned by small farmers to demonstrate the efficacy of fertilizers. It also introduced the crop insurance scheme on an experimental basis with the assistance of IDBI, which under-wrote the risk of crop- failure and the Bank of Baroda, which provided loans to farmers, while all technical inputs and supervision was provided by GSFC. It was for the first time that such a well coordinated tri-partite scheme was introduced in the country.

In essence, the Book narrates a fine story of industrial enterprise in Gujarat, manufacturing fertilizers to begin with and subsequently emerging as a multi-product company by undertaking manufacture of new petrochemical products, which were earlier imported. It is also an inspiring in-depth case study of a corporation set up in the early phase of India's industrialization focusing on the role of its top management in introducing various innovative techniques, which contributed significantly to the growth of the company. The book also describes vividly the top management's role and approach in tackling various expected and unexpected challenges and finding out appropriate and often unique solutions for them under the prevailing circumstances during those times, which helped the company to emerge as one of the most profitable industrial units in India, yielding direct and indirect benefits to the farmers, to other industries, to the consumes and to the common man in the country. GSFC represents a significant example of the benefits of inclusive growth. While many new enterprises and companies which were incorporated in the Sixties are not operational today for various reasons, GSFC is still going strong yielding benefits to all its stakeholders after nearly five fruitful decades of its existence.

The story of an Indian corporation that could achieve so much within a short span of two decades under most difficult circumstances during the early stage of India's industrialization should inspire today's young managers and engineers to do even better while facing formidable managerial challenges posed by the business environment of the 21st century. I hope the book will prove to be a valuable reference material for researchers and teachers of management in developing countries.

I congratulate Shri D. C. Gami for his commendable effort in writing such an insightful book and for sustaining his enthusiasm till the ripe age of eighty to ensure its effective completion.

Bakul Dholakia
Former Director
Indian Institute of Management
Ahmedabad & Director Adani
Institute Of Infrastructure
Management

⌘　⌘　⌘

Preface

I started writing this book four years ago as my wife and daughter were constantly goading me to write about my experiences. I came to Gujarat primarily to attend to my family duties, I being the eldest after passing away of my father, to educate my three sisters, Gita, Jyotsna and Shobhna who were in high school and two brothers Vinod and Jagdish who were in college, and to arrange for their timely marriages.

We were a big family with five brothers and seven sisters. Jagdish, the youngest brother, went to USA for further studies in engineering and settled there. While I got very busy with my work, my mother Kashiben looked after my sisters' school and college education and later their marriages from Nadiad and my wife Kokila looked after my two brothers and our three children at Vadodara. My third brother Ramesh, who was already in the USA from 1961 returned to India in 1968. He was staying with me and looked after the various other family duties. My two brothers Chandravadan and Vinod, being engineers, devoted their entire professional careers to fertilizer industry, and I also spent most of my productive career in the fertilizer industry.

This book shows how practice of "Innovative Management" ensured success to the manufacturing company for more than two decades. In fact it is still operating successfully after four decades. This is the case study of its management practices over two decades. The success of the company had become a household word in Gujarat and quite well known in India and many countries in Europe and Japan. Indian Institute of Management at Ahmadabad (IIM A) had made a case study of the success of its first project. However only a few persons know that while achieving this success, the company had set many precedents, through innovations, taking decisions involving heavy risks and facing challenges, such as (1) Joint sector constitution of the public Limited Company which led to tremendous industrial development, not only in the country but also in foreign countries, by adopting this approach and modifying the same from time to time, (2) taking calculated risks in adopting new technologies, and (3) setting up projects with much larger capacities than prevailing demand/consumption for the first time in the country. Further what went behind the success is known only to a very few and is now revealed in the book.

My object in writing this book is to show, to Future Entrepreneurs. and Foreign Companies interested in making investment in India, how innovative management practices made the Company successful for more than two decades. How such precedents impacted (a) company growth, (b) industrial development, and (c) change in thinking of political leaders on control of enterprises. The success was achieved after facing a large number of problems, specially those peculiar to Indian environment and finding simple and at times innovative solutions to ensure success at each stage. One chapter is also devoted to show the relevance of management practices described in the book to today's management, and a section deals with 'Spirituality in the Management as practiced'. The last chapter is on the opportunities for investments in India for Indian and foreign companies.

As the book provides details of management practices, negotiations with foreign licensors and contractors, strategy for growth and similar topics of management interest, it will be valuable both as a guide and reference for making investment and managerial decisions for: (1) All companies/entrepreneurs, in India as well as in Foreign countries, interested in investment in any large projects, especially in the fields of petrochemicals, chemicals, fertilizers, and engineering. (2) All Indian and Foreign engineering companies doing projects, large contractors, and management companies (3) all associations such as Federation of Industries and chambers of commerce India (FICCI), Confederation of Indian Industries (CII), management associations, Various professional associations such as Fertilizer Association of India (F.A.I), Indian Chemical Manufacturers Association (ICMA), Association of Synthetic fiber India (ASFI), Federation of Industries and Chambers of Commerce in different Cities, and (4) educational institutes such as Indian Institutes of Management (IIMs), Indian Institute of Technology(IITs), and engineering colleges and (5) business schools, and many others interested in the entire gamut on management.

I like to thank all my former colleagues with whom I had the opportunity to discuss the subject matter for their valuable suggestions. I would also like to specially thank my friends DR.YVS Murthy for his valuable suggestions, Mr. Ghanshyam Sodha and Mr. L. Rajagopalan for editing the manuscript, Mr. M.J Dholakia for technical discussions and assistance particularly in writing section (a) Engineering research under chapter 8, and my friend and former colleague Mr. H.B.Parikh for general review on the financial aspects brought out in the write up and Mr. P.R. Mankad, an old colleague who became Yoga teacher, for contributing to the section on 'Spirituality in the Management as practiced'.

Dhirajlal Gami
dcgami@gmail.com
www.journey2corporateindia.com

⌘ ⌘ ⌘

Introduction

There are a number of books published by Indian and American authors on "Doing Business in India". These books provide general information on culture and customs, dealing with Indian partner, understanding the way Indian do business and developing business plan to create interest in doing business in India. However no book gives hands-on Management practices that can be followed to make the enterprise successful in India. 'Journey to Corporate India' fills this gap. It describes practical approaches to managing industries in India, and facilitates corporations and entrepreneurs to take-part in the multi billion dollar investment opportunities unfolding within infrastructure, manufacturing and service sectors. .

This book provides details of the innovative management practices followed by the Indian manufacturing Company which made it successful for more than two decades. It is still successfully operating after four decades. The company carried out several innovations such as (1) ownership structure, adoption of similar structure for developmental organizations by Gujarat State and later by practically all Indian States led to the establishment of thousands of industries in all fields (2) managing company with fresh school and college graduates after providing innovative training (3) providing innovative services for marketing of fertilizers as well as industrial products, specially to customers to help them grow their produce/products, introducing at that time concept of "customer is the king" which is now a key Mantra for all marketers, (4) procurement, construction and project management using simplified Project Evaluation and Review Technique (PERT) system and innovative techniques such as pre qualifications, bringing all tenders on equal technical footing, negotiating with lowest bidder to reduce price, devising special motto to motivate all, target setting, solving conflict using win-win method: result-fastest completion of the project, receiving bouquets from National Press (5) The company implemented CSR (Corporate Social Responsibility) policy, which was not even heard off at that time and which is now practically compulsory for all corporations to report in their annual accounts and balance sheets.

The company made several decisions involving high risks in (1) selecting technologies with very little or no experience in the world, (2) selecting and producing products for the first time in the country, (3) taking up expansion before the production had started in the first project and that too without availability of funds. (4) Establishing very large capacity (many more times than the demand of the products at that time) projects. The management practices followed by the Company have relevance to the modern day management. A separate chapter gives details of this relevance.

Gujarat State Fertilizers Company Limited (GSFC) was born in 1962 in an unconventional manner and remained unconventional for a period of at least twenty years. This probably was the main reason for its success. To start with, Dr. Jivaraj Mehta, the then Chief Minister of Gujarat, its promoter, took an unconventional decision not to make it a Government company or a private one. He decided that Government would take 49% equity in the Company and the balance to be given to the public, (that means, it is neither a Government nor a private company), with prominent persons and industrialists as directors of the company with Mr. Jayakrishna Harivallabhdas, prominent Gujarat industrialist, as Chairman to manage it in a businesslike manner with public interest being the driving force. This was an innovation in the ownership of the company, as earlier it was either Government owned or by private sector owned. This new concept was introduced for the first time in the country, and later on came to be known as joint sector. It was modified from time to time and contributed substantially to the industrial development of the country. This was further modified under the concept of "Public Private Partnership" (PPP) which has gained ground since 1990 in several countries including India and projects worth several billions of dollars have been implemented in U.S.A., Australia, Canada, U.K., India and other countries with several benefits.

The Government of Gujarat had the power to nominate 4 directors including the chairman and managing director. It had power to order Controller and Auditor General (CAG) audit, as technically the Company was Government Company till 31st August 1967 when public issue was fully subscribed and paid up. In practice all directors were nominated by the Government. Government however did not interfere with the management of the company and all decisions taken by the Board were immediately implemented by the management and no decision was communicated to Government for approval, ratification or even information. Government directors were fully aware of and were party to all the decisions. This became known as "Self denial ordinance", as Government voluntarily did not use its powers.

This created political controversies for the Company as many political leaders wanted it to be a Government Company. The very leaders who wanted it to be a Government Company, after coming to power in late 1972, did not press for the same and forgot about it by 1974. This was not the only political controversy the company had faced but many followed on marketing distribution, fertilizer pricing, project execution, feed stock selection, and technology selection for the Gujarat Narmada Valley Fertilizers Company Limited (GNFC) project. Two industrial groups also lobbied to influence Government of India to take decisions which were not only against the interest of the company but also against the national interest. All these controversies lasted till 1980.

The Board of Director took several decisions involving risks such as (1) not having overall project consultant but only for preparation of project report and specifications and helping the company in negotiations and finalization of foreign contracts, this too only for the first project. All other activities, namely, planning, contracts with Indian companies, execution and management of the entire project was entrusted to the executives with full responsibility. For large projects in those days there was always an overall consultant from the concept to the completion, and normally that consultant would be a foreign company, (2) Selection of ICI (Imperial Chemical Industries) steam reforming process for Ammonia and single stream concept for all fertilizer plants. Though the Fertilizers Corporation of India (FCI) experts and the Government of India were reluctant to approve this selection and concept, as there was no experience on this process and earlier partial oxidation process and multi stream plant concepts were used for fertilizer plants in India. All future gas/Naphtha based Ammonia plants adopted this technology. (3) Technologies for phosphoric acid, DAP and Ammonium Sulfate from by-product gypsum were new technologies adopted for the first time in the country. If any of the decisions had failed, the Company would have become a sick company. To ensure that all decisions become successful, it was necessary to adopt innovative management practices which included systems of contracting, purchasing, organization, training, marketing and strategy for growth.

The lead thus provided by the Company was followed by all future Ammonia plants (more than 30 gas or naphtha based plants) who adopted ICI stream reforming process and single stream concept and most complex fertilizers manufacturers adopted DAP/ASP as product (14 plants) and a few adopted Nitro phosphate as product (4 plants).

GSFC completed its first project in 25 months, considered at that time to be the fastest completion. To achieve this it had to discard old management philosophy and bring new innovations in management not only for project execution but also for planning, procurement, contracting, civil works, financing, manpower planning and Human Relations (HR) policy. Simplified PERT system was used in monitoring and coordinating all activities not only of GSFC but also of all contractors as well as activities of outside parties such as railways, Gujarat Electricity Board etc.

In view of the unsatisfactory working of the fertilizer industry at that time, financial institutions were unwilling to provide term loans. The Company had to persuade, for a long time, at the highest levels in Government as well as in financial institutions to obtain approval of term loans, as without this approval the Company would have folded up even before it could start the project work. Finally, financial institutions could be convinced only after the Company sold Rs. 10 million worth of equity shares, within a period of two months, to 25,000 farmers and Co-operative societies to show that farmers were interested in buying fertilizers and they were prepared to take risk in buying equity. GSFC successfully completed the largest public issue (both equity and preference shares) of Rs.58.8 million in the country (1966). At about the same time Mr. Chakrabartty of Coromandel fertilizers and Mr. Ghosh of FCI had said in a seminar, in 1966, on cost and financing of fertilizer projects "In the context of the present capital market conditions in India, perhaps nobody could imagine a more difficult task in the financial field than arranging a large equity issue for any project and the position becomes critical for a project in the fertilizer field, where prospects for dividend for the share holders for initial 6-7 years are very dim". Thus successful completion of largest public issue in the country can be considered as a feather in the cap of GSFC

Company decided to recruit manpower required only for the operations of the plants and deployed this manpower for planning and execution of the project. The objective was to see that no surplus person is required to be retrenched later. Most of these people were fresh high school graduates, Industrial Training Institute (ITI) certificate holders, diploma holders, science graduates, and fresh engineering graduates, (they were taken as management trainees and trained separately in India as well as in foreign plants) with a few experienced officers, managers and executives. These fresh graduates, ITIs were trained in the company's Training Centre for a period of two years. These trainees from Gujarat constituted 90% of GSFC technical staff, a desire of the Chief Minister of Gujarat, which was thus fulfilled by the Company.

HR Policy required that workers' union will be "company Union". If any outside person was to be taken as a leader, he should get 75% vote of all employees. This was not liked by organized union leaders. One prominent labor leader, who later became the Finance Minister of Gujarat, was a bitter critic of GSFC and persistently attacked GSFC for this policy. Company had a liberal HR policy, besides good salary, it paid, provident fund, bonus, gratuity, pension, and company also provided house at a rent of 5% of basic salary in the Fertilizer Nagar, practically free electricity and water, free maintenance of house, school, free medical facilities including hospitalization, shopping centre, bus service to go to the City, temple for all religions, free access to sports such as: table tennis, badminton, tennis, billiards, cricket, etc. In addition to this the Company provided loan, at low rate of interest of 6%/year, for building house in Vadodara or at the employee's native place.

In the first year of operations (8.5 months of 1967-68), the company produced 117,500 .M.T. fertilizers, earned cash profit of Rs.15.7 million, but after providing full depreciation of Rs.31.9 million resulted in a loss of Rs. 16.2 million. Local newspapers next day published with front page headlines that GSFC made huge loss. This became the talk of the town, condemning GSFC and giving brick bats for the loss and ascribing reasons for the same. This was the common man's reaction. On the other hand national dailies such as Financial Express, Indian Express and monthly technical journal Chemical Engineering World gave "bouquets for achieving the miracle" (quote from Financial Express- 19-4-1968).

GSFC provided education and training to farmers and demonstrated the advantages of the use of fertilizers by carrying out demonstrations (thousands of them) in farmers' fields, providing fertilizers free of cost for a period of five years from 1962 to 1967 before it sold its first fertilizer product to the farmers. This was an innovation in marketing at that time. Thus the 'present day' concept of "customer is the king" was implemented by GSFC 40 years ago. I do not think any company in India, till today, would have provided such a long customer service before placing its products for sale.

GSFC was in a hurry to grow. It, therefore, took up expansion of its Ammonia-urea plants, before the first phase of plants had gone in operations. This Rs.225 million expansion project was completed in 23 months with no additional equity. The Company did not have funds, but it could organize deferred credit of Rs. 132 million from Japan and a loan of Rs.25 million, balance Rs. 67 millions was met from internal generation. GSFC has set up 3 fertilizer projects and is operating them, and one very large project for GNFC for which the Company selected site, technology and signed contracts with foreign companies. According to technology supplier this technology was selected, for the first time in the world, and was used to set up world's largest ammonia plant on this technology. GSFC obtained approval of Foreign Exchange loan from KFW and Rupee loan from Indian Financial Institutions. Project was then handed over to GNFC for execution and operations.

GSFC diversified into projects, building seven projects related to fertilizer operations, either utilizing intermediates from fertilizer plants, or fertilizer products or produced downstream products. Caprolactam, melamine and MEK oxime were produced for the first time in India. Not only this, GSFC is still the only producer of melamine and MEK oxime after 25 years of each plant's operations. It was also the only producer of Caprolactam for 15 years till FACT came up with the second plant. Techno economic integration of all plants was a new innovation which allowed preparation of techno-economic model for higher profitability.

The company established an Application Development center (ADC), a new concept for marketing of industrial products. ADC undertook development of new grades, new uses and new products from Nylon engineering plastic and melamine being manufactured by the company. It also helped in the development of a number of new industrial units to manufacture new products from GSFC Nylon and Melamine and made melamine a household product, even in villages, and nylon one of the important components for a number of industries. This ensured rapid growth of Nylon and Melamine.

The company also had three pronged strategy for developmental research (1) development of engineering technology for production of indigenous components and also fabrication of equipment which were hitherto being imported. It also imparted technology to a number of engineering fabricators and as a result better quality equipment, equaling international standards, could be manufactured in the country (2) Use of indigenous reformer tubes and reformer catalyst in place of imported ones for the first time in the country. Subsequently all ammonia producers started using indigenous tubes and catalyst 3) development of process for new products such as (a) Bio fertilizers, (b) MEK Oxime and (3) SAN resin and set up plant for the production of MEK Oxime, 90% of which is being exported, and bio-fertilizers.

The Company, in this manner, through its new concept of Joint Sector, created and established Fertilizer and basic industrial products. Further its Development & Research (R&D) activities contributed immeasurably to the social and industrial development of the country. As large numbers of companies from all over the world have and are interested in making investment in India, a chapter on "opportunities for investment in India" describes opportunities available for investment in different sectors of Indian economy. This will be valuable to Indian as well as foreign investors interested in making investment in India.

While considering various aspects of management, the theories propounded by various management Gurus of the period like (1) Peter Drucker on innovation, marketing, management structure and organization, (2) Abraham Maslow on motivation and human relations, (3) Henry Fayol on management, (4) Douglas McGregor on employment Practices, (5) Fredrick Herzberg on motivation to work, (6) Mary Parker Follett on dynamic administration and conflict resolution, (7) Igor Ansoff on corporate strategy, (8) Alfred Chandler on strategy and structure, (9) Hamel and Prahlad on strategy implementation, (10) Ted Levitt on innovation in marketing, and (11) Philip Kotler on market leadership, have been compared with the Company's management practices in the respective areas, at appropriate places in the text. The correlation of theories and practical aspects of management as practiced at GSFC will provide insight/guidance to the readers on implementation of theories on various aspects of management. Relevance of Management practices followed at GSFC to the modern day management is also given in a separate chapter.

GSFC had established latest available process for gaseous pollution treatment, though at that time there were no pollution laws. Even in USA pollution laws for fertilizer industry was enacted in 1973 six years after the company' fertilizer plants went into operations. It had established liquid effluent treatment plants and had helped Government of Gujarat to establish a common effluent channel for disposal of liquid effluents from all other large as well as medium size units from the surrounding area to the sea after appropriate treatment for the first time in the country. This led to the concept of Central Effluent Treatment Plants (CETP) for different industrial areas or group of industries. Such CETPs have been established at Ahmedabad, Ankaleshwar, Padra District and Vapi.

As GSFC is basically a fertilizer company, the book will not be complete without writing about fertilizer subsidy. The substantial increase in oil prices as a result of second oil shock in December 1973, prices of practically everything went up and Government had to introduce above scheme to supply fertilizers at reasonable price to farmers and at the same time provide reasonable return to the fertilizer industry. Till today Government of India has not been able to satisfy Fertilizer Industry, Politicians or Economists, even though it is continuously tinkering with the subsidy scheme, practically from the beginning, yet paying continuously increasing subsidy bills which are now amounting to more than Rs. 1000 million for 2008-9.

While doing this the Government was fixing prices of different nutrients in such a manner that farmers used more and more nitrogen (N) nutrient and lesser Phosphorus(P) & Potash(K) thereby using unbalanced quantum of N.P & K. Government also neglected to promote fourth important nutrient "S"(Sulfur) and neglected the production of Single Super Phosphate (SSP) in spite of the fact that it supplies two nutrients namely S. and P. As a result of unbalanced fertilization, neglect of Sulfur (S) nutrient and other micro nutrients, soil productivity started going down from the production of 15 kg food grain/kg Nitrogen in 1970, to 10 kg food grain average during decade of 1980-90 and to 6.6 kg Food grain/kg Nitrogen during the decade of 1990-2000. This means that, if soil productivity was maintained at 1970 level, Country would have been using only 40% of nutrients for the present level of food grain production than what it is using today and would not have to spend nearly Rs. 1000 million on subsidy estimated for 2008-9.(which was Rs.85.2.million in 2003-4) Government has announced new fertilizer policy in June 2008, which it is hoped would take care of some of the problems. The Government however has not tackled problems, especially of reduced fertility of soil experienced practically in the entire country on account of the use of unbalanced fertilizers and deficiency of micronutrients.

It is not expensive to improve soil fertility and crop productivity to 1970 level but requires strong will by the Government of India and dedication by State Governments and fertilizer industry to provide good extension service on the basis of Site Specific Nutrient Management System (SSNM), including establishment of large number of properly staffed soil testing laboratories within 50 KM reach of any farmer, educating farmers on use of balanced fertilizers including bio fertilizers, sulfur and micro nutrients. I had prepared an 'action plan' based on this to increase food grain production from 200 million tons to 350 million tons in seven years and had sent this in

December 2007 to ministries of fertilizers and agriculture and some prominent persons. The new policy of June 2008 have accepted some of the suggestions but have not forcefully advocated establishment of proper soil testing laboratories to make it possible for the farmers to receive appropriate recommendations based on SSNM system to increase farm productivity and agriculture production.

While writing this book I have talked to a number of former colleagues and present executives of GSFC, have relied for facts on GSFC & GNFC annual reports, their publications, FAI newsletters and other publications, a number of articles published in magazines, news papers and in seminars and a book "Politics and Economic Development in India" by Howard L. Erdman". What I have written is my perception; some other person may have a different perception of the same topic. Finally more details of all that is described above and details of other topics not mentioned here are given in the book.

From the above it will be seen that GSFC faced lots of problems from outside, especially due to the resistance to innovative concepts, whereas it had minor problems from within, either from plants or from employees. All types of problems, which are typical for Indian manufacturing sector, faced by the company are discussed in detail in the book. While overcoming the external problems and continuing innovations, GSFC set up 10 projects, operated plants profitably, increased fixed assets from Rs. 371 million after first project to Rs. 1626 million in a period of fifteen years, and reserves of Rs. 1008 million on equity base of Rs. 90 million plus bonus shares, and payment of dividends to increase share holder value. Thus it earned blue chip status in stock exchange by 1982.

Dhirajlal Gami
dcgami@gmail.com
www.journey2corporateindia.com

⌘   ⌘   ⌘

Chapter 1
Earlier History

Gujarat State was carved out by bifurcation of the former Bombay State on May 1st 1960. The first chief minister of Gujarat, Dr. Jivraj Mehta had on top of his mind the priority of increasing the food production in Gujarat. He wanted Gujarat to become self-sufficient in the production of food grains. Till then, Gujarat was buying food grain from other states. He was firmly convinced that lesser production of food grain was due to scarcity of fertilizers. He therefore thought of establishing a fertilizer factory in Gujarat so that adequate quantities of fertilizers are available to help farmers to produce sufficient food grain.

He appointed in May 1960 a committee called 'Gujarat Fertilizer Committee' to determine the feasibility of producing Nitrogenous fertilizers in Gujarat, as at that time single-super-phosphate was being produced (in small factories) to supply the phosphate nutrient. Dr. C.B. Patel, who was the Director of Industries, was named the secretary of the committee. The committee submitted its report in August 1960.

In the original terms of reference, the committee was asked to report on possible sites, types, and quantities of fertilizers that could be manufactured, raw materials required for the product mix, cost and the estimated personnel required and making suggestions for the implementation of the committee recommendations.

The committee report was primarily techno-economic in character. For example, it noted the recent Central Government emphasis on nitrogenous fertilizer production; it noted that the cost estimation per unit of production would permit a far lower selling price than that prevailing in India at that time; it emphasized the appropriateness of the fertilizers recommended for the soils, and crops of Gujarat. It addressed itself to the foreign exchange question, and made some efforts to indicate ways in which the foreign exchange component could be reduced. It further observed that the likely finding of crude oil would require production of petroleum products in the State which was likely to contribute essential attributes to the fertilizer facilities.

In view of the power situation in the State, it recommended independent power plant as part of the fertilizer plant. The committee considered that desirable level of nitrogen consumption in Gujarat was far higher than those set by the Government of India. Thus it noted that there was a need for two nitrogenous fertilizer plants, one to be established immediately. The report stated that in case the project needs to be undertaken by the private sector, the Government of Gujarat should play a major role in acquiring the necessary land, acquiring rights for the necessary pipe lines, providing aid in transportation (roads, and railroad sidings), and in guaranteeing the adequate quantity of water so that fertilizer production is achieved in the shortest possible time. The committee did not go into details of financing of the project and who will own the project, whether the Government of India, the Government of Gujarat, or the private sector. The committee estimated the project cost for annual capacity of 80,000 M. T. nitrogenous fertilizer plant to be Rs. 380 million.

The committee did not consider the following three important aspects:

The agency which would own, establishes, and operates the facility

The means of finance (how to raise total funds for the project)
Marketing of the fertilizers

While trying to fix the above three, lots of difficulties, time, and controversies were created. These will be discussed later.

The Government of Gujarat in December 1960 constituted the Board for the state fertilizer project with prominent Gujarat industrialist Mr. Jaykrishna Harivallabhdas as chairman with four government officers, and seven prominent persons, mostly industrialists as directors. The Government officers included Mr. V. Isvaran I.C.S, the chief secretary of the Government of Gujarat, and Mr. K. R. Srivatsa I.A.S, the deputy secretary of the Industries Department. The board was to take steps required to implement the Fertilizer Committee's recommendations.

The Government of Gujarat originally in its third five year plan did not provide for the fertilizer project, while Government of India in the revised third year plan provided for the 80,000 metric ton nitrogenous fertilizer project in the state. Dr. Jivraj Mehta, the Chief Minister desired the project to be established by the Government of Gujarat with state industrialists contributing their business acumen as he wanted the fertilizer project to be operated in a business-like manner. Then it was considered that no private sector corporate house in Gujarat was capable of or interested in taking such a capital intensive project. Further a single private sector house could not be considered to take a major role in such a project as in such arrangement private sector would demand the management control by it. This would go against the desire for the effective control of the project in the public interest.

Thus, the responsibility for the promotion of the project, and arranging full finance fell on the Government of Gujarat. In 1960-61, the Government could only provide a nominal amount. Considering the project cost, at that time, of Rs. 280 million, the equity portion was kept at Rs. 100 million and the balance amount to be raised by borrowing. As the full equity amount could not be contributed by the Government of Gujarat, a new innovative idea was born, while keeping the Government contribution to less than 50%, the balance equity may be obtained through public participation in the equity. Accordingly, while drafting the article of association for the company, Mr. V Isvaran and Mr. K. R. Srivatsa decided to keep the contribution of the Government of Gujarat at 49% equity or less. This would mean that it would not be a Government company, which necessitates minimum equity holding of 51% by the state. If it was a Government Company financial institutions, at that time, could not be approached to provide loans as they were specifically debarred at that time from giving loans to a Government Company.

Thus by keeping equity at 49% or less, and balance with the public the Government created an innovative ownership structure for the establishment of the fertilizer factory for the first time in the country. The idea of establishing a fertilizer factory was to meet the needs of farmers (customers) and to encourage more of them not only to use the fertilizers but also to make them use more and more fertilizers for higher crop production. This was the practical demonstration of the theory of Management Guru Peter Drucker as expressed in his book "Practice of management" (1954). He states "there is only one definition of business purpose: to create customer. Markets are not created by God, nature or economic forces, but by businessmen". He further argues that since the role of business was to create customers, its only two essential functions were marketing and innovation.

This was done by innovation in the ownership structure of the company so that farmers (customers) would have more confidence in the product, being produced by a Government sponsored company. Company also adopted innovating marketing practice by providing various services and free fertilizers, five years before the company put its products in farmer's hand. Thousands of farmers started using fertilizers produced by GSFC and the number of farmers and quantum of fertilizers used by them are continuously increasing since last three decades and yet only 70 percent of the farmers use fertilizers. The Company had done many such innovations such as (1) selection of technologies, (2) project management, (3) tools and methods of training. (4) Marketing services to customers of fertilizers and industrial products, (5) social development and industrial development through the services of Application Development Centre. As the Company is profitably operating even after 20 years and growing continuously, it has fulfilled the requirements postulated as above by Peter Drucker.

Birth of G.S.F.C.

The company was incorporated as Gujarat State Fertilizers Company Ltd. in February 1962. The Government of Gujarat appointed the following Directors on the Board:

Mr. Jayakrishna Harivallabhdas	Chairman
Dr. Vikram Ambalal Sarabhai	Director
Mr. Madanmohan Mangaldas	Director
Mr. H. M. Patel I.C.S. (retd)	Director
Mr. Arvind Navinchandra Mafatlal	Director
Mr. Arvind Narottam Lalbhai	Director
Mr, Dhirendrakumar Nanji Kalidas	Director.
Mr. Ramanbhai Bhailalbhai Amin	Director
Mr. V. Isvaran I.C.S.(retd)	Director
Mr. V. L. Gidwani I.C.S	Director
Mr. F.J. Heredia I.A.S	Director
Mr. K. R. Srivatsa I.A.S	Managing Director

It was expected that each industrialist director would contribute Rs. 1.5 million towards the share capital of the company. Though Mr. Arvind Mafatlal agreed to the figure, other directors did not agree. After discussions, it was considered reasonable that each director may contribute between Rs. 0.25 and 0.5 million towards the share capital. Mr. Madanmohan Mangaldas did not agree on principle to contribute to share capital stating that this was excessive and further he could not contribute from personal finance. He further stated that when he was asked to become a director, it was expected that he would contribute his business acumen but not finance. Further, he felt that prospects for the company were not bright. Therefore, he resigned from the Board of Directors of the company.

The precise impact of this cannot be gauged adequately, but one may safely assume that such a posture on the part of one of the leading industrialists of Ahmedabad had a deterrent effect on others, many of whom shared doubts expressed by Mr. Madanmohan Mangaldas about the profitability of such a venture, as earlier fertilizer projects did not show profitability. Certainly, on the face of this set back, there was some nervousness all round, especially, after some contractor's selection had changed, target for making contracts effective was not certain, and the public issue could not be launched as originally planned. Thereafter, businessmen and others started to have some doubts whether the project would come up.

Despite various claims that the industrialists justified their presence by bringing their business acumen, but not large sums of money, there were those who asked how well they could serve a company in which they had rather little confidence and a limited financial involvement. Similar hesitation was expected among outside investors; and it seemed unlikely that a decent financial package could be put together to place before the general investing public and the public lending institutions. Thus in early 1964, there were serious doubts about the viability of the project. There were doubts whether the company would fold up before it starts production. It is at this juncture that I decided to join the company.

I had completed my Master's degree in Chemical Engineering from the University of Michigan in 1951 and had worked 3 years at the institute of gas technology, Chicago, for research and development related work to obtain physical and thermodynamic data for Nitrogen and Methane mixtures at cryogenic temperatures. I returned to India in August 1954 and joined the Department of Atomic Energy, initially to work on the design of the first nuclear reactor.

After the completion of the reactor, I had the choice to become the Superintendent of the reactor or form a new heavy water group. Heavy water is required as the moderator in nuclear reactor fuelled by natural Uranium. Since India did not have enough Uranium, Dr. Bhabha had the idea to utilize thorium through a three stage cycle so that thorium can be converted to use as a fuel for the Nuclear Reactor. For this type of reactor as well as natural uranium fueled reactor, heavy water is required as a moderator. I therefore opted for the heavy water group. The easiest source to produce heavy water in India, at that time was the Hydrogen gas (synthesis gas), an intermediate in the production of ammonia, a basic raw material for fertilizers. Thus, the production of heavy water was linked up in India with the fertilizer plants till an independent Hydrogen Sulfide-Water process was developed in India. Even after this heavy water plants continued to be established in association with fertilizer plants.

The Department of Atomic Energy had organized with the Government of India that a representative of the Department of Atomic Energy should be associated with the planning and execution of all fertilizer projects. Thus, as a representative of the Department of Atomic Energy, I had the privilege to be associated with the following fertilizer projects:

1) Rourekela fertilizer project where the deuterium concentration in the coke oven gas was found to be too low to be economical to produce heavy water.

2) The fertilizer project to be established near Mumbai for the selection of the site. The committee selected the site at Trombay. (now Rashtriya Chemicals and Fertilizers Limited)

3) Nangal fertilizer project:

Fortunately, the Bhakra Dam had a very large capacity to produce power and they did not have customers to utilize this power. Dr. Bhabha had organized with the Government of India to provide 164 megawatts of power for the fertilizer cum heavy water project so that Hydrogen can be produced from water. This was economical at that time as the price of power was negotiated at 1.35 Paisa per unit. (The price of power today is at least 200 times higher) Hydrogen can be enriched in Deuterium through the arrangements of electrolyzers in cascade formation, from which heavy water can be produced, and hydrogen depleted in deuterium can be used for the production of fertilizers. I was associated with this project from the stage of site selection and planning, to project execution and operation. Thus, because of integrated planning of fertilizer and heavy water, I was associated with both fertilizer and heavy water and was in charge of heavy water. This fertilizer project was commissioned in 1960 and heavy water in 1962.

Joining GSFC

Basically, I was interested in coming to Gujarat as my brothers and sisters were growing up and my mother (I lost my father in 1958) was insisting that I should come to Gujarat to look after the education and marriage of brothers and sisters who were growing up. I therefore decided to come to Gujarat and was looking for opportunity. I had talked to my boss Mr. Sethna, who later became chairman of Atomic Energy Commission, to transfer me back to Bombay, but he said this will take a year or two. In the meantime GSFC had advertised for suitable posts for their fertilizer complex. I had talked with my cousin Chandubhai Gami who was a businessman in Ahmedabad. He told me that as per Ahmedabad Business circles there was doubt whether GSFC would come up because of the financial problems, though Government of Gujarat was very keen on the project. As I was keen to come to Gujarat for family reasons, I applied to GSFC even though there were apprehensions about its future.

I was called for interview in February, 1964 at Ahmedabad. There were 5 candidates for 3 positions, General Superintendant Technical, General Superintendant Production and General Superintendant Maintenance. Before I was called for interview, I found that committee members were leaving. I therefore talked to Mr. S.R. Modi who was administrative officer looking after the arrangements. He immediately talked to Mr. Srivatsa – Managing Director and Mr. Nat Parikh – General Manager about this. They told him that they will interview me. After about half an hour of interview they told me that I was selected. After about a fortnight I received the appointment letter, which however indicated much lower salary than advertised. I, therefore, wrote to them that this was not acceptable to me. Lot of correspondence ensued and finally in June, 1964 they revised the appointment letter in accordance with what I had asked. I wrote to them that I would resign from the Department of Atomic Energy and would join GSFC on being relieved by them.

I sent my resignation to Mr. Sethna, who later became Chairman of Atomic Energy Commission. However he did not agree to relieve me. As I was going to Bombay quite often to report on progress of the heavy water project, I took the opportunity to discuss with Mr. Sethna who was my boss. He told me to go to administration department and find out. When I went there the undersecretary told me that I had very good confidential reports and therefore I have very good chance of going up very high and it will be foolish on my part to resign. Since I was very keen to come to Gujarat I then sent, after about fifteen days, a telegram to Mr. Sethna that if I am not relieved by end of October, I will relinquish the position. To which he replied by telegram stating that I was a Government Officer and cannot leave my post till I am relieved. If I do leave, strict disciplinary action will be taken against me. I again met him in October and talked to him. This time he was more amenable and told me that he will relieve me in November. I was finally relieved in mid November.

In the mean time GSFC was not pressing me to join early as, perhaps, they were not in a hurry as the project was not making progress or they did not need me badly. I think the former was the fact as I found out when I joined GSFC in late November, 1964. The actual work on the project had not started as there ware financial difficulties and they were waiting for the approval of the term loan from the financial institutions. Other necessary agreements such as joint water supply scheme with Gujarat refinery, for supply of electricity with Gujarat Electricity board, for providing marshalling yard and railway siding, pipeline for supply of naphtha etc. were signed. Architect for township, Adm. Building, workshop, canteen guest house etc was appointed.

⌘ ⌘ ⌘

Chapter 2
Innovations in Management Practices

During those days projects were taking long time for completion and over runs in cost and time were of routine nature, GSFC had to devise new management philosophy for projects, procurement and construction, personnel policy, marketing innovations, finance management and operations management. Following management theories provided guidelines to decide on how to organize new management practices for these functions.

Henri Fayol in his book "General and Industrial Management" (1949) created a system of management. He put management at the centre of the organization. He divided all activities to which industrial undertakings give rise can be divided into six groups: (1) technical (2) commercial (3) financial (4) security (5) accounting and (6) managerial. Fayol noted that the management function was quite different from the other five essential functions. "To manage is to forecast and plan, to organize, to command, to coordinate and to control. The maxim, "managing means looking ahead", gives some idea of the importance attached to planning in the business world, and it is true that if foresight is not the whole of management at least it is an essential part of it".

Peter Drucker in his book "The Practice of Management" (1954) argues that management has central role in the twentieth-century society. He places management and managers at the epicenter of economic activity. He also lays the foundation of Management by Objectives (MBO) in this book. He says that ' a manager's job should be based on a task to be performed in order to attain the company's objectives'. He further states that a manager should be directed and controlled by the objectives of performance rather than by his boss. To perform his task the manager must know and understand what the business goal demand of him in terms of performance and his superior must know what contribution to demand and expect of him and must judge him accordingly. Peter Drucker establishes five basics of the managerial role: to set objectives; to organize; motivate and communicate; to measure and to develop people. Gary Hamel himself a business guru of the 21st. century wrote in 1994 "I would like to set a challenge for would-be management Gurus: try to find something to say that Peter Drucker has not said first, and has not said well".

Details of the management for project, procurement and construction are given in following paragraphs. While going through the details one will observe that the principles enunciated by Fayol and Druker, namely setting objectives, organizing, coordinating, motivating and developing people are followed as indicated in the systems and procedures established in GSFC and detailed bellow. It will also be observed that individual managers were given tasks to be performed and were judged by their performance.

Project Management

Normally a new company, in those days, would select a foreign company as project consultant who will carry out all work including issue of tenders, procurement, selection of licensors, and contractors, and erection supervision till the commissioning of the plants, normally in consultation with the company. This was necessary as the normal organization in a new company would not have the required experts to carry out project work. Considering that earlier projects were invariably getting delayed causing over run in the cost and time, it was thought that we had to innovate management practices which would ensure that (1) company management have a complete control in the management of the project, (2) execute the project within time and budgeted cost and (3) operate the plant at high level of capacity utilization while keeping in mind the principles of management Gurus as indicated above.

It was therefore necessary to have an interim organization for project execution as activities during the project are quite different from those required for the management of the company with operating plants. Many of the project activities have to be done only once and not to be repeated. For example selection of site, selection of process licensors, contractors, procurement of equipment and materials, bringing in power, water, railway siding, facilities for handling raw materials, administrative building, workshop, stores, township etc are required to be done only once. However these activities have to be coordinated and completed in time and within the cost estimates. On the other hand, for the running of the plants there are repeated and continuous activities such as procuring raw materials and spares, production, and marketing of products etc, which requires different types of expertise and consequently different type of organization, is required. (See under "operation Management").

Considering these aspects, as there were three major divisions of the company namely 1) Ammonia – Urea 2) Phosphatic group and 3) Electrical & Utilities, and there were three general superintendants, each one was asked to look after one group and take full responsibility with authority for completing the work in time. I was asked to look after Ammonia – urea group, Mr. Jaganathan the Phosphatic Group, and Mr.Subaraya to look after the Electrical and Utilities. Each one had to keep close contact and coordination with each other to ensure that all activities are completed in time and within the estimate. In the past in most of the public sector enterprises, delays and cost over run were the norm as there was no proper coordination and timely decisions and actions were not taken. It was, therefore, necessary to devise a system for such coordination and control.

I took upon myself to devise a simplified Project Evaluation and Review Technique (PERT) to meet these objectives.. First of all distinct activities, required for completion of the project and start up of the plants, were listed in as much details as possible. These were divided into contracts, delivery periods, third party activities etc. Time required for each such activity was evaluated. Project cost estimates were divided into cost for each activity. There are a number of activities which cannot be started before the completion of some other activities. All such activities were studied to work out the required sequence of completion of different activities. Estimate of time required for all such activities which are required to be completed one by one, was prepared. Total time required for completion of such group of activities was then calculated.

The longest time required for the completion of any group of activities is the time required for the completion of the project. The project was required to be completed in 24 months. The completion time required for some group of activities had to be curtailed to ensure completion of the project within 24 months. Such group of activities for which time of completion had to be curtailed became critical activities. Any delay in completion of any of this group of activities would delay the project. These activities, besides the normal activities had to be specially monitored every month. Most of the activities would only be partially completed every month. The percentage completion of activities was derived on the basis of percentage of the actual cost incurred to the total estimated cost of each activity. The current established practice, however, is to do physical measurement of quantities.

To properly monitor, these activities were depicted in graphical form on a big chart which was hung on the wall so as to be visible to any one wanted to look at the progress. Vertical lines showed the months from start up to the completion. The Horizontal lines listed all activities. The actual completion of each activity was shown by a black horizontal line indicating the percentage completion in that month. If the progress actually was less than that required for the month, the line will be short to the extent of delay in completion in that month. This gap will be filled by red lines indicating the extent of the delay. A pendulum with string was hung on the wall and moved from month to month so that on a given month to what extent actual progress is behind schedule can be noted by seeing the red lines.

Such delays would be discussed with all concerned and contractors and ways and means of bringing the activities for target completion would be discussed. In most cases it would be shortage of indigenous material such as steel, cement, piping etc. as these were controlled and were in short supply in those days. There could be also delays from contractors, either by not keeping enough skilled people or due to delay in receipt of drawings/materials or misinterpretation of drawings. This would be discussed with the contractors. In the meeting who caused the delay would not be discussed but what caused the delay would be discussed to find the solution to overcome the delay. In case of financial problem of the contractor he was helped as discussions were held to find solution. Normally a positive result always occurred. As contractors were pre-qualified (for details see below "procurement and construction") very few incidents of delay occurred. As Mr. Srivatsa was keen to complete the project in time, he would approve open market purchase or help the contractor once he was satisfied that this will bring the project schedule in line.

There were lots of activities which were to be done by third parties such as bringing 66 KV power line from Gujarat Electricity Board (GEB), railway siding to the company premises, naphtha pipe line from Indian Oil Corporation Ltd (IOCL), gas pipe line by Oil and Natural Gas Corporation (ONGC), water pipe line from Mahi river as a joint project with Gujarat Refinery. All these activities were monitored by a separate group and discussions were held with authorities undertaking these activities and continuously expedited for timely completion. In fact the agreements and contracts for all these activities were executed far ahead (some time one year) of the effective date of the foreign contractors. This gave much more time to the agencies to complete the work in time. All such activities were completed in time.

In order to make sure that there was no shortage of finance, all activities were assigned priorities. All those activities directly connected with completion and commissioning of the plants were on top priority, others, such as Administrative building etc, were given lower priority. Further Mr. Srivatsa had expertise by which he would get money from the Government of Gujarat early enough before the requirement and also manage to get loans from the Government. In fact at the end of every year there was lot of money in bank deposits (Rs. 15 million at least) till the commissioning of the plants. Finance Department managed to get disbursement of money from financial institutions as soon as agreements were signed. The expenditure was slowed down during the uncertainty period: May 1964 till October 1965.

Thus by closely monitoring the progress, controlling the delays and by quick management decisions, the project could be completed in time. In fact this project was completed in record time and Indian Institute of Management, Ahmadabad, had made a case study to find out how this was achieved. More details are given under phase 1 project.

Procurement and Construction

The indigenous procurement of machinery and material for the project was very important and critical as any defect in any machinery or material could cause problems in the commissioning of the plant which is very costly, specially, for a new company. Similarly any delay in supply could lead to cost over run which company can ill afford. It was, therefore, very essential that proper care was taken in the selection of suppliers, vendors as well as contractors so that they would supply quality material with good workmanship and equipment as per specifications and deliver them in time. Similarly, selection of the contractors for civil works, erection etc. had also to be done carefully. Therefore a new system and procedure was required to be established. The following procedure and system was established.

The machines and materials to be procured and items for which contracts were to be given were listed. These were then divided into three different categories depending upon sophistication, complexity, delivery schedule and cost. Different teams of engineers were formed depending upon the technical expertise required. Each team would visit the potential manufacturer, supplier, vendor or contractors and assess their capacity in terms of technical capability, material processing (stainless steel, alloy steel etc) material handling capacity, finance capacity and records of past supplies, contracts etc. On the basis of the data collected, contractors would be grouped in appropriate category. There were three categories, large, medium and small capacities.

Normally there would be listing of 10-12 parties for each category. From this list, enquiries were sent to 5-6 parties in each category. Tenders were invited in two parts one technical and second financial and commercial. First technical discussions were held and if there were any deviations parties were asked to modify to conform to the specifications. In this manner all parties were brought as far as possible on the same technical level. As these are pre- qualified parties, normally technical rejection would not occur unless the party was not prepared to revise his tender specifications. Whenever any technical modifications are done the party can change its commercial and financial bid. After this, negotiations were started on commercial aspects. In order to ensure that the company got a reasonable price, the cost estimate for each item were prepared by company engineers in advance (keeping in view total project cost) on the basis of total work required to be done by the contractor.

The company followed Herzberg's and McGregor's principals, and the aim of the company was to bring the price of the bidder lower than (by 2 to 3%) the estimated price by the company. Negotiations were held with two lowest bidders to bring down the price. Our aim was to see that contractors/ suppliers made reasonable profit and did not lose, but at the same time did not make excessive profit. In the negotiations also Gujarat parties were given preference if they were amongst the lowest two or three bidders. They were given the opportunity to bring down the price by two or three percentage lower than the lowest. If they could do so they were given the order. All prices were compared on the basis of cost at site. If they could not, order will go to the non Gujarat party who was the lowest after negotiations. Special instructions were given to make payments to contractors within one week of passing bill by appropriate authority, which in turn was required to pass the bill without any delay

We had no difficulties in following the procedure and Board also approved the same. However in one case when order was given to a Bombay party, the Managing Director of Gujarat party, who did not get the order, complained to Mr. H.M. Patel our Director who was also the Chairman of that company. He was visibly upset and talked to our chairman. The chairman talked to me and told me that Mr. H.M. Patel was upset with me and we should meet half an hour before the next Board meeting in his office to settle the problem. When we met, Mr. H.M Patel told me that he thought that I had always favored Gujarat parties but in one case instead of giving the order to a Gujarat party I had given the order to Bombay party where one of my uncles was the chief engineer. I immediately understood what he was driving at.

I asked Mr. H.M.Patel whether the complainant Managing Director told him that I had called him in my office and asked him to reduce the price if he wanted to get the order. At that time he had said that he could not afford to reduce the price as in that case he would lose money. I told him that I could not give him the order at his price by making our company lose money. Mr. H.M. Patel asked me to confirm that I had called him in my office and had these discussions with the Managing Director. I told him yes, he then said he will find out. At the time of the next Board Meeting Mr. H.M. Patel came to my office and told me that he was sorry that he had doubted my integrity without verifying the facts. He told me that he had discussed the matter with the complainant Managing Director and asked him whether I had called him to my office. When he confirmed this, Mr. Patel got angry with him and told him not to complain in future without telling him full facts.

Motivating People: Human Resource Policy

Douglas McGregor in his book 'The human side of enterprise' (1960) states that people can be trusted, people want to do the right thing, people are capable of imagination and ingenuity. According to Gary Hamel (1994) these were McGregor's fundamental premises, and they underline the work of modern management thinkers from Drucker to Deming, and the employment practices of the world's most progressive and successful companies.

Fredrick Herzberg, in his book 'Motivation to Work' (1959), separates the motivational elements of work into two categories- those serving people's animal needs (hygiene factors) and those meeting uniquely human needs (motivational factors). Hygiene factors - also termed maintenance factors - are determined to include supervision, inter- personal relations, physical working conditions, salary, company policies and administrative practices, benefits and job security. 'When these factors deteriorate to a level below which the employee considers them acceptable, then job dissatisfaction ensues', observes Herzberg. GSFC always ensured, through policy measures and practical implementation of policies, that these factors remain at a high level of satisfaction.

Herzberg says true motivation comes from achievement, personal development, job satisfaction and recognition. The aim should be to motivate people through the job itself rather than through rewards or pressure. The company followed Herzberg's and McGregor's fundamental premises and provided policy measures which would also provide job satisfaction, recognition and personal development through higher levels of opportunities, training and promotion to GSFC employees to give their best to the company. Following paragraphs outline the policy details of training and facilities provided to employees.

GSFC had made arrangement for training of engineers and officers in plant operations in Japan at Japanese contractors' works. Further it had also made arrangement to train about 100 technicians in fertilizer plants in India. However this would not be adequate as training would be for a short period of three months. GSFC planned to employ 700 persons in the plants for the 1st phase of fertilizer plants. There are 8 plants employing high pressure, high temperature technologies as well as processing hazardous and flammable gases and liquids and corrosive fluids. Further it was for the first time that new technologies and single stream concept was used in the country. Earlier the Company was to have at least two streams in each plant, so that for any reason one stream was out, at least plant can produce at 50% level instead of zero production if there was only single stream. It was therefore necessary to impart theoretical training for about a year as well as practical training to fresh graduates etc for about a year making a total training for two years.

It was considered necessary to have a large training centre, as there were only two years left before commissioning of plants, which could train 250 persons every year. The training centre should start by June, 1965 so that first batch with theoretical training on Carmody process trainer and practical training at other operating fertilizer plants can be fully completed and second batch given one year theoretical training on Carmody process trainer and practical training during erection and commissioning of plants, and also to other operating fertilizer plants.

During those days steel and cement were not readily available, it was therefore decided to procure fabricated steel structure and construct silo type six halls to be used as training centre and one hall for administrative office where all officers including Managing Director would sit. These were completed in June 1965, within a 4 months period, started recruiting training officers and training superintendent from February 1965, recruited 250 trainees and started training from June, 65.

In order to make sure that trainees were from Gujarat, we decided not to advertise, as my feeling was that due to lack of communication skill in English of Gujarat students, they will find it difficult to compete with others. This feeling was confirmed when we started interviewing students, many times we had to ask questions in Gujarati as they were not able to explain in English though they knew the subject. We wrote to all Gujarat schools, colleges as well as Industrial Training Institutes, to send us the names and addresses of 1st 10 graduating students with at least 50% marks so that we can call them for interview. The selection process consisted of written papers and those who passed were orally interviewed. As long as a student had passed from school or college in Gujarat, he was considered Gujarati irrespective of where his parents came from.

As these were sophisticated plants, verbal, theoretical and practical training would not be adequate. I was therefore looking for some method of training which could give more practical bias. As airlines were training their pilots through simulators, I thought there could similarly be simulators for training of process operators and technicians. On search I found that M/s Carmody Corporation of USA made simulators for training of Chemical plant operators. They had two models - one automatic which was very expensive and the second semi automatic which required a supervisor to control the operations. We selected the semi automatic model. This was an innovative way of training and perhaps for the first time that such simulator was used for the training of process plant operators in the country.

In this model any process or section of the process can be set up on the panel with necessary instrumentation as per the Process & Instrument Diagram of the process. Various process variables such as pressure, temperature, flow can be set at the control point and master controller is given to the supervisor. Supervisor changes one process variable and asks the student to bring back the process condition to the control point by manipulating any other control valves. If the student takes correct action by adjustment of any of the controller, variable will come to normal point indicating that student has taken the right action. On the contrary, if he selects the wrong control valve or adjusts the controller in a wrong position an alarm will ring indicating that he has made a mistake. Supervisor will explain to him the consequence of such a mistake. In this manner the student would learn how to control the process correctly and also the consequences if he does not do so.

In the school or college if a student gets 70% marks he is considered to have passed with distinction. This means that he does not know 100%. However for the operation of the process plant his knowledge has to be 100%. I was looking for whether there were any books / systems which can teach 100% correct operations/maintenance. I found that M/S Dupont of USA had printed a series of books, titled "self learning series" which gave a step by step instruction for start up, operations and maintenance of any equipment such as pump, motor, reactor, distillation column etc. I wrote to them and they were nice to send me a complete set of 70 books, though strictly they were to be used for training of employees of M/S Dupont only. These books were very good especially for High School and ITI graduates and diploma holders. I also got some of the books translated in Gujarati so that such students, who were weak in English, could learn to start/operate the equipment in 100% correct manner. Language knowledge was not absolutely necessary as all instructions were through diagram of parts of equipment and right and wrong answers were also indicated again by diagram.

First year training was theoretical and trainees were taught chemistry, fertilizer processes, equipments, safety, Factory Act etc. required for fertilizer plants. Maintenance technicians were trained on maintenance aspects of all above and given rigorous workshop practice so they exactly learn how to use all maintenance tools. After successful completion of

1 year training students were selected and assigned for work in specific plants and then they were given training for that specific plant, first on Carmody process simulator and then sent to Fertilizer factory such as FACT for further training. For the 2nd batch students, after completion of theoretical training, the practical training was given on Carmody process trainer and then at GSFC plants which were under construction or commissioning so that they can see the actual equipment as well as controls. They were also sent to operating fertilizer plants for 2-3 months. 1st batch students were also given practical training at GSFC Plants under construction and commissioning.

Fresh engineering graduates from colleges in Gujarat were taken as management trainees, trained about a year in training centre and assigned the plant where they will work and then sent for three months specific training to Japan. For the recruitment of experienced persons for the positions of shift engineers and above advertisements were issued and persons recruited with experience in steel plants, engineering industry, petrochemical plants etc. They were also sent for training to Japan for a period of three months. Here no distinction was made between persons from Gujarat or outside. Here we could get at least 50% of the persons from Gujarat. Practically all persons were from Gujarat for all other departments such as finance, material management, Human Relations, security, administration etc. For marketing department most persons were agronomists who were fresh graduates from the Gujarat Colleges. Thus we could fulfill the desire of the chief Minister of having at least 90% employees from Gujarat for running the company.

Training Centre continued to recruit persons for manning of expansion projects of the company and till next 15 years the trainees continued to rise in position so that it was not necessary to recruit any experienced person from outside even for higher positions. Training centre was also utilized for training of persons from other fertilizer companies such as ICI, FCI, FACT, EID Perry, DCM, State Fertilizer Manufacturing Corporation of Ceylon etc.

Abraham Maslow's book "Motivation and Personality" (1954) is best known for its 'hierarchy of needs'- a concept which was first published by Maslow in 1943. In that book Maslow argues that there is an ascending scale of needs which will have to be understood if people are to be motivated.

First are the fundamental physiological needs of warmth, shelter and food. Next on the hierarchy are social or love needs, and ego and self-esteem needs. Ultimately , as the man moves up the scale, with each need being satisfied comes what Maslow labels 'self actualization', when the individual achieves his or her own potential. Maslow's hierarchy of needs contributed to the emergence of human relations as a management discipline and to a sea change in how motivation was perceived..

By recruiting fresh students and training them at the training centre, GSFC provided motivation to all workers by first meeting their basic needs and further meeting their higher levels of hierarchy of needs through upgrading their knowledge which gave them opportunity for growth. Some trainees reached the level of Executive Director, some to general manager level after a number of years of service and others at different levels of responsibility; thus most of them achieved 'self actualization', that is achieving their own personal potential. Because of this approach there was hardly any turnover of workers or managers and most retired at the end of their service in GSFC. There was hardly any recruitment from outside for next 15 years from 1967, except trainees, to meet personnel requirement for expansion and growth of the company.

As explained earlier most of the workers and junior officers were trained in the Company's training centre and more experienced persons specially managers and above were recruited from outside and trained in foreign country and other Indian fertilizer plants. To minimize turn over of personnel, it was considered desirable to have a town ship for these people, as during those days Baroda did not have sufficient housing accommodation available at reasonable rent.

In the first phase 800 houses were constructed and in the second phase additional 500 houses were constructed. Mr. Balkrishna Doshi (Vastu Shilpa) of Ahmedabad was appointed as the architect for the entire township which included, besides houses, shopping centre, school, hospital, sports complex, temple etc. The township was unusual in the sense that it was circular with shopping centre and school in the centre and temple, hospital and sports complex on the periphery. Mr. Doshi won a special award from Switzerland for the architecture of the township which is called Fertilizer Nagar. It was administered by the Council. called Fertilizer Nagar Council (FNC), with managing director as president and vice president and six members all to be nominated by the Managing Director of GSFC and six members to be elected by the residents.

FNC had full responsibility and the authority to administer and manage the township. It was again a new innovation for the management of township. The council made plans for operations, maintenance, beautification, additional facilities and prepared budget and obtained financial approval of GSFC to carry out all the work. Thus the workers and officers of GSFC were fully involved in the administration and management of the fertilizer Nagar. I was the fist vice president of the FNC. I believe it to be the best township with thousands of trees, keeping temperature 2 degree lower than the temperature in the city, completely clean and absolutely safe for children.

The employees were given other benefits. Besides Provident Fund, employees were paid bonus and a pension scheme was introduced in 1971. This was unique in those days as employees got all three benefits namely, Provident Fund, Bonus and Pension. Fertilizer Nagar had sufficient houses to accommodate all workers, managers, executives and Managing Director. Even then company decided to provide housing loans at a very low interest of 6% to the employees to build their own homes in Vadodara or in their native place. This was to ensure that worker will have a home when he retires. Any employee with two years services was eligible for the loan. He must build the house within 18 months from the date loan is taken and should vacate the township and live in his own house if built in Baroda. He was also paid house rent allowance for this.

Thus an employee who worked for 20 years in the company would practically get the house free of cost without spending any money from his pocket. If he worked for more than 20 years there will be an additional gain, as he would continue to get house rent even though his house loan has been completely paid. Initially the company was financing such loans from its own funds but later on made arrangement with Housing Development Finance Corporation (HDFC) to obtain loan. HDFC extended the loan to employee who will mortgage the house to it. GSFC would deduct interest and repayment amount of the loan from the employee's salary and pay to HDFC. As a result HDFC got practical guarantee for the repayment and interest. As HDFC was charging higher interest rate, the difference in the interest charged by HDFC and 6% to be charged to the employee, as per Company scheme, was paid by the company.

During 1970's there was good demand for skilled workers in the Middle East. In order that our people can gain additional experience and also make and save more money, when I became Managing Director in January 1977, I formulated a scheme by which an employee can take two years leave to go to Middle East for work. He would pay 10% of the salary to the company for keeping his position in GSFC. In this manner every year 30 persons were allowed to avail of this advantage. A large number of employees took advantage and on their return when I talked to them I found that they were enthusiastic and motivated to work harder, as they realized how hard they had to work in the Middle East. Besides they also learned other skills as each one had to do all work whether operation, maintenance, instrumentation etc. Their contribution to the company after such visit did improve substantially. This scheme was innovative and continued till 1983 and was discontinued after some time by my successor. I thought this was a very useful scheme for the company as it improved the skills of workers which added to the technological pool and it was giving monetary advantage to workers.

The company carried out assessment of each employee, workers, officers, managers and executives each year and promoted them as per the recommendations of the heads of the departments, after personal interview if found necessary. Company set up 10 projects by 1982, but did not recruit any experienced person from outside, as we trusted the people to do the right job as suggested by Douglas McGregor. The Company took number of trainees in different categories as per the requirement of additional number of workers/officers every year. Freshly trained people will be posted in existing plants and for new plant experienced people will be drawn from existing plants along with some fresh trainees specifically trained for new plants. In this manner employee got opportunity to learn new skills in new plants as well as opportunity for promotion. Thus they achieved personal development through job satisfaction and recognition as required as per the theory of Herzberg and others as stated above.

Motivation through Human Relations policy and training provided additional benefits which were not envisaged earlier. The distinct culture of GSFC based on its slogan "Faith, Discipline, Hard Work and Success" and its motto "Basic to India's Progress" got firmly established in their minds. A learning environment was created generating fresh views/ideas. Both way communications, from top to bottom and bottom to top, induced dynamism among all concerned.

The traditional Indian laziness, exemplified in attitude "what needs to be done today can be done tomorrow" changed to "what needs be done to morrow can be done to day". A number of examples of this can be found in the section "How GSFC accomplished fastest completion" The best example is the achievement of the dates of production and dispatch of fertilizers, which were announced months before the schedule dates.

The word 'faith' in the slogan meant faith in oneself and faith in God. Worship and celebration by workers and offices would precede initiations of any major activity. This provided additional confidence to all for successful completion of the task.

When we view Human Relations Policy and specially training retrospectively, we find forty five years later, that is today, that this is a must for any corporation in view of the shortage of skilled manpower not only in India but in practically all parts of the world.

Win Win solution on Strike by workers

In spite of the above facilities given to the workers, there was a strike by them during my 1st year as Managing Director. The strike lasted for seven days. I talked to the officers and convinced them to maintain and continue production in spite of the strike. The officers agreed and operated the plant by themselves and all plants except those handling solid materials were kept operating. The bagging plants as they require large work force were shutdown and the production in bulk was stored in silos.

During the strike period, the Chief Minister also paid visit and he told me to be generous to the workers. I explained to him that we have to give to workers what is appropriate and otherwise every time their demand would go up. The management had also made counter demands to the workers; the important one was to cut down staff in each plant by 10%. Government had sent Mr. R. Basu labor commissioner for discussion and negotiations. I had explained to workers that there was some surplus staff and if 10% of staff is reduced I was prepared to give them increment. In the beginning workers would not agree and sought clarification as to what will happen to those members who are removed from the plants. I told them that they will not be discharged but would be transferred to training centre and train them for new plants such as Melamine, Nylon chips etc. which will come up shortly and for which we require people. After training they would be posted in these new plants. Till then they will remain in the training centre and would not be allowed to go to their old plants.

I had also called the officers and told them to list 10% of the staff in each plant and hand over the list to the personnel department, so that as soon as union agreed, we can immediately transfer the workers to the training centre. After some discussions union people agreed to my proposal and we signed the agreement and immediately transferred 10% of the people to the training centre, while granting all workers 10% increment. This was the first time in GSFC that number of persons in each plant was reduced. It has not happened again till now (2008) in GSFC. I thought the agreement was a win - win situation for both the management and workers. GSFC could reduce the man power bill for the existing operations and simultaneously get trained persons for new plants while workers got the increment as well as surety of the job. My handling of strike was greatly appreciated by the corporate world.

Marketing Innovations

Customer is the king for the fertilizer marketing

In recent times all corporations shout from the roof top that "customer is the king". However way back in 1962 GSFC implemented this without shouting about it. GSFC started taking action in 1962 to please its customers, 5 year before it started production. This was a new innovative concept in marketing to woo the customer 5 years before placing products in his hand.

To start with, the company undertook programs of agronomic studies, fertilizer trials and demonstration and intensive propagation in collaboration with the institute of agriculture, Anand and the Director of Agriculture Gujarat. This arrangement was for a period of three years. At that time the company was planning to produce nitro phosphate fertilizer which was later on changed to the production of Diammonium Phosphate (DAP) and/or Ammonium Sulfate Phosphate (ASP) in 1963-64. The company provided the staff and the funds for the programs. After 1963-64, demonstrations were undertaken using Ammonium Sulfate Phosphate and urea on ten different crops in the districts of Baroda, Surat and Kheda. The progressive farmers were given the required quantity of fertilizers free of cost. The company's agronomists frequently visited the farms and rendered technical services. The company also started a demonstration cum research farm at Fertilizer Nagar in 1964.

The Institute of Agriculture, Anand, through field trials established efficiency of DAP, ASP and Urea on yield as well as quality of some important crops of Gujarat. Total 1960 trials were undertaken to show the quantum of increase in the production of crops. Large scale field trials in 72 progressive farmers' fields in districts of Kheda, Bharuch, Surat and Baroda were also carried out by the company.

The company participated in the third National Agricultural Fair at Ahmedabad where more than 100,000 visitors from all over India including Gujarat visited the GSFC stall. Useful literature was distributed freely to all the visitors to create awareness about fertilizers and their use among the farmers. Mass contact of farmers was made in villages, newspaper supplements and radio talks were arranged. Further demonstration programs on new crops were carried out. Large scale demonstrations were carried out in the district of Bharuch. A seminar was organized at the company premises where 300 farmers participated.

In the 5 years period the company distributed more than 13,000 M.T of fertilizers (urea, ASP, DAP) to the farmers free of cost. All the cost towards research, demonstration, field trials, seminar, literature etc was born by the company. The company also started a special magazine for farmers in Gujarati language. It was named "Krishi Jeevan". This was, and still is, one of the most popular farmers' magazines in Gujarat. Company had also designed special jingles which were regularly aired over the radio. These became very popular among farmers as they gave them entertainment as well as education on how to improve farming and increase food production.

All the above was done during the period of 5 years from February 1962 to July 1967 before the commissioning of the plant. Thus farmers were wooed for a period of 5 years before the company put its products for sale in their hands. Thus farmers were educated; as a result they understood the advantage of using the fertilizers and accepted that fertilizers would increase production in their farms. Naturally, with this knowledge farmers took to DAP and ASP, which they had never seen or heard of before and to urea which was relatively new, in a big way. In this way GSFC products became the darling of Gujarat farmers. The proof of this is that during the first 2 years of operation, farmers consumed 200,000 M.T of GSFC fertilizers and produced nearly 1 million M.T. additional food grains. Further 5000 – 6000 farmers would attend every annual general meeting and the main questions were shortage of fertilizers in some remote corners of Gujarat. GSFC production capacity was quite large and after meeting the Gujarat farmers' requirement it was marketing fertilizers in other states of India.

After the role of GSFC was established as above, GSFC started opening its own depots from 1967-68 to further improve services to the farmers- its customers. The depots were later renamed "Farmers Information Centre"(FIC) in 1969 -70 when they numbered 100. Each centre was manned by an agronomist. The FIC sold all inputs such as fertilizers, seeds, pesticides etc, provided soil testing free of cost to farmers and rendered technical services at the centre in addition to frequent visits to farmers' fields where they gave advice on how to use, the quantity to be used and the time when to use different inputs. These services are continuing today also.

Insurance for the customers

The company was the first one in the country to introduce crop insurance for selected crop for the farmers on experimental basis. This was named by the company four "P" program (package of practice with plant protection). Under the plan, the company provided to farmers fertilizers and pesticides for the cultivation of hybrid cotton crops and use of fertilizers and spraying of pesticides was carried out under the supervision of the company. The agricultural officers of the company went to the spot to make study of crop conditions and guide the farmers. The Life Insurance Corporation (LIC) and Bank of Baroda were associated with the scheme.

The LIC insured the cost of inputs for crops cultivated under the scheme and Bank of Baroda provided funds required for agricultural inputs to the farmers. The scheme was tried on 200 acres of high breed cotton during 1971-72 and 1000 acres of land in Baroda and Surat districts in 1972-73. The first year was successful. In the second year however due to adverse climatic conditions LIC incurred heavy losses. Therefore they did not extend the scheme further. This was because in a limited area same agro climatic conditions could prevail. If the areas selected were large and dispersed, agro climatic conditions could be different, the risk would be lower which would mean lower insurance premium and probability of insurance Company making loss would be lower.

Recently Government of India has formulated "Modified National Agricultural Insurance Scheme (MNAIS)" to be covered in 100 districts from 2007 onwards. According to Economic Times this scheme runs the risk of taking crop insurance further down the road to becoming localized drought relief for 100 of the most backward and drought prone districts in the country.

Next to the extension services being provided by the state governments and fertilizer industry, crop insurance is the single largest need of the agricultural sector, especially when the farmers are required to diversify from the traditional cropping pattern. It is best if the insurance is organized and implemented by the Government of India at the national level as it can spread the insurance in very large areas over different agro climatic regions. Fortunately in India the agro climatic conditions in various regions are very much different. This is an advantage as it will reduce the premium due to reduction in risk for insurance of the crops in the areas with very divergent agro climatic conditions. The present scheme (MNAIS) covers the risk and area base crop failures. The insurance should be provided and it is necessary to the extent that scheme covers more crops and all states.

Industrial Products Marketing – Application Development Center

GSFC with a motto of "basic to India's progress" concentrated on manufacturing products which were basic and which would provide scope for further industrial development. This meant taking up of products which were not yet produced in the country and which had potential to further increase industrial development. This placed greater responsibility and meant more hard work for the marketing team and also to D&R departments. D&R had to select products properly and Marketing people had to convince customers to buy products manufactured for the first time in the country in place of imported products, and also render technical and other customer services associated with marketing of products.

GSFC produces a number of industrial products such as 1) Ammonia 2) Technical grade urea 3) Sulfuric Acid and oleum 4) Methane 5) Argon gas 6) Oxo syngas 7) Caprolactam 8) cyclohexanone, 9) Nylon Chips 10) Melamine and 11) MEK Oxime. After 1983 more products were added with the amalgamation of Polymer Corporation of Gujarat and Gujarat Nylon Ltd. GSFC did not export products for the first 20 years as there was a large potential domestic demand compared to availability. The Company decided to establish Application Development Center to convert potential demand to actual demand and succeeded in doing so. All products fell in different categories in different markets and therefore marketing was carried out through 1) direct sales to customers where the consumption is large 2) Through the distributors 3) Through stockist and 4) through dealers. The product pricing is fixed by the company. Discounts, rebates, credits etc are determined by the marketing department in consultation with the finance department and with the approval of the managing director. These change from time to time depending upon market conditions such as changing needs of customer, imports, change in government policy on taxes, excise etc.

For some products such as Melamine, Nylon Chips and Argon, the production capacity established by the company for each of the products was 10 to 30 times more than the consumption in the country at that time as the potential was very high. Further, markets for these products were growing slowly due to 1) import restrictions 2) Lack of knowledge of the new products which could be produced from GSFC products and 3) Lack of knowledge on the process to manufacture new products. The Application Development Centre developed new grades of products from Melamine resins and Nylon chips, newer applications and provided services to customers not only on how to use GSFC products but also application of the same in the new products and the manufacturing method of new products from the GSFC products. This was a new concept. This method of development was a slow process to start with but gained momentum with more knowledge and experience. Details of marketing of industrial products are given in the chapter on diversification.

Strategy for Growth

It was considered necessary that selected products should have long life, provide continuous growth opportunity and remain profitable over a period of at least 20 years. At the same time each selected product should have some synergy with the company's operations. It should be possible to techno-economically integrate plants of such products with the existing plants. The company could have continuously grown with fertilizers, as demand of these is continuously growing even after 40 years. The company established 4 fertilizer projects, all working profitably. As prices and marketing of fertilizers are controlled by the Government of India, it was not advisable to grow in fertilizers only.

Synergy with existing operations was considered as important criteria, besides opportunities for growth. Selected products should use intermediates or finished products from the existing plants or should produce product or byproduct which can be used in fertilizer plants. There should be possibility of techno-economic integration of all plants. For details see chapter 7 Diversification and Growth.

Finance Management

The basic philosophy of financial management was 1) application of funds in the most productive manner, 2) to expend economically aimed at cost reduction and taking advantage of the competitive market, 3) provide liberal services to customers, 4) be a good model employer, 5) distribute reasonable dividend to shareholders, 6) maximize investment in new projects, 7) minimize interest burden on term loans, 8) take maximum advantage of available tax benefits, and 9) accelerate loan repayments to the extent possible.

Project financial management

Every cost conscious management has to ensure that works are completed not only as per the specifications, within the time period with good workmanship but also within the cost budgeted for the works. To ensure that the project will be completed within the budget, detailed cost estimates for all items of work required to be completed were prepared. Further, to provide flexibility for unforeseen items, contingencies were provided, to be backed by adequate cash resources to avoid any hold ups in project execution.

Project budget was divided into annual budget and annual budget was further detailed out into quarterly budget. This was done by making use of data available through Project Evaluation and Review Technique (PERT) management system which had not only sub-divided cost of individual items but also linked with the time schedule for satisfactory and timely completion of each major item. This style of budgeting was reviewed from time to time and was compared with physical progress every month as per the PERT monitoring system. Another salient feature of budgeting was estimation of costs remaining to be incurred on the balance items to be executed. This was done to avoid overruns on the project.

The review system gave clear idea as to whether funds provided were adequate to meet physical targets and further ensuring that budgeted funds will be expended during the specified period. The idea was to avoid imbalances in budgetary funds by way of either surplus or shortage for the remaining physical work. Since GSFC was a public limited company with accountability as to resources management and general limitation of resource constraints, it was also expedient that ways and means position of the company was clearly brought out for continuous review and corrective actions in time. Finance Department had the responsibility to prepare ways and means position every month and project the funds requirement in the next quarter for enabling the company to raise required resources by way of equity contribution from the promoters- Government of Gujarat and if required look to raising funds from other available sources.

These financial statements were reviewed by the Managing Director. The whole budgeting system ensured that required finance was available for the project and that too in the relevant period. It was the basic practice of the company to regularly associate finance department personnel in various activities directed towards the execution of the project with a view to minimize the effective cost and investment for the project and further ensure meeting the financial parameters. Details of actual project financial management are given under fertilizer plants phase 1."

Operating Financial Management

The company took up the expansion of the fertilizer plants even before the first phase of plants had gone into operation. After the commissioning of the first project there was sizeable requirement of funds for expansion project finance and working funds for operations. The company organized funds for expansion from Japan.

Development and research division was established to conceptualize, identify, plan and implement all new projects including expansion of the plant facilities established and in operation. This division was drawing specialists from operations and technical departments and had a permanent member from the finance department. The said division after finalizing main contracts would prepare project cost estimates as also detailed cost estimates, similar to the practice followed in the first project, and taking support of PERT system. The finance department would ensure that required funds were tied up and made available for execution of the new projects. Close co-ordination between development & research division and finance department was assured by inclusion of one finance member in the project team.

The agreements for the expansion project were signed in July 1967 and the project was completed in two parts, that is urea plant was completed in March 1969 and ammonia plant in September 1969. Actual data on project and operational financial management are given under phase 2 Ammonia Urea plants.

With the satisfactory establishment of the two projects, internal generation had started flowing and company's credit worthiness was of high rating. Further, encouraging operational performance made it possible to raise term loans etc for financing of the new and diversified projects envisaged for continuing the sustained growth of the company. A good feature also was availability of tax incentives on capital expenditure on projects. This helped in increased quantum of generated resources. The tax incentives available were (1) first five year tax holiday (2) provision of 35 % development rebate and (3) no tax on income equivalent to 6% of capital employed for expansion or grass root projects. The continuous growth of the company through new and diversified projects and conscious tax planning, the company had no tax liability for a long period till the year 1974-75.Since the company had tax free profits; the shareholders were also rewarded with tax free dividends in those years.

Caprolactam was the first diversification project. The Government of India approved the project including the foreign exchange component in May 1971. The payment in Swiss franc was made to Inventa through Rs.30 million (US$ 4 Million) loans from ICICI and the balance foreign exchange requirement of Rs.90 million was released from the French credit available with the Government. The project was completed in March, 1974 and marketing started in August 1974. For details of finance management of the project, please see under Diversification, Caprolactam.

The company took up additional projects from 1975 onwards as given below.

Project Name	Cost in Rs. Million
Purge gas recovery	Rs.100.00
Phosphoric Acid de bottlenecking	Rs.30.00
Oxo Syngas	Rs. 27.70
Ammonia 3 plant	Rs. 45.00
Nylon Chips	Rs.180.00
Melamine	Rs.150.00
Sulphuric Acid Plant 400 M.T / day	Rs.100.00
Effluent Channel Project	Rs.22.00
SAN	Rs. 2.50
MEK Oxime	Rs.15.00
Total	Rs.672.20

The details of financing of these projects along with actual finance management are given under diversification.

Operations Management

Peter Drucker in his book "The Practice of Management" (1954) provides an evocatively simple insight into the nature and raison d'etre of organizations: Organization is not an end in itself, but a means to the end of business performance and business results. Organization structure is an indispensable means, and the wrong structure will seriously impair business performance and may even destroy it. The first question in discussing organization structure must be: What is our business and what should it be? Organization structure must be designed so as to make possible the attainment of the objectives of the business for five, ten, fifteen years hence."

Organization of the operations management is practically (as most people are in operations) the organization for the whole company when it is a manufacturing one. Following paragraphs give details of the GSFC organization. The very fact that the company has fulfilled its objectives for more than twenty years is an ample proof of the adoption of correct organizational structure. Peter Drucker recommends seven layers as the maximum necessary for any organization. GSFC had fulfilled these criteria, in fact with lower number of layers. Different designations among workers were not hierarchical but mainly as recognition of proficiency as all worked in parallel and not reporting to any higher level worker. There were four layers among managers and officers.

When GSFC started production, earlier fertilizer plants were not doing well and producing at low capacity as a result companies were making losses. Some of the reasons for this were inadequate knowledge of repairs, maintenance and lack of knowledge for the requirement of very good workmanship. Further as fertilizer plants are specifically designed and tailor made any defects during fabrication of equipment at suppliers works would also show up during operations. Thus different fertilizer plants had problems on different equipment causing maintenance problems. The latter even vary from year to year for different equipments. These problems got substantially diminished in the later plants, as engineering companies, equipment manufacturers and plant personnel had acquired adequate experience, and plants could be operated at 100% or even better.

In case of GFSC this was further complicated as the company had adopted new sophisticated process and equipment for the first time in the country and for which very little experience was available even in foreign countries. It was therefore necessary that organization for plant operations is properly determined and adequate advance steps are taken to ensure high level of production. To start with, the company ordered spares for three years operations along with the signing of the main contracts so that spares are delivered along with the equipment. Further in addition to normal guarantee test runs of seven days, the company asked process licensors and plant suppliers to operate the plants for four months along with GSFC personnel and demonstrate average 60 % production in the four months after the guarantee tests are conducted. This enabled operating and maintenance personnel to understand equipment behavior and to take appropriate steps to maintain high level of production.

Even before the contracts became effective, GSFC had established a large training center capable of annually training 250 operating, maintenance, safety and quality control personnel. Training center was equipped with, workshop for mechanical, electrical and instrument maintenance, laboratory, and special imported process simulator for training of operators for the first time in the country. And a set of "self learning books" specifically designed by M/S DuPont of USA, to acquire 100 percent knowledge, for their maintenance personnel, which they were kind enough to send to us. Thus fresh trainees were given two years training, one year theoretical on fertilizer processes, equipment, safety, environment, quality control, factory act etc, and second year specific training in the selected plants of fertilizer factories in India, workshops, Carmody Process Trainer, and some bright trainees were also trained abroad for a period of three months, further training was given during erection, commissioning and initial 4 months operations of the plants. All managers and officers were sent abroad for training in suppliers' plants (more than 90 persons were trained abroad) as well as in Indian fertilizer plants and during erection, commissioning and operations of the Company's plants under the supervision of foreign technicians and managers.

Number of personnel in plants was kept to lowest for Indian conditions but more than what they employed abroad. This was necessary as in India we experience a number of power failures, voltage fluctuations, adverse weather conditions such as humidity, high temperatures, storms, heavy rains etc. All these cause either plant shutdowns or malfunctioning of equipment, which requires more people to tend to as well as for restart of plants. Separate safety, quality control and technical departments, independent of production and maintenance, on one side to see that no safety and quality norms are violated and on the other side to help operations by providing guidance in process, technical, safety and quality matters.

A group of equipment and facilities producing products, by-products and waste products (liquid, solid or gaseous) is defined as plant. There were more than ten such plants. Each plant is headed by a plant manager for production and plant engineer for maintenance. If any plant is not large enough, a group of plants will have one plant manager. There will be daily meeting of all plant managers, engineers and heads of technical, safety, quality control departments to discuss achievement of daily production, problems encountered, and to find solutions. If problem can not be solved immediately, technical department will be asked to study it and suggest solution as early as possible. The proposed solution will be discussed with concerned plant manager, plant engineer, workshop personnel along with safety and will be implemented if approved. Finance was never a constraint for any productive purpose.

No data were considered secret from staff and officers and daily, monthly and yearly target for production and actual production were displayed prominently at every plant. This helped in achieving targets and helped in developing good team spirit, tendency of complaining against one another and finding faults of individuals was curbed. On the other hand cooperation among all was encouraged. Multidisciplinary approach for solving problems was developed. How good team spirit and cooperation among all saved considerable amount of production can be seen from two examples.

In 1969 rotating preheater of Ammonia one plant got destroyed because of internal fire (within preheater). This resulted in shutdown of the entire ammonia plant. Preheater was a special design and Japanese contractor said it would take minimum 90 days to fabricate it in Japan and further time to dispatch by air and install the preheater. This would have been a very long shutdown. Our experts from production, maintenance, engineering, workshop, and safety discussed with

Japanese technical experts with a view to minimize the time. Our suggestion was that Japanese may airfreight all raw materials such as plates, tubes etc (a full Boeing plane load materials) and company will fabricate the preheater in the workshop and install it within 45 days. Japanese were reluctant and said this was not possible but agreed to the proposal after heated discussions on the basis that entire responsibility will be that of GSFC, however they will fully cooperate with GSFC. The job was completed in 45 days which allowed the company to produce Rs. 20 million worth of more fertilizers and correspondingly increased profit.

Second example is when titanium lining of the reactor (250 MT weight) of the second urea plant developed leakage in February 1974. This resulted in complete shut own of second urea plant. Japanese said it was not possible to repair this reactor in India and a new reactor should be ordered. The company took the challenge to repair the titanium lining, however to be on safe side the board of directors decided to order a new reactor which had a long delivery period of two years. With the cooperation of all departments, the reactor lining was repaired, reactor was installed and plant was commissioned in 93 days from the day of leakage. The plant operated at full capacity till new reactor arrived and commissioned in March 1976. By taking up this challenging repair job, the Company produced Rs. 400 million worth more fertilizers (400,000 MT of Urea). If challenge was not taken up, loss of production for two years could have made Company a sick company. Incidentally this was the first such repair job done in India and necessitated learning of titanium welding by GSFC technicians. Afterwards GSFC helped a number of fertilizer companies to do such repair jobs.

As the time passed by and GSFC started growing, new requirements started cropping up. For example it was found that imported spares were expensive, an import substitution cell was constituted to develop indigenous spares. This cell together with workshop developed indigenous spares which was a tough job (details are given at paragraphs on indigenous development and fabrication of spares and equipment)

Here again company sought cooperation from Government of India and Technical Development Committee (of the Government Refineries and Fertilizer Companies). In this manner large amount of money and foreign exchange was saved as cost of indigenous spares was only one fourth to one twentieth of the imported spares. As problems due to corrosion were increasing, a corrosion cell was established. This cell not only helped solve corrosion problems but also earned valuable foreign exchange. (for details see Research: corrosion cell). As technologies were changing fast, need arose to establish modernization department for introducing new developments in the existing plants. This created a need for design department: then it became necessary to do more than two projects at a time due to delay in clearance by Government, new project department was established. Earlier technical and development & research departments were already established.

Thus organization at GSFC was flexible yet compact and need based, considering that company was very large and complex in terms of technology and investment, and continued to evolve organization as new problems/requirements cropped up to solve the same. Main emphasis was on self reliance, compact organization and economy. This helped in continuously maintaining profitability.

Spirituality in the Management as practiced

Spirituality is India's heritage, yoga an offshoot of spirituality, is India's gift to the world. Yoga is an important, perhaps one of the most important needs for any management. This is slowly being realized in recent years. Yoga is subdivided in many types. Important ones are (a) Action (Karma), (b) Devotion (Bhakti), and (c) Knowledge (Gyan).

All these three types of yoga were practiced at different levels of management at GSFC. Look at the first Board of Directors of GSFC. It would not be an exaggeration to say that, it was a grand group of Yogis of knowledge (Gyan). and action (Karma). Yoga is defined as balance and skill (in Sanskrit:- Samatvam Yoga Uchyate: Yogah Karmsu Kaushalam) and this Board symbolized these values.

Devotion (to work) came from workforce; most of them were trained at the training center. In addition to technical training, Yogis, out of their inner abundance, communicated and taught carefulness, joyfulness and inner management. Spiritual training was considered necessary for the raw youths and managers on whose shoulders lay the responsibility to establish and operate the prestigious largest fertilizer project in India. Some aspects of these spiritual training are described below.

1. Shri Pandurang Shastri, Magsaysay award winner, inculcated value system for successful management. A large group of GSFC personnel became his devotee and would regularly meet for self development and also go to villages to teach yogic lifestyle to village people.

2. Swami Adhyatmananda and Swami Bhumananda of Shivanand mission, Rishilesh, camped thrice at Fertilizer Nagar and trained more than 100 employees in Patanjali Yoga. Wives of the employees also took advantage of these camps. A group of them continued the teaching of yoga.

3. Kayavarohan is a famous Yoga Complex near Vadodara. Shri Rajarshi Muni of this yoga complex also camped at Fertilizer Nagar and taught advance Yoga to a large group.

4. Transcendental Meditation, TM as it is popularly known as, is the most researched meditation method till date. Volumes of technical data with results are available. It is having deep impact on corporate managements. Maharshi Mahesh Yogi, the well known Yogi and the originator of TM method, was in Vadodara during 1965-66. Mrs. Anandaben Srivatsa, the wife of the first Managing Director, and few executives were trained personally by him. They along with authorized teachers trained a large group of GSFC employees.

5. Mrs. Susan Heredia, the wife of the second Managing Director, conducted moral science classes at Fertilizer Nagar School for a

period of two years and for a further period two years by other executives.

Every member of the Swiss commissioning team, licensors of Caprolactam process, was trained for TM. This, they said transformed their views on work and life. These trainings translated into (the minds of employees) Samatwam (balance) and kaushalam (skill) both of which are necessary for the success of any enterprise. It is difficult to quantify the benefits of all these teachings but it can certainly be seen in the change in attitudes of diverse groups while solving technical and human relations problems.

Following are examples of practice of faith and discipline – a part of GSFC's slogan "faith, discipline, hard work and success". (faith in God and in self) Some examples are given bellow.

a. A Director performed ground breaking ceremony by performing "Bhumi Puja"
b. The first employee (worker) was given the honor of commissioning the caprolactam plant.
c. All major activities were followed by a Puja Ceremony. Such practices are not known in Western World, though they are prevalent in Japan and some other Asiatic Countries.

These gave added confidence to people and eliminated unnecessary and harmful stress. It is believed that practice of Yoga, as taught to GSFC people, provided intuition to predict failures in advance. People operated, without fear, such hazardous plants in complete black out during 1971 Indo-Pak war as plants were very close to the border. There was no major dispute between GSFC and licensors, contractors, vendors and suppliers in the span of twenty years. There was not a single legal case by either side. This speaks for the approach adopted.

⌘ ⌘ ⌘

Chapter 3
Finance from Financial Institutions

The agreements with Japanese contractors for supply of all plants were made during August-September 1964 and Government of India had assured availability of Foreign Exchange in 1964 from the 3rd Yen credit and onwards. Government of India approved the contracts and yen credit for the same on 14th. April 1965. However in absence of term loan approval, the company did not have sufficient funds to make contracts effective and start project activities, as first payment had to be made to Government of India to make contract effective under the yen credit arrangement.

Dr. Jivraj Mehta Chief Minister (CM) of Gujarat was very keen that the project should be implemented by Gujarat and not by the centre. It was also his assessment that no Gujarat Industrialist would come forward to take up this project in view of large capital cost and requirement of massive funds. Further even if an industrialist was interested, CM thought such an arrangement would require private sector's own management team, which he thought would be against the effective control in public interest. This view was fortified when

Mr. Madanmohan Mangaldas, director of GSFC, a leading industrialist and president of Indian Chamber of Commerce and Industry (FICCI) resigned from the board of directors stating that he was willing to bring his business experience and talent to the GSFC board, but did not have amount of money (Rs.0.5million) to invest personally, specially in a venture which he did not consider as particularly promising.

Considering the above the Government of Gujarat decided to take up the project with public participation. The Chief Minister did not want it to be government company, and therefore decided to contribute 49% (Rs.58.5 million) equity and balance equity to be obtained from the public. The article of association was prepared on this basis. This required a public subscription of 51% of the shares (Rs.61.5 million) which will provide a total fund of RS. 120 million after the public issue is made. Project cost was estimated at RS.300 million. Thus there was wide gap of Rs. 180 million. This gap could only be filled by obtaining term loan from financial institutions.

Financing of project can be done through (1) equity which can be contributed by promoter- foreign company or Indian, (2) term loan in Rupee from Indian financial Institutions, Banks-foreign or Indian and For payment in foreign currency for import of equipment and/or technology, it is necessary to obtain Government of India approval. Government may provide foreign currency from its own source or from bilateral credit; it may have negotiated with foreign countries. It is possible to obtain loans in foreign currency from International Finance Corporation, Asian Development Bank, U.S. Aid, German Banks such as DEG and KFW, Overseas Private Investment Corporation (USA), long term suppliers/buyers credits, some Indian and foreign banks.

Financial Institutions were reluctant to provide term loan. Mr. H.M Patel, former Finance Minister of the Government of India, our director, and a Swatantra Party leader, who had big clout in the Union Finance Ministry and influence among the politicians, used his good offices by special visits to Delhi. Mr. Narayana Swami Finance

Advisor of the company, who had recently retired as Additional Finance Secretary, Government of India also tried his influence with officials of the finance ministry. Mr. V. Ishvaran chief secretary of the Government of Gujarat and Mr. Srivatsa Managing Director made several visits to Delhi and Mumbai to convince the finance ministry as well as financial institutions for grant of term loan. However the reaction was not still positive, perhaps due to following position of the fertilizer consumption, production and capacity as given in Table1.

Table 1

The position of the consumption and production
of fertilizers was as follows.

Years	Consumption M.T	Production M.T	Capacity M.T	Short fall M.T
1963-64	376,100	126,100	NA.	250,000
1964-65	551,240	148,000	349,000	410,000

From the above it may be seen that there was increase in the consumption of fertilizers with increase in production, but capacity utilization was low at about 42% resulting in substantial short fall of fertilizers which was increasing from year to year. The public sector fertilizer industry was not operating well and was not profitable. At that time there was no private sector plant for the production of nitrogenous fertilizers.

Government of India had planned for expansion of public sector enterprises, inviting private sector participation and suggestion of fertilizer activity on the part of the state governments themselves. In view of this, state Government of West Bengal had proposed state / private sector fertilizer factory at Durgapur and also provision for state government facility. Andhra Pradesh Government had also proposed to sponsor a fertilizer plant but that did not fructify in public sector and was transferred to private sector. Further experience of the public sector undertakings in the fertilizer field was not encouraging. Raising funds was difficult.

In spite of various trips to Delhi and to financial institutions it seemed that Industrial Development Bank of India (IDBI), perhaps in view of what is stated above, may not perhaps approve term loan to GSFC. At this time Mr. Arvind Mafatlal, a leading industrialist of Mumbai, director of GSFC and director of IDBI started personal discussions with chairman of IDBI to find out why IDBI was reluctant. The feeling in IDBI was that with high capital cost of the project, the cost of urea would also be high and the farmers may not buy fertilizers at such price. Mr. Mafatlal stated that Gujarat farmers want more fertilizer as there is acute shortage and they would definitely purchase fertilizers even if the price was high as they have understood the advantage of using fertilizer in terms of higher crop production. He further wanted to know what would satisfy IDBI chairman to convince him that farmers would buy fertilizers.

After some thought IDBI chairman stated that if farmers contribute Rs.10 million towards the equity of GSFC he would be convinced that Gujarat farmers would buy fertilizer and he would approve the term loan. This was in June 1965. As soon as Mr. Mafatlal conveyed the news to GSFC, the Government of Gujarat as well as GSFC management got galvanized. Government of Gujarat stated that it would provide loans to any cooperative societies which are interested to buy GSFC shares. And GSFC management sent out all employees, except some technical persons, under the leadership of Dr. C.B Patel to villages to canvas for GSFC shares. About 20 persons went round, from village to village, canvassing with various farmers. It was astonishing that no farmer asked about the price. On the other hand all farmers wanted to have guaranteed supply of fertilizers if they contribute to the equity.

They were explained that capacity was many times more than the requirement of fertilizers in Gujarat and therefore they surely will get the fertilizers. Within 2 months farmers purchased equity worth Rs.10.3million more than the target of Rs. 10 million asked by IDBI. More than 25,000 farmers contributed to the equity. Thus truly speaking GSFC was the first genuine farmers cooperative. Indian Farmers Fertilizer Cooperative Ltd (IFFCO) and Krishak Bharati Coperative Ltd. (KRIBHCO), fertilizer entities in the Cooperative sector, came much later. The IDBI and other financial institutions approved the loan and the agreements were signed on 27th October, 1965. This was the highest quantum of term loan IDBI had approved to any company till then.

If the company would not have been able to sell Rs.10 million worth equity to farmers, IDBI would not have approved the term loan and GSFC would have been folded up even before the project work started. Financial problem was still not over. The company had to raise equity of Rs.61.5 million from the public. Since the capital market was not buoyant it was necessary to underwrite the shares. According to executives from Coromandel Fertilizers and FCI, it was almost impossible to raise funds through equity considering the prevailing conditions then. Again Mr. Arvind Mafatlal came to the rescue. He again convinced IDBI and other financial institutions to underwrite GSFC shares. GSFC floated public issue in 1966 the shares were fully subscribed; however 30% of the shares had to be taken up by the underwriters. This can be considered as a feather in the cap of GSFC. The Japanese Trading company Toyo Menka converted Rs.0.9 million, which was confiscated by the Govt. of India during World War, into GSFC equity after due permission from the Government of India. Directors and friends contributed equity worth Rs.3.5 million. Total number of share holders worked out to 35,000.

On June 6, 1966 Government of India devalued Rupee as a result the Rupee cost of foreign currency went up by Rs.44.2million. The company approached IDBI for further loan. IDBI was gracious enough to approve additional loan of Rs.40 million to meet this requirement. Thus the total amount of loan from financial institutions worked out to Rs.220 million; of this Rs.180 million from IDBI, Rs.20 million from Industrial Finance Corporation of India (IFCI) and Rs.20million from Life Insurance Corporation (LIC). Govt. of Gujarat also provided additional loan of Rs.30 million. Management of GSFC should be thankful to Mr. Arvind Mafatlal for using his good offices with IDBI to ensure continuation of the company.

⌘ ⌘ ⌘

Chapter 4
Fertilizer Projects

For the first project the company had appointed consultant for limited scope such as preparation of the project report and drafting of specifications of plants for inviting tenders, selection of technology and selection of contractors. Planning and implementation of the project and conceptualization, planning and implementation of all subsequent projects both for fertilizers as well as others were the responsibility of the company (D & R Department) itself.

GSFC has implemented four fertilizer projects and operated 3. (1) Phase I consisting of Ammonia, Urea, Sulfuric Acid, Phosphoric Acid and DAP plus ammonium sulfate or ASP (2) Phase II consisting of Ammonia and Urea Plants (3) Ammonia 3 plant in joint venture with department of Atomic Energy at the same site (4) New fertilizer project in joint sector with Government of Gujarat for the new company, Gujarat Narmada Valley Fertilizer Company Ltd. (GNFC), at Bharuch for which all conceptualization, planning, contracting, site selection and land acquisition was done by the company and handed over to GNFC for construction and operation of the plants, of course experts not only for construction and operations but also for finance, Company Secretarial work and marketing were either loaned or transferred by GSFC to GNFC..

a. Fertilizer Plants Phase I

The certificate of commencement of business was obtained by GSFC on 15th February 1962. The company after careful consideration selected M/s. Kuljian Corporation of Philadelphia and Dr. John van der Valk and Associates of New York as consultants for preparation of project report. Project report was submitted in November, 1962 and after discussions and making modifications, the final report was submitted and approved by the Board of Directors in February, 1963.

The same companies were appointed as consultant for drafting bid specifications for plants, machinery and equipment including auxiliaries for inviting quotation, evaluation and selection of plant suppliers and other jobs. While inviting tenders, the consultants were asked to keep open processes for different products in bidding documents so that the latest technologies can be offered by the bidders. As the company had not yet decided on the type of complex fertilizers to be produced, consultants were asked to include in the tender scope for plants for Nitric Acid, Nitro Phosphate, Sulfuric Acid, Phosphoric Acid and Ammonium Sulfate Phosphate in the bid documents. In the mean time various interested process licensers and plant suppliers were visiting the company and discussing their processes for plants in which they were interested and providing technical information. The specifications given in the tender documents were modified to include some of the suggestions made by Licensers of various Processes and plants suppliers and which were acceptable to the consultants and the company.

There was good response to the invitation to the tenders which were received in July-August, 1963. Toyo Engineering Corporation, Japan, Humphrey and Glasgow, U.K., Bechtel Corporation, USA, Glexa, France, Hitachi Ltd. Japan, Snamprogetti, Italy, Dorr-Oliver

SARL, France, and Hitachi Shipbuilding, Japan, submitted their bids. Before receipt of the tenders the project cost was estimated at Rs.300 million with foreign exchange requirement of Rs.150 million. Government of India had indicated that the foreign exchange may be available for the proposed plants from Belgium, Canada, France, Italy and Japan.

The Ammonia plant was to be based on Naphtha as feedstock available from Gujarat Refinery and Associated Gas which would be available from Ankleshwar oil field to be supplied by Oil and Natural Gas Commission (as it was then called). As the quantity of Associated Gas which would be available was not known nor it could be ascertained, the plant was to be designed to accept mixture of both Naphtha and Associated Gas as feedstock with any ratio between 80-20 % of Naphtha and 20-80 % of Gas in any proportion in this range. For complex fertilizers Sulfur and Rock Phosphate were to be imported.

Government of India had originally given letter of Intent to GSFC in July, 1962 for manufacture of products as follows:

Ammonia ------------------ 96,000 MT in terms of Nitrogen
Urea ----------------------- 40,000 MT in terms of Nitrogen
Complex Fertilizer -------- 36,000 MT in terms of P_2O_5

However company wanted to put up larger capacity plant and requested Government of India in 1962 to approve larger capacity as follow:

1. Ammonia -------------- 150,000 MT (120,000 MT N_2)
   Including 20,000 MT for sale
2. Urea -------------------- 100,000 M.T (46,000 MT N_2)
3. Complex Fertilizers --- 249,600 MT

The Government of India approved the above revised capacity.

> To undertake manufacturing activities, the company requires industrial license from Government of India. Now most products do not require license. Government of India first issues Letter of Intent and after it is satisfied with the progress of the project, industrial license is issued to the Company. Indian Company is required to submit Industrial Memorandum of Understanding and foreign company to approach Foreign Investment Promotion Board to obtain clarification and information on the requirement of the Industrial License.

Tender evaluation was done by the consultants, the engineers of Fertilizer Corporation of India and GSFC. After negotiations, M/s. Dorr-Oliver (India) Ltd, And M/s. Dorr Oliver, S.A.R.L, France was selected for the supply of Sulfuric Acid and Phosphoric Acid technologies and plants, and Letter of Intent was issued to them. The Government of India had also indicated the possible availability of French credit. However actual contract for above plants was signed with Japanese firm M/s. Hitachi Ship Building and Engineering Co. Ltd. which had offered Chemico (USA) technology for Phosphoric Acid. When I asked Mr. Srivatsa reasons for the change, he stated that M/s. Dorr Oliver were not willing to provide performance guarantees and quality of phosphoric Acid as per the requirement of GSFC.

They were very stiff in contract negotiations and looking at everything from legal angle. They did not want to make commitments and take responsibility arising out of operations of the plants in the future and GSFC would have to take full responsibility and liability for anything which may arise from plant operations in future. This was not acceptable to GSFC management. After days of negotiations and finding that there was no possibility of arriving at solution acceptable to both the parties, the contract negotiations were terminated with them and in their place M/s. Hitachi Ship Building and Engineering Ltd were selected and contract signed with them.

My guess is that what perhaps M/s. Dorr Oliver had in mind was not to take any responsibility for any problems arising out of the production of byproduct Gypsum and emission of Fluorine vapors out of the plant. Both these would create problems of pollution. Till that date, even in USA there was no pollution laws for fertilizer industry, it was enacted in 1973. No solution was found for disposal of Gypsum by USA industry and gypsum was dumped in artificial pond created near the plant and recovery of Fluorine vapors was not yet practiced. If M/s. Door Oliver wanted to settle the issue they could have provided appropriate performance guarantee and suggested possible future work for solving these problems and accept the responsibility for the same.

The company had issued a letter of intent for the supply of electrical equipment and utilities plant to M/s. Hitachi Ltd. The General Manager of Hitachi was to come to India to finalize negotiations in May 1965 and sign the contract. Mr. Srivatsa called me and asked me to participate in the negotiations. I told him that I was not an electrical engineer and Mr. Subaraya who was General Superintendent (Electrical and Mechanical maintenance) is the right person to participate. He told me that he would like me to participate and lead the discussions and Mr. Subaraya would also be in the meeting. He said that he would ask Mr. C.G. Patel, chief electrical engineer, to acquaint me with the scope and specifications and would report to me for the purpose of these negotiations. He told me that my aim, during the discussions, should be to show that M/S Hitachi was not supplying the latest equipment with new technology. Fortunately I had some knowledge on electrical aspects as I was first going to electrical equipment section during my daily visit at Heavy Water plant at Nangal when it was under construction and therefore had acquired some basic knowledge.

Mr. Kitani – General Manager of Hitachi Ltd. came for negotiations. He was staying at Ahmedabad as there was no guest house or good hotel in Baroda at that time. Therefore discussions were limited from 10.0 A.M – to 5.0 P.M. Discussions started smoothly and Mr. Kitani did agree to make some changes in the scope and specifications. This went on for 7 days and on the 8th day, after discussions for about an hour on Switch Gear, he got up, thumped the table and said "I am not proceeding further with the discussions and leaving the meeting right now and will go back to Japan". I was shocked with this sudden development which I never expected or anticipated. As soon as he left I told Mr. Srivatsa that I was sorry that I upset Mr. Kitani to the extent that he was threatening to leave for Japan. Mr. Srivatsa told me not to worry. On the other hand, he said I deserve congratulations. He closed the meeting. All of us were rather surprised and did not understand what Mr. Srivatsa was driving at. Mr. Srivatsa told me to follow him to his office. When we both reached his office he told me that I had touched Mr. Kitani's sense of pride and prestige and therefore he was upset, but he would not go back to Japan but would stay back in Ahmadabad. If he went back to Japan he would feel ashamed of losing the contract which would bring down the prestige of his company. He would, therefore, stay and try to find a solution. It was now a game of testing of patience. We had therefore to wait for him to return to the negotiating table.

After about a week Mr. Kitani rang up Mr. Srivatsa and told him that he was prepared to come for negotiations provided it was started a fresh and Mr. Gami did not come to the table. Mr. Srivatsa told him "I cannot ask Mr. Gami not to come as he is a technical person but I can ask him not to speak and instead I myself will lead the negotiations". Mr. Kitani agreed to this. Afterwards Mr. Srivatsa called me and told me about his conversation with Mr. Kitani and said that he would now handle the negotiations. And perhaps would have to say something about technical experts not being realistic to Mr. Kitani.

Next day when Mr. Kitani came for discussions, I told him that I had not meant to offend him but I was only trying to discuss in the interest of our company and I am sorry if he had felt offended. Mr. Kitani said let us forget that and restart the discussions. He told us that earlier he had agreed to certain changes but he would now like to withdraw the same. Mr. Srivatsa said that it was not fair to go back on what he had agreed to. After some discussions, finding that Mr. Kitani did not want to change his stand, Mr. Srivatsa said' "if you want to maintain the original scope and specifications, it will be difficult for me to convince my board in view of the reservations from the technical people". I know technical people are always very idealistic and do not appreciate commercial and financial aspects. But we both are commercial people, we can, therefore, discuss the commercial and financial aspects provided you agree that you can give some monetary concessions. In that case I would be able to convince the technical people and also my Board to accept the same scope and specifications, in view of reduction in price even though they might have some reservations (Mr.Srivasta had earlier asked me to find out whether the original scope and specifications were acceptable and would be able to meet performance guarantees and that whether the plant would work smoothly. I had told him that I had checked up with Mr. C. G. Patel and he was satisfied.) After this, discussions started on the price and ultimately Mr. Kitani agreed to reduce the price by Rs.10 million on the condition that original scope and specifications would be maintained.

M/s. Toyo Engineering Corporation had offered Imperial Chemical Industries (ICI) steam reforming process for the production of Ammonia with single stream. At that time ICI had recently developed the process and were operating the only plant in the world using Naphtha as feed stock. M/s. Toyo Engineering had taken license and was planning to build the plant at its Chiba factory. The Fertilizer Corporation of India and the Government of India had reservation on selection of this process as there was very limited experience. Further partial oxidation process for Ammonia was used in India till that time. They also had reservation on the single stream concept.

During that period in India the Fertilizer plants were installing minimum two stream plants as, if one stream, for any reason, has to be shut down, the plant could still produce at 50% capacity. At that time Gujarat Refinery was also building three streams refinery with each stream of 1 million tons/year. The fertilizer factory at Nangal was also built on three streams with each stream Ammonia capacity of 100MT./day. As against this, GSFC was planning to build a single stream Ammonia plant with capacity of 450 MT/day. Selection of single stream ICI (Imperial Chemical Industry) steam reforming process for Ammonia was therefore a decision involving high risk.. If plant would not have worked well it would have meant substantial losses and perhaps the chance of Company becoming sick as most of the equipment would have become redundant. One of the main reasons for adopting multi stream plants in earlier projects was weak maintenance due to lack of knowledge of machinery and also lack of operating experience. Multi stream plants increased capital cost of the plants.

Adoption of single stream plant was not only an innovation, but at the same time adopting ICI steam reforming process was a big risk requiring strong will of an owner company and a big challenge to the management to operate it successfully. It would have been suicidal for the company if these decisions do not turn out to be successful, Before taking such a risk, innovative management practices had to be evolved not only on technical aspects and contractual conditions but also in all spheres of management and administration as detailed under "Innovation in Management Practices" The single stream means if any problem any where in the plant occurs, the entire plant will have to be shut down and production will come to zero. After due explanations, the Government of India, after considering that capital cost, power consumption and operating costs were substantially lower than those of the conventional partial oxidation plants, accepted the new concept.

For the phosphatic fertilizers (N&P) company decided to adopt Diammonium Phosphate (DAP) plus Ammonium sulfate (AS) or ammonium sulfate phosphate as products and not Nitro Phosphate. DAP again was selected as phophatic fertilizer product for the first time in the country. This was a marketing risk as farmers had no knowledge of this fertilizer.

The following companies were selected for supply of know how, plant machinery, erection and commissioning on turn key basis and letters of intent were issued to them and contracts were signed with them.

Ammonia Urea Plants – M/s. Toyo Engineering Corporation, Japan
DAP plus AS. (ASP Plant) - M/s. Hitachi Limited, Japan.
Sulfuric Acid and Phosphoric Acid Plants – M/s. Hitachi Shipbuilding and Engineering Company Ltd. Japan
Utilities – M/s. Hitachi Limited, Japan.

The Government of India approved the contracts and also made available yen credit, for payment in foreign currency for which necessary formalities were completed by the company (in April 1965). For Sulfuric Acid and Phosphoric Acid plant M/s. Hitachi Ship-building & Engineering Company Ltd. had offered deferred credit however Yen credit was selected, which was also approved by the Government of India. Deferred credit was not selected as it would have required providing bank guarantee for the full amount which was not possible at that time.

There were certain features of the plants which were unique at that time. For example ICI steam reforming process was for the first time adopted in India and subsequently all Ammonia plants (numbering 30) operating on Naphtha or Gas as feedstock adopted the same process. Thus GSFC provided lead to the country for adopting most modern and economical process. DAP again was being produced for the first time in the country and most of the subsequent phosphatic fertilizer plants adopted DAP or ASP as product. Ammonium Sulfate was produced from byproduct Gypsum as the main raw material. This was the first plant based on byproduct gypsum in the country, and probably in the world. Earlier FACT had a small ammonium Sulfate plant which was based on natural Gypsum. As FACT had problems in this plant they had asked GSFC to provide consultancy to improve the Ammonium Sulfate plant operation which was carried out successfully by GSFC.

A new technique for Water supply

One non process special feature of the complex was the scheme for drawing water from the river. Company had made experiments with drilling bore wells. However the quantity and quality of water was not adequate. Company needed 9 Million Gallons of water per day. At the same time Gujarat Refinery was also looking for scheme for bringing water from Mahi River. We had made an agreement for a joint water supply scheme with Gujarat Refinery. Unfortunately there was no perennial flow of water in the river throughout the year. A French company Celanese had developed a process of digging a well in the river to bring water from the underground as it was considered that there was always an underground parallel river with constant flow below the bed level of the river. They had set up a number of wells on this basis in France, but perhaps this was for the first time being done in India. The GSFC Refinery joint water supply scheme gave contract to agent of M/s. Celanese. The scheme is as follows.

A well about 25 Ft in diameter is dug in the river to the depth 10 ft. bellow the underground level of the water flow. The well is extended from underground to a height above ground up to which flood water can rise so as to prevent flood water entering the well and damage the pumps which are installed in side the well at underground water level. Few feet above the bottom of the underground water level, the radial pipes with special nozzles are introduced in horizontal direction all round outside the well in the river bed. The special nozzles are so designed to keep laminar water flow so that only water can enter inside the pipe but not the sand. The number of pipes and diameter of the pipe is designed to ensure very low velocity of water so that it doesn't drag sand with it.

The water through the radial pipes enters the well. The pumps with appropriate capacity are installed inside the well so that they can pump out the water from the well to the company boundary, in our case to the boundary of the fertilizer factory as well as refinery. In this manner each well would give 10 millions gallons of water per day. Water would be good potable and bacteria free. As the river was only about 30 kilometer from the sea, during high tide hydraulic pressure exerted by the sea water would contaminate the underground water during the severe draught condition. We had experienced this several times during the years 1972 -74 when quality of water from the well had deteriorated. To solve this problem we had started building temporary check dam, costing about Rs.0.5. million located downstream of all wells. This will ensure some surface water on the river bed. This would counter exert hydraulic pressure so that during high tide there will not be any deterioration of water quality. This worked very well for many years. One year there was such a high flood that water entered the wells and damaged the pump motors. This caused shut down of plants for 4 days till the motors were repaired.

Barring this incident good water is available from this since last 41 years. With the expansion of the company the additional requirement of water was also met with similar scheme by establishing additional wells in the river.

Horton sphere fire

The erection and commissioning progressed smoothly and there were no major problems except the fire on the Horton Sphere (Ammonia Storage tank) while it was being insulated. Just about when insulation was being completed, probably spark from welding machine ignited insulation which caused a big fire as insulation was polystyrene foam which ignites very quickly. As the steel of Horton Sphere was special quality to withstand low temperature. It was not advisable to extinguish fire by water and we had to allow the fire to extinguish on its own when all the insulation had burnt out. There was a fear that Micro structure of the steel might have been affected. These were investigated by both Japanese as well as by the company through department of Atomic Energy and M.S. University. Fortunately it was found that there was no damage to micro structure of the steel and the Horton Sphere could be used after insulating it again. There was no delay in commissioning on this account. The production and marketing of fertilizer started in August 1967. Horton Sphere provided satisfactory service for about 20 years, when it was replaced by a larger storage tank as demand for Ammonia storage had increased considerably.

Erratic Electricity supply

After commissioning of the plants, Ammonia plant was working relatively smoothly, however there was problem on account of quality of electricity supply in terms of voltage and frequency, as a result large synchronous motors with capacity up to 6 M.W. were tripping and the whole plant would shut down. In some months there could be as many as 10 shut downs on this account. Apparently Gujarat Electricity Board (GEB) had no previous experience for supply of quality electricity supply for such motors. Power was supplied at 66KV and GEB considered that at such high voltage no disturbance from other consumers would affect voltage and/or frequency at GSFC. As neither GSFC nor GEB could find the cause for such tripping of motors, after lots of discussions and hot arguments, it was decided to appoint Indian Institute of Science, Bangalore as consultants to recommend remedial measures. Both parties agreed to accept the recommendations which may be made and to bear the cost of changes required in each of their respective facilities. The report of the Institute recommended changes in relays at GEB as well as at GSFC and upgrading the electricity supply voltage to 132 KV. After this quality of electricity supply was good for continuous operation of the motors.

Synthesis Gas Compressor Fire

During initial operations synthesis gas compressor suddenly caught fire. The flames went up to the ceiling of the compressor house. Operation was immediately stopped. On checking it was found that piston rod had broken, damaging the metallic packing which had gone through the end cover. Gas emitting from the suction pipe also caught fire, fortunately no one was injured. It was the responsibility of the contractor to replace damaged parts and repair the compressor. Since contractor did not have the spares, GSFC provided the same, as it had ordered the spares along with plant and equipment, and the compressor was repaired and restarted.

How GSFC accomplished fastest completion of its fertilizer complex

As there are many parties working together to complete a project, there are bound to be disagreements and conflicts. Mary Parker Follett in her book "Dynamic Administration" (1941) says "I do not think we have psychological, ethical and economic problems. We have human problems, with psychological, ethical and economical aspects and as many others as you like". Follett advocates giving greater responsibility to people. "Responsibility is the great developer of men." There is also a modern ring to Follett's advice on leadership. "The most successful leader of all is the one who sees another picture not yet actualized." Follett suggests that "a leader is someone who sees the whole rather than the particular, organizes the experiences of the group, offers a vision of the future and trains followers to become leaders."

Underpinning all of her work is the importance of relationships, not just transactions, in organizations. She pointed to the reciprocal nature of relationships, the mutual influence developed when people work together. She specially explores conflict. She argues that as conflict is a fact of life 'we should use it to work for us' Follett points out three ways of dealing with confrontations: namely (1`) domination, (2) compromise, or (3) integration. The last requires in-depth understanding. She concludes integration is the only positive way forward. This can be achieved by first 'uncovering' the real conflict and then taking the demands of both sides and breaking them up into their constituent parts. The Company had adopted this approach with contractors and suppliers throughout the project management period. According to her our chances of business success largely diminishes when our thinking is constrained within the limits what has been called an either-or situation. This therefore should be avoided.

It will be seen from the following paragraphs that the project was viewed upon as a whole and not in parts and that conflict was not allowed to be developed and the problems solved in an integrated manner while maintaining relationships. By following Follett's theory in a meaningful manner, GSFC could accomplish fastest completion of the project.

It would be worthwhile to know first the conditions prevailing at that time. There were no telex, or fax. To make long-distance call from Vadodara to Mumbai it would take 3-4 hours. Engineering standards were old ones, for example. Boiler code still specified Riveted construction where as all boilers abroad were fabricated by welding. It was very difficult to get approval of welded boilers from inspector. For civil works, such as digging, foundations and concreting only human power was used. There were manual concrete mixers and concrete was poured by bringing it in the buckets by human beings, transport of material within site was by donkeys. There were no trucks and no cranes/derricks.

In the words of Mr. Kanagawa who was project engineer of Toyo Engineering "We could never say that we could not construct without crane, we could not say that we could not bring things because we did not have a truck, but we had to use our intelligence, think about the Indian conditions and somehow find a way out ." Under these conditions it was time consuming to do construction and project work. It is amazing that such complex project was completed in 25 months considering the limited availability of infrastructure at that time.

As indicated in "Innovation in the management practices" GSFC had determined the organization not only for the project but also for personnel as well as finance so as to complete the plant in shortest possible period. Some details as to how this was achieved are given below.

At first GSFC coined a special motto "Faith, discipline, hard work and success" and drilled the slogan in the minds of all to follow it regularly. Sign boards were placed all over the site to remind every one of this.

Delays caused in earlier projects by other companies were mainly due to lack of coordination between contractors, detailed engineering company, the consultants and the owner and rigid attitudes of all. Further foreign consultants had their own views. This resulted in delay in taking decisions: all these added to delays. Therefore earlier projects needed special staff in project division. First decision was therefore to exercise control on the project by the Company and all decisions also to be taken by the Company. It was decided to recruit people only for the requirement of the operations for the plants who could also be used for project execution. This required innovative way of contracting so that expertise in every discipline is not required. Each contractor was given complete responsibility for civil works till completion including mechanical, electrical and instrumentation. Several teams were formed from the available persons for supervision of the contractors. Each team was given specified and specific responsibilities for the planning, execution and all aspects of the project.

Project was divided into three groups. 1) Ammonia Urea plants 2) Phosphatic group of plants and 3) Electrical and utilities plants. Each group had a Japanese contractor. There were three Indian contractors 1) for cooling towers 2) For water treatment plant and 3) for inter connecting pipe lines between each group of above plants. Separate groups were also formed for 1) Import license - clearance of goods to be imported 2) Indigenous procurement including expediting of the deliveries 3) Progressing of work of all including Indian contractors 4) execution work of sub station, utilities, township, workshop etc and 5) arrangement of supply of raw materials.

Following special conditions were incorporated in the contracts with the foreign parties namely 1) Provision for cancellation of contract, 2) demonstrate Production performance for first 4 months in addition to normal seven day guarantee test runs. 3) Guaranteed completion period and 4) fixed price contract in Rupees with respect to all works in India including civil works, material supplies & erection.

PERT was mainly used as reporting technique, where as the actual decisions on how to solve the bottle necks were taken by the management. Since there were Government controls on supply of cement and steel, in the beginning these techniques were used for progressing, allocation and the requirement of cement and steel. The requirement of cement and steel was collected from all the contractors and on the basis of desired progress of work, the requirement of cement and steel as a function of time were determined. Data such as quota of cement and steel applied for, released and the quantity received were noted. These requirements were reviewed and forecast revised.

Similarly data were collected on fabrication of equipment, shipping, erection, testing etc from each contractor and were put on a PERT form of net work. A master control net work for the entire project was prepared. This not only included activities which were to be performed by GSFC or its contractors but also by other agencies such as Gujarat Electricity Board, Railways etc., so that overall progress of the entire project is kept in view. This information from the chart is first used by each team to monitor the progress and discussed with other concerned teams and when necessary it is also reviewed by the Managing Director and if required by the board of directors. As Managing Director was very dynamic, practically all controversial/difficult decisions were taken by him to ensure quick solution of the problems as they were encountered.

The PERT information gave opportunities to engineers to discuss with their counterparts of the contractors and sub contractors. These discussions revealed a number of difficulties which contractors were facing and which may give rise to delay in progress. Such difficulties were immediately reported to the top management and invariably GSFC management gave helping hand to the contractors in their difficulties. Some points in which help was given, were 1) arrangement for special wagons for over dimensional cargo, 2) obtaining special permits from railways and other government authorities 3) Speedy clearance of imported materials 4) Help in obtaining derricks for heavy erection job 5) Using good offices to persuade sub contractors to do the job speedily and economically for the contractors 6) Maintaining list of mischievous laborers and seeing that contractors did not employ them at site 7) Helping in labor trouble etc.

In spite of all above a number of difficulties and pitfalls were encountered in the execution of the project. Where these were related to items, such as township, administration building, workshop etc, not connected with the operations of the plant, were not rigorously followed. On the other hand those items of work which were directly related to production effort, the contractors were regularly chased up, In spite of such efforts it was found for example that urea silo was getting further delayed, management then pressed the contractor to put in service extra set of shuttering without any extra cost to bring it to the scheduled construction. This was successfully done. In case of indigenous equipment especially electrical, considerable delays were encountered partly due to non availability of copper and partly due to over booking of the vendors. This was resolved by constant personal persuasion by senior officers with the higher officials of the sub contractors/vendors and by utilizing social pressures. In some cases we had to help main contractors by importing equipment on their behalf. The company also helped the contractors by chasing sub contractors to see that they delivered goods in time.

We had also devised special technique of "stage wise" completion time schedule and "stage wise" penalty clause for the civil works contractors. For this purpose contractors had to give detailed schedule divided into identifiable stages and give the time schedule for completion of each stage. Any delay in any stage would call for penalty and would be discussed and bring it to the required completion date. Our interest was not collection of penalty but to ensure that delays are absolutely minimized. For our future projects similar technique was developed for fabrication, manufacture and erection of equipment and piping.

Another method called "target setting" was also used to speed up the work. Especially where 1) it was desired to complete the job earlier than the scheduled time. For example it was found that it should be possible to complete Ammonia Urea plant by January 1967 instead of target date of June 1967. On the other hand in the period July- October, 1966 it was found that progress was not picking up. Therefore a target completion date of 25th January, 1967, eve of the republic day, was announced and each one was motivated to complete the job by that date. This way the ammonia urea plants were completed on January 25, 1967 instead of June, 1967. This target setting technique was also utilized to recoup the time on the works which were already delayed. For this purpose some functions were organized before which identified activities were to be completed. Such motivations always worked.

Fertilizer Marketing

Till 1966 Government of India was controlling price and marketing of nitrogenous fertilizers which was heavily regulated. In 1966 Government of India adopted liberalized policy allowing free pricing and marketing of nitrogenous fertilizers for a period of 7 years from the date the plant went in production. The phosphatic fertilizer was till then completely free for pricing as well as marketing. Nitrogenous fertilizers were controlled through the "Central fertilizer pool" which set price and allocated both imported and indigenous fertilizers to several states. All state governments could set their own distribution procedure. Gujarat practiced fertilizer distribution through cooperative societies on exclusive basis.

Government of India had appointed a committee on fertilizers in 1965 under the chairmanship of Mr. Sivaraman. The report of the committee, called Sivaraman Committee report, had expressed considerable doubts whether cooperatives were organizationally, financially, and temperamentally adequate for the task of marketing higher quantum of contemplated fertilizer output through aggressive salesmanship, which would develop demand, not merely satisfy existing demand. It was therefore widely held that greater reliance was needed on business minded marketers – either manufactures net work of depots or through private distributors.

GSFC in its prospectus for the public issue during 1966 had stated "under the pricing and distribution policy of Nitrogenous fertilizers recently announced by the Government of India, Ministry of Petroleum and Chemicals (Department of Chemicals), the company will be free to price its products and to arrange its own distribution for a period of 7 years from the date of commencement of commercial production, subject to the conditions that it shall sell to the government at latter's option up to 30% of the products at a price to be settled between it and the government".

Considering above, GSFC was interested in the distribution of fertilizers by itself whereas Gujarat state cooperative marketing federation (GSCMF) wanted to exclusively market GSFC fertilizers. GSCMF was dominated by political leaders. Gujarat Government as well as political leaders, especially agriculture minister Thakorbhai Desai wanted the same. There was therefore a divergence of views between GSCMF and the company. Government of Gujarat did not issue any formal directions though official directors conveyed concern for the marketing arrangement to be employed by the GSFC. Lot of pressure from politicians and GSCMF were brought on the company to entrust 100% marketing of products to GSCMF. Fortunately for GSFC Swatantra party made a strong showing in 1967 election. Mr. H.M Patel and Mr. R.B Amin directors of the company wanted free marketing, whereas other directors were inclined towards the cooperatives. There were lots of discussions between GSFC and GSCMF and finally consensus evolved. GSFC agreed to market fertilizes through GSCMF and simultaneously open its own depots with emphasis on supplementary character of the depot rather than competitive character.

GSFC opened 29 depots in 2nd year, marketing small quantities through depots and most through GSCMF. GSFC was the first fertilizer company in the country to have its own depots called Farm Information Centre (FIC) for marketing of fertilizers.

As production increased, Shri H. M. Patel, our director suggested that GSFC fertilizers should have brand name. He suggested "SARDAR", (after the name of Sardar Vallabhbhai Patel, Iron man of India, and first Deputy Prime Minister of India) as brand name for all GSFC fertilizers. Brand was registered and henceforth all GSFC fertilizers were sold under SARDAR brand. When the production outstripped demand in Gujarat, GSFC started marketing its fertilizers outside Gujarat after meeting requirement of Gujarat. It marketed fertilizers outside Gujarat through Rallis India Ltd and through Cooperatives in other states. At one time the company had opened maximum of 200 FIC in Gujarat. It had also opened 15 FIC in Haryana, U.P. and Rajasthan. GSCMF would make agreement for quantum of fertilizers to be marketed by it during rabi and khariff seasons. As cooperatives were efficient in distribution of fertilizers, most of the GSFC fertilizers in Gujarat were sold by it. GSCMF was getting 10% commission which included cost of storage, freight and distribution.

Each FIC was manned by agricultural science graduates. As brought out (in Para "customer is the king") they were providing various services such as technical advice, soil testing, farm management, water management, selection of fertilizers and selection of seeds and pesticides: also supplied all these inputs to the farmers and carried out demonstrations in farmers fields to demonstrate efficacy and method of application of company's fertilizers.

The company prepared a report, at the request of the State Government, for the optimum use of water from Kadana Dam so that all farmers around Kadana dam can obtain maximum advantage of the water when the dam is built. The company along with State Government sponsored Kadana Development Association to undertake all agricultural related activities around Kadana Dam area. The company established "leap forward project" to improve the standard of living of Adivasis. This program was carried out in Chhota udepur, (Baroda District) and Santrampur and Lunawada of Panchmahal district. Action program for optimum use of water and fertilizers was carried out in Banaskantha and Gandhinagar districts.

The company had developed process of bio fertilizers and started production and marketing of the same with technical advice on method and use of bio fertilizers and selection of each bio fertilizer for different crops.

Government of India imposed 10% excise duty on fertilizers. There was considerable talk of withdrawing or reducing it as a result the marketing of the fertilizers nearly stopped. Cooperatives/ Dealers therefore held back orders pending clarification from the Government. To ensure smooth marketing and distribution of fertilizers so that farmers can get fertilizers when they needed, GSFC advised its dealers and cooperatives to place orders as usual, with company assurance that if the excise duty was eliminated / reduced a proportionate rebate will be given. For similar reasons, during shortage of closed railway wagons, the company would dispatch fertilizers in open wagons along with its security staff so that fertilizer reached safely to the destinations and in time.

Marketing of Urea was no problem, as first of all farmers were familiar with it to some extent; it was cheaper and gave very good and quick results in increasing production. Farmers had experienced that urea increases crop production. On the other hand, Diammonium Phosphate (DAP) was the product being introduced for the first time in the country and farmers had no knowledge of its usefulness as they were using Single Superphosphate (SSP) since many years. DAP was more expensive than SSP. GSFC had seed-marketed imported DAP for some years and had educated the farmers. Even then it was very difficult to convince farmers to use DAP as price of DAP was three times the price of SSP.

GSFC therefore had kept DAP price lower than what it should be as per the cost of production. And besides educating farmers, the company had carried out promotion through advertisements and demonstrations in farmer's fields and distribution of technical literature. The DAP become popular in 3 years' time as 90% of its production could be marketed in Gujarat by then. The company increased price of DAP in 1971 specially in view of increasing price of raw materials and also to bring it in line with the cost of production. This created lot of controversies perhaps due to timing of its increase as it was just before the start of the season for the fertilizer consumption. GSFC Chairman in his annual speech had explained, in details, the reasons for increasing the price of DAP.

Subsidy

Government of India was levying charges on fertilizers which were credited to the Central Fertilizer Pool which in turn was used to subsidize imported fertilizers till 1974. This indicates that indigenous fertilizers were cheaper than imported ones till 1974. After the 1st oil crises which increased crude oil price substantially in November, 1973, there was large increase in price of hydrocarbons and related products. These necessitated increasing the price of fertilizers. As input prices were increasing, the Government of India appointed a Committee under the Chairmanship of Mr. S.S Marathe to introduce a rational system of pricing of fertilizers with a view to ensuring a reasonable return on investments and facilitate the healthy development and growth of the fertilizer and agricultural sectors. In May 1977 the committee submitted the 1st part of its report covering nitrogenous fertilizers. On the basis of the recommendations made in the report, the Government of India introduced a system of retention price for individual units in the nitrogenous fertilizer sector with effect from 1st November, 1977.

The retention price, at that time, was based on capacity utilization of 80% and combination of normative and actual cost in regard to consumption, maintenance, marketing and other costs, and post tax return of 12% on net worth. As a result of introduction of retention price system (RPS) if the retention price allowed to a particular unit was lower than the uniform ex-factory price fixed by the government, the manufacturer was required to deposit the difference with the Government of India. On the other hand when retention price was higher than the ex-works price fixed by the government, the government would pay the difference to the fertilizer manufacturer. The Government of India introduced RPS for phosphatic fertilizers on 1st February, 1979. RPS is effective for a period of 3 years and it is reviewed every 3 years to fix revised prices considering the prevailing costs. However in practice review never happened in time.

Practically all fertilizer manufacturers found that RPS did not provide 12% post tax return as envisaged in the scheme, perhaps mainly due to non allowance of various legitimate expenses. The Government of India appointed a fertilizer industry coordination committee (FICC) consisting of 7 members, two of whom were selected by the Government from the fertilizer industry, to go into the various points raised by the fertilizer industry and to fix the retention price for individual units. Even though Government of India is modifying the scheme from time to time with a view to reduce subsidy, it has neither succeeded in reducing subsidy nor satisfying fertilizer industry, economists or politicians.

When one analysis the impact of RPS over a period of time, one finds that productivity of crops and fertility of soil have gone down considerably from 15 kg food grain/kg nitrogen in 1970, to 10 kg average during the decade of 1980-1990 and further down to 6.6kg average during the decade of 1990-2000. This is mainly due to unbalanced use of fertilizers, neglect of major nutrient "Sulfur" and micronutrients and neglect of extension services by State Governments. This had happened mainly because of lopsided pricing policy of the Government of India. It made Urea relatively much cheaper than phoshphatic and complex fertilizers and completely neglected SSP which supplied two nutrients namely P and S.

This resulted in two bad consequences (1) the farmer had to use more fertilizers, to compensate for reduction in fertility of soil, increasing his cost of production of food grain and (2) increasing the subsidy bill for the Government which is expected to increase to Rs. 110 billion in 2008-9 from Rs. 85.2 billion in 2003-4. These facts are very well known to the Government, but they are busy in thinking about how to reduce subsidy on Urea, rather than thinking about how to increase soil and crop productivity, which will indirectly reduce fertilizer subsidy. For the same quantum of food grain production, farmer has to use now nearly 2.25 kg Nitrogen instead of 1 kg nitrogen which he was using in 1970. Farm productivity can be easily increased by the following steps.

(1) Insisting on State Governments and fertilizer industry to provide efficient extension services on the basis of the results of soil testing laboratories established with in 50 KM distance of any farmer and make recommendations following Site Specific Nutrient Management

(SSNM) system (2) Encouraging use of materials/fertilizers containing "S" such as SSP, Ammonium Sulfate, gypsum, pyrites to reduce sulfur deficiency and zinc sulfate to reduce both sulfur and zinc deficiency. Nearly 50% of the soils are deficient in both these (3) Promoting production of SSP rather than DAP (4) promotion of essential (at present mainly zinc, Sulfur and Boron) micronutrients (5) promotion of Bio fertilizers and (6) promotion of potassium chloride. To do this efficiently rigorous soil testing of all farm lands and appropriate recommendations of fertilizers and other inputs using SSNM system is required.

I had prepared an 'Action Plan' to increase food grain production to 358 million metric tons by 2016 from 216 million metric tons in 2005-6 utilizing technique and fertilizers as stated above and without any additional use of Urea and DAP. This 'Action Plan' was sent to the Ministries of Fertilizers and Agriculture and some prominent persons. The new policy announced in June 2008 has accepted some of the suggestions, but most important, that of establishing proper and sufficient number of soil testing laboratories and providing full extension services is not forcefully advocated. There are sufficient scientific data available to show that in the above manner soil productivity can be increased. The rate at which soil productivity can be increased will depend upon firmness with which both Government of India and State Governments and fertilizer industry take the above steps.

Farmers of Gujarat, knowing that Government is not likely to tackle their problems, they (even small farmers) have started engaging consultants to advise them on improving productivity of soils and thereby increasing production in their farms. This is really the role of the State Governments and fertilizer industry, which is being neglected, forcing farmers to engage consultants. Some farmers have already become consultants in addition to doing their own farming. Ammonium Sulfate fertilizer is decontrolled but farmers are willingly paying Rs. 30/kg N for this fertilizer as against the controlled price of Urea which is only Rs. 10/kg N. A farmer would not pay such high price unless he finds that it is profitable to do so. This action of farmers indicates that State Governments should improve and increase their agricultural extension services to educate them on balanced use of fertilizers and need to remove micronutrient deficiency by providing micro nutrients to the soil.

Actual Project Financial management

The project was completed and production operations commenced in July 1967.The estimated project cost was Rs.410 million (July 1967 completion) with means of finance as Rs.120 million equity, Rs.220 million term loans from financial institutions (including Rs. 40 million additional cost of imported equipment due to devaluation of rupee) Rs. 50 million loan from Government of Gujarat and about Rs. 20 million from internal generation. The table 2 indicates how the funds were raised, expenditure incurred and loans received (both secured and unsecured) from year to year along with corresponding value of creation of fixed assets.

Table 2

Rs. milion

At the year end	Equity	Loans	Total finance	Expen diture	Cash & Bank Balance	Gross fixed assets
1962-63	5.045	-	5.045	1.51	3.49	0.061
1963-64	20.045	-	20.045	4.668	15.377	3.357
1964-65	41.950	-	41.950	13.725	28.225	8.060
1965-66	66.052	38.541	104.593	89.646	14.946	71.944
1966-67	85.120	240.635	325.755	308.234	17.521	299.048
1967-68	119.226	315.952	435.178	419.764	15.414	371.218

Source of Data: GSFC annual reports and balance sheets

From the above it will be seen that the company did not borrow any money till 1965 (October) and started borrowing in small measure only in 1965-66 and bulk of the funds in the two subsequent years 1966-68 and completed the project as originally envisaged with production commencing from July 1967.The interest cost for the entire project was Rs 19.7 million which was less than 5% of the project cost. This was considered most economical by any standard especially when the charging rate of interest for long term loans was 12%. The company expended Rs. 419.7 million as on 31st. March 1968, and created fixed assets worth Rs 371.2 million and along with current assets and other items the project. completion cost was within the project estimate of Rs. 414.2 million as of July 1967, inclusive of providing for Rupee devaluation impact of aboutRs.44.2 million.

GSFC was perhaps one of the few public limited companies which had been able to maintain the progress of work and complete it without taking recourse to additional funds for overrun or similar purposes. In fact during that period there had been substantial increases in the prices of various materials and as a consequence most of the companies executing large projects had to seek additional funds, beyond what was originally contemplated. The monthly review of ways and means position, effective and appropriate controls on the progress of the project, strict budgetary control and judicious deployment of funds were the prime factors for completing the project as envisaged in terms of cost, time-frame and more important, of producing and marketing of products-much needed fertilizers to the farmers. These innovative and vigilant approaches made it possible for the company to earn cash profit even in the first year of operation (8.5 months) and further pay dividend in the third year of operations. This unique performance of GSFC was greatly appreciated by the national press for creating new land marks particularly in the fertilizer industry.

The first year's performance - Brick bats and Bouquets

In the first year 1967-1968 (8.5 months) GSFC had produced 117,500 M.T of fertilizers and made cash profit of Rs.15.7 Million. After providing full depreciation of Rs. 31.9 million it made a loss of Rs.16.2 million. This news was given next day in all local news papers in front page headlines condemning performance- loss of Rs 16.2 millions- and throwing brick bats at GSFC. It became a talk of the town, every body interpreting giving reasons for such loss. Even my mother scolded me and told me that all employees should not take any salary till company makes profit. She thought Rs.16.2 million was such a large sum that it will be difficult for the Company to recover. This was the general public feeling especially in small towns and amongst most people in Gujarat.

On the other hand the national press eulogized the performance of the company. The daily news paper Financial Express stated under title "A miracle" in the editorial of 19th April, 1968 as follows.

"The Gujarat Fertilizers company deserves bouquets for achieving the miracle of bringing one of the largest fertilizers complexes in Asia to fruition in a short time and ending the shortage of chemical fertilizers in the state. It is indeed a miracle that this project could be completed in less than 25 months from the date on which the contract became effective and only 900 workers, mostly locally recruited and trained could produce in a short period 8 month and ½ nearly 1.17,000 M.T. of fertilizers in addition to various chemicals. The total sales during this period have been of the order of Rs.100 million and have saved the country about half the foreign exchange it has spent on its creation. The company's expansion program and caprolactam program do not visualize any foreign collaboration and it is refreshing to know that after the expansion is achieved the company will have an annual turnover of Rs.1700 million as a result of labors of some 1700 operators".

"Judged by past experience, the future is assured. To that extent the experiment of establishment of this company in the joint sector is fully justified. In a country where such a high breed project pattern has potential of creating complication in organizational matters, it is heartening to note that speedy decision and decentralization which are features of private sector have been combined with code of conduct, procedures, and controls and institutional and government audit associated with the public sector. Could it be that the homogeneous board of management having a majority of top private industrialists working hand in hand with government officials can produce better results then one or the other sector exclusive?"

A letter written to the Indian Express on 9th May, 1968 under the title "Public Sector" reads as follows.

Those who have been criticizing the public sector over the years should not feel happy now when reports of the Parliamentary Committee on Public Undertaking fully document the charge of inefficiency and gross mismanagement of national funds. The question before the country today is; having put a lot of money – estimated at around Rs.30000 million – in these undertakings, how can country get a decent return of at least 10% on them? Unfortunately, the public sector seems to have become a society for rehabilitation of the politically crippled, and nest of power and patronage for politicians and government officers. Both should be compelled to release their grip over the public sector, before it can be made efficient and productive."

"The central government can borrow a leaf from the Gujarat Government's Book. The Gujarat State Fertilizer Corporation is a happy example of a truly public sector. The government own 49% shares, and has nominees on board of the company, but reportedly they do not interfere with the affairs of the company. 51% of the shares are held by public (cultivators in this case, as also institutions). The chairman is an experienced industrialist from the private sector. The corporation is autonomous in its working. Results: an enterprise which combines public policy plus profits, and yields handsome dividend to the state government."

"The best course, for the Central Government, is to throw open 51% shares of all its enterprises to the public for subscription, and persuade successful industrialists to manage these companies on 25 year lease, on commission basis."

The monthly magazine chemical engineering world in their first issue of 1968 on the publisher's page wrote as follows:

"The first issue of chemical engineering world in 1968 starts with a searching look at India's biggest fertilizers complex - GSFC. The Gujarat State fertilizer company limited has some rare distinctions to its credit. The GSFC fertilizer complex went on stream before the schedule and at the savings of millions of Rupees. These are unique achievements. In India where all other big fertilizers complexes till now have been invariably delayed and their budgets are always to be stretched out considerably, the achievement of GSFC gains special significance."

"The purpose of this special issue is to examine how these magnificent achievements were forged into reality and what lessons could be learnt from the GSFC story. If there are any lessons to be learnt – and there are definitely many – it is important that they are revealed. We felt, it we could describe and show, how, why and under what circumstances certain decisions were taken, what were the consequences etc. It would be more revealing and educative then just to glorify the achievements."

b. Phase II Ammonia Urea Plant

Mr. Srivatsa Managing Director was very keen that the company should generate high profit. He had estimated that with the likely selling price of Urea it would make good profit. However it would be difficult to make profit on DAP, as it would be a slow process to market full quantities of DAP as its price would be more than 3 times the price of SSP which was phosphatic fertilizer used by the farmers for many years (SSP in the country was introduced as early as 1903 and the first SSP Plant in Gujarat was established in 1938). He was therefore thinking that if Ammonia Urea Plant can be expanded, the profitability of the company can be increased. He therefore called me and we had detailed discussions on the feasibility of setting up another Ammonia Urea plant at the same site. This was also an opportune time as Government of India had rejected proposal of Bechtel to set up a series of 10 fertilizer plants. On the other hand GSFC did not have funds and it was not known from where the required funds would come. It was therefore risky even to think about expansion.

My colleague Mr. B. K. Shridhar had made a wonderful layout for the entire complex visualizing future expansions in fertilizer and petrochemical fields and also considering the requirement of the treatment of pollution from the plants. The lay out visualized the expansion of fertilizer facilities as well as diversification into petrochemicals. The utility facilities such as power, steam, water, (These were in a separate bloc centrally located to extend utilities to all future plants), railway sidings, bagging plants and roads were so arranged that the extension of each could be achieved and facilitate easy movement of raw materials and finished products even in future. In fact, the thinking had gone far beyond and layout of individual plant was so arranged that not only each plant could be expanded but standby equipment of one plant could be utilized for expansion plants and thereby providing the scope in reduction in the cost of expansion. Similarly raw material storage area was far away with ample provision of storage of new raw materials.

Company decided in 1967 to start a new department, called Development and Research, whose main functions would be to conceptualize, plan and implement expansion as well as diversification projects, in addition to undertake developmental research for indigenous development (import substitution), process and product development. I was made in charge of the new department in addition to my existing duties.

Selection of the Technology

At about the same time technology for manufacture of centrifugal compressor was coming into advance stage. M/S M.W. Kellog had put forward an idea of combining, utilization of centrifugal compressor for synthesis gas compression with low or medium pressure synthesis process for the production of Ammonia. This combination promised further reduction in power and fuel requirement and also the reduction in capital cost.

The smallest size of centrifugal compressor is determined by the maximum allowable tip speed which was about 1000 feet/second. With the above limitation it was found that a minimum capacity of 600 Metric Tons/day Ammonia plant is required to use these compressors. Though these are 10% cheaper in capital cost, their efficiency was at that time 10% lower for 600MT/day plant and 5% lower for 1000MT/day plant. Other disadvantage was that minimum capacity of the plant at which it can be operated safely was 80–85% of the installed capacity. With the technological developments in India those days, it was felt that a spare installed centrifugal compressor or at least spare rotor was necessary to assure adequate stream factor. Considering these and several other aspects – such as failure of this technology, initially caused such losses in U.S.A. that insurance companies stopped insuring this technology for 2-3 years till Kellog could improve upon this technology. Further limitation was that at that time maximum capacity single stream urea plant was 800 Metric tons/day. It was therefore considered too risky and uneconomical to adopt centrifugal compressor technology at that time.

The Company therefore decided to maintain reciprocal compressor technology and go ahead with 500 MT/day Ammonia and 800 MT/day urea plant for expansion. As additional quantity of gas was not available, Naphtha was to be used as feed stock. Initially Government of India indicated availability of process Naphtha which ICI were reluctant to use. Fortunately when plant started, straight run naphtha was available. After 7-8 years, large Ammonia plants (900-1300 MT/day capacity) did come up in India with centrifugal compressor technology. The first 900 MT/day Ammonia plant in India faced some hiccups for two-three years before working well. Subsequent 1300 MT/day plants worked well.

It was also considered essential to incorporate the latest technology as well as to utilize lay out prepared earlier as expansion Ammonia and

Urea plants were much bigger. Certain technical changes such as higher pressure reformer, vetrocoke purification without MEA scrubbers, pneumatic drying and melting at the top of the prilling tower, addition of carbon dioxide gas holder interconnecting all gas lines and important equipment between 1st phase and expansion, etc were incorporated.

Negotiations and Selection of Contractor

Company had informally found that Japanese credit will be available for this expansion and therefore tenders were invited from Japanese company with the informal approval of the Government of India. M/s. Toyo Engineering and M/s. Hitachi Shipbuilding quoted for the same. After discussions both the parties were nearly equal. It was found that M/s. Hitachi Shipbuilding was very keen on the contract. Mr. Matsuoka had come for negotiation on their behalf. Mr. Srivatsa asked me to find out whether Matsuoka would be interested in reducing price further. On one social evening when Matsuoka, Srivatsa and I were sitting together, Matsuoka showed great interest in the contract for the expansion plant. On indication by Mr. Srivatsa I asked Matsuoka whether he would be prepared to reduce the price to get the contract. He asked me how much he will have to reduce. I told him Rs.10 million. He stated that he will have to consult his head office and come back to us.

After couple of days he confirmed that M/s. Hitachi Shipbuilding would be reducing the price by Rs. 10 million and he will give the letter accordingly. On the basis of this we selected M/s. Hitachi Shipbuilding as main contractor. I have a feeling that both companies had some mutual understanding that if one is selected as main contractor other would act as a subcontractor Toyo Engineering became sub contractor for Urea plant to Hitachi Shipbuilding. In Japan there is understanding that Miti (Ministry of trade) decides the contractors when YEN credit is provided. Yen credit is Government to Government credit and requires payment of money by the company to the Government of India as per contract terms. The owner has to pay cash and he does not get credit.

> For payment in foreign currency for import of equipment and/ or technology, it is necessary to obtain Government of India approval. Government may provide foreign currency from its own source or from bilateral credit it may have negotiated with foreign countries. It is possible to obtain loans in foreign currency from International Finance Corporation, Asian Development Bank, U.S. Aid, German Banks, suppliers/buyers credits from foreign supplies or buyers, some Indian and foreign banks.

The company had no surplus funds, as available funds were already applied for completion of the first phase project. Further, there were no prospects then to have additional long term borrowings from the financial institutions and recourse to another public issue was not considered feasible. At the same time, it was considered expedient to embark upon expansion of the fertilizer plants and to meet this objective; the company approached M/s Hitachi Shipbuilding of Japan to arrange for the deferred credit to finance the expansion project. However, as per the Japanese Government's norms for the deferred credit the recipient had to arrange at least 10% down payment, which was also not possible for the company to organize. The matter was pursued with Hitachi Shipbuilding to find a way in resolving the stalemate and with their efforts loan of 10% down payment was organized from M/s Marubeni Ida of Japan. In this manner, deferred credit was finalized and expansion contract was made effective. The deferred credit was a direct credit by Hitachi Shipbuilding and Marubeni Ida to GSFC, requiring balance payment in installments spread over a period of about eight years.

Commissioning

The expansion of Ammonia Urea plant was to be commissioned in July, 1969. However there was delay in construction of steam plant as well as Ammonia plant. On the other hand Urea plant was getting completed earlier. Since we had surplus ammonia from first plant (remember, we had kept unconverted Ammonia for future Caprolactam and Acrylonitrile plants) we were interested in starting Urea plant so that we can produce more Urea as fertilizer season was approaching. We discussed this with M/s. Hitachi Shipbuilding who stated that they could handover the Urea plant after its completion, provided we give them proportionate bonus for early completion of Urea plant. They of course will be prepared to pay penalty for late completion of Ammonia plant.

It became necessary to split the contract into two, one for Ammonia and second for Urea. We calculated that company will gain substantially by this due to additional production of Urea giving additional profit even after payment of bonus for earlier completion of urea plant. Further gain would be availability of more fertilizers. Note was prepared to the Board for approval for the splitting of the contract. Board approved the same. The Urea plant was completed earlier in March, 1969 and Bonus was paid to M/s. Hitachi Ship Building. On the other hand, the ammonia plant was delayed and completed in August 1969 for which M/s. Hitachi Ship Building paid appropriate penalty.

The earlier single contract had provided for bonus / penalty clause for early / late completion. Later on, after few years, in 1973-74 (In late 1971 the board of directors had accepted audit by Controller and Auditor general (CAG) .The CAG raised the issue of paying Bonus to M/s Hitachi Shipbuilding and loosing substantial quantum of penalty by splitting the contract and stated that even the Board of Directors did not have the power to split the contract as original contract was approved by the Government of India. At that time Mr. M.D. Rajpal was the Managing Director, Mr. Rajpal and I discussed with the Auditor General and explained to him the rational of splitting the contract and the monetary advantage company got, even after considering loss of penalty. He however did not agree and stated that he would put adverse remark. This would be politically very embarrassing to GSFC. Mr. M.D. Rajpal therefore suggested to CAG that they may discuss the issue with the Chief Minister. After long discussions between the Chief Minister, CAG and Mr. Rajpal, Chief Minister stated that though CAG may be technically right, however GSFC has actually gained substantial financial advantage and more important was that farmers got more fertilizers when there was shortage and therefore he should not put an adverse remark on the report to which CAG agreed.

The commissioning of the plants was done by the Company personnel and not by the Contractor. During the commissioning of Ammonia plant, it was found that centrifugal process air compressor was not delivering the volume or the required pressure. Further it was surging at lower flow. The cost of replacement was estimated at about Rs. 10 million. After long discussions, M/s Hitachi Ship Building finally agreed to replace the compressor at their cost.

In the mean time we were able to operate the plant at 100% capacity by utilizing air from standby compressor of the first Ammonia plant. Since ammonia 1 plant was operating at lower pressure we had to use a booster compressor to bring up the pressure. This was provided as part of interconnection of plants. We also purchased an additional booster compressor as a standby. Thus interconnection of pipes between plants helped in maintaining production in new plant at 100% capacity.

Operating finance management

The company took up the expansion of the fertilizer plants even before the first phase plants had gone into operations. The pattern and systems developed for project financial management were followed with suitable modifications, in seeing that the expansion project is completed with utmost efficiency in terms of cost and time frame. The company repeated its earlier encouraging performance even in the execution of the expansion project. The agreements for expansion project were signed in July, 1967 and project was completed for economic reasons in two parts; Urea plant in March, 1969 in 20 months time and Ammonia plant in September 1969 in 26 months time. The following Table 3 gives data on the funds available, loans (secured, unsecured and deferred credit), and the gross fixed assets created with the completion of the expansion plants.

It was not possible, at the time of writing, to identify separately the year wise expenditure for the project and the operating plants.

Table 3

Rs. Million

At the Year end	Equity + Reserve	Loans	Total finance	Cash & Bank Balance	Gross fixed assets	Dividend During the year
1967-68	119.226	315.952	435.178	15.414	371.218	NIL
1968-69	119.678	426.738	596.416	8.324	534.033	NIL
1969-70	146.120	438.732	584.852	46.503	589.402	18.054

Source of Data: Annual reports and Balance sheets of GSFC.

It will be seen from the table that increase in loan is Rs. 122.8 million practically to the extent of differed credit of about Rs. 120.0 million; No additional loan was required to be taken for completion of expansion project of Rs. 230.0 million. This could be made possible by substantial internal generation of funds through operations. In the year 1969-70 the Company also declared maiden dividend.

The differed credit for expansion project was in foreign exchange (Japanese Yen). During that period Yen was a stronger currency in relation to Indian Rupee and therefore while paying the installments in foreign exchange, the company had to absorb the impact of foreign exchange variation in rupee term over the installment repayment period. This was an adverse feature of the differed credit, though this element was insignificant in relation to the total benefits accrued to the Company from the expansion plants.

⌘ ⌘ ⌘

Chapter 5
New Fertilizer Project

As there was huge supply demand gap in fertilizers, the company started consideration of further expansion of its fertilizer capacity. Government of India issued letter of intent to GSFC on 16th. April 1974 for the manufacture of annually 4,45,000 M.T. of Ammonia and 5,28,000 M.T. of Urea. There was a substantial gap (1.5 million tones of Nitrogen requiring 5 more large capacity Urea plants) between the demand and production of Fertilizers. There was indication that large quantum of residual fuel oil (RFO) would be available from Gujarat Refinery and for which Government of India was looking for an outlet. This could form a very good feed stock for manufacture of fertilizes.. The company named this as "New Fertilizer Project". (NFP)

D & R department prepared a preliminary project report which showed the estimated project cost of around Rs. 2700 million in June 1974. This was considered very high as compared to Rs.620 million spent by company for both - its first phase and second phase fertilizer plants which also included ammonium sulfate and DAP plants Total capacity was almost equivalent to the capacity of NFP. Expansion plant, which had 40% capacity of NFP, was completed with a cost of Rs. 225 million. Thus NFP was at least 5 times more expensive per annual Metric Ton of product.

When note was put up to the board of directors of GSFC for the approval of NFP, the directors felt that risk to GSFC for establishing such high cost project would be very high, if the project is established as a division of the company. In case of failure, as the cost of production would be very high, this would mean incurring high losses, and could wipe out GSFC reserves and perhaps make it sick. At that time Government had not yet formulated subsidy scheme. There are several advantages for establishing project as a division. This included availability of large quantum of loans and depreciation amount which could enable GSFC to grow by investment of these funds, and the tax shelter it will provide for years. I was personally in favour for setting it up as a division. As per our finance advisor Mr. H. B. Parikh, Chairman of Industrial Credit and Investment Corporation (ICICI) was also in favor of implementing it as division. However considering the risks, the board contemplated to set up project in a new company, which GSFC would promote along with the Government of Gujarat. GSFC can contribute 25% equity of the new company and Government of Gujarat could be requested to contribute 26% equity to make it real joint sector project. This necessitated approval of the Government of Gujarat.

Mr. L. R Dalal, who was the Chief Secretary of the Government of Gujarat and the director of the company, felt that even as a joint sector project risk was very high and he will not be able to recommend it to the Government.

During the discussions I requested the Board to look at the project from altogether different angles such as:

(1). Gujarat and the country need more fertilizers to augment availability of food grains to more than 200 million tons by the year 2000. (2) This would necessitate establishment of several such fertilizer projects. Thus the proposed project will not be the last project to be established.(3) New fertilizer projects, coming up in future, will be more expensive than the one GSFC is considering now.(4) There is no other project at present in Gujarat which would bring such large amount of funds from financial institutions. The availability of the funds would trigger further development in Gujarat.(5) The sales tax available to the Government of the Gujarat would mean larger return to the Government on its investment of equity in the new company. Thus even if the company is not profitable it will still give Government good return.

These arguments, though appealed to all other directors, they still did not appeal to Mr.. L. R Dalal. He was adamant and said he would not approve the project in Joint Sector with participation of the Government of Gujarat. His approval was absolutely essential to get yes nod from the Government of Gujarat. At that point of time Mr. Jayakrishna, Chairman of GSFC, requested the Board of Directors to let him have private discussions with Mr. L.R. Dalal. He then took aside Mr. Dalal to a different room and had discussions with him for 10-15 minutes time. After the discussions Mr. Dalal agreed to give approval to the project. Chairman did not reveal how he convinced the Chief Secretary.

My guess is that he may have used two arguments 1. Government of Gujarat takes risky decision. Look at the risky decision on GSFC, both industrialists and financial institutions were reluctant to support the decision, however GSFC people converted it into a successful decision. 2. To feed additional population in 2000, fifteen new fertilizer plants of this capacity are required to produce required additional food grain. Government of India cannot allow these plants to become sick as long as their owners/management operate and manage them efficiently. GSFC people are capable of managing the proposed new plant efficiently. Thus without this diplomatic move by the Chairman, new fertilizer project would not have fructified..

Mr. H. M. Patel suggested that word 'Narmada' should appear in the name of the new company. The name "Gujarat Narmada

Fertilizers Company Ltd". was suggested. Registrar of Companies (ROC) did not approve this name as there was a fertilizer company with this name; Mr. H.M. Patel then suggested the name as Gujarat Narmada Valley Fertilizers Company Ltd. (GNFC), which name was approved by ROC.

In mid 1975, Chairman told me that he is discussing with the Chief Minister to make me Technical director (whole time director on the board). As per Articles of Association of GSFC, only Government of Gujarat can appoint whole time director. The Government of Gujarat agreed and I was made Technical Director of the company effective from 29th December 1975.

I had suggested that as a joint venture partner, GSFC should have a right to nominate Managing Director and both Government of Gujarat and GSFC should have equal number of directors with powers to the Government of Gujarat to appoint the chairman.. Board did not agree to this, the Government Directors stated that Government may direct GSFC to nominate a particular person as Managing Director Therefore this would only be a theoretical right for GSFC. Further they did not even agree to equal number of directors, but 3 to be nominated by Government of Gujarat and 2 to be nominated by GSFC from amongst its board members only. In practice this was also not followed and I had to remind in every board meeting to nominate GSFC representatives on the board of Gujarat Narmada Valley Fertilizers Company Limited (GNFC). And further that as Whole time Director/ Managing Director (from January 1977) of GSFC, I should be on the board of GNFC. After reminding a number of times I was nominated on the board of GNFC only in November 1977, though GNFC board was constituted in May 1976. I have a feeling that Mr. Capoor, who was at that time chief Secretary, Government of Gujarat, did not want me as Director of GNFC, as he wanted it to be operated like a Government Company, rather than joint sector and independent company like GSFC. Since then only one Director is nominated by GSFC, that too Managing Director of GSFC, who is since 1983 a Government officer. In 2007 Managing Director of GSFC was not a nominee Director of GSFC on the Board of GNFC, but as an elected director of GNFC shareholders.

GSFC invited tenders for new fertilizer project for know how, basic engineering, supply of imported equipment, supervision and commissioning of 1350 MT/day of ammonia and 1600 MT/day urea plants from world renowned foreign companies in June, 1974. As project would use residual fuel oil as feed stock it was necessary to adopt partial oxidation process. Earlier fertilizer plants in India, adopting partial oxidation process, were not operating satisfactorily, it was therefore necessary to investigate technologies thoroughly before deciding on the same. The company received tenders from 5 foreign companies in November 1974.

Selection of Ammonia Technology

The company deputed the team of D.C Gami and V.A Sanghani to visit all licensors plants with a view to appraise the technology in the operating plants. The team visited plants of all the 5 bidders. This included the visit to the pilot plant of Texaco Corporation for the new process which was located at Montebello, California. This was a very high pressure – 85 kg per cm2 for gasification. Pilot plant was operating continuously and showed that plant worked smoothly over a long period without shutdown. Further Texaco people stated that the process can be operated on any Hydrocarbon feed stock as long as it can be converted to liquid. Further plant can be modified to operate on solid feed stock such as coal or wood.

After detailed discussions with various bidders, M/s. Linde of West Germany was selected as a contractor in March 1976 by the Board of Directors of GSFC with Texaco high pressure partial oxidation process. This was a risky decision, as this very high pressure process was only proven in a continuous pilot plant. The normal partial oxidation process, operating at much lower pressure, uses oxygen compressor, which had in the past created problems of fire and explosions. Further oxygen compressor also experienced a lot of maintenance problems. Alternative was to use liquid oxygen pump. M/s. Linde had perfected technology for liquid oxygen pumps requiring cryogenic operations. They had supplied small liquid oxygen pumps working at even higher pressure than 100 kg per cm^2 and very large liquid oxygen pumps, larger than required for this plant, operating at much lower pressure. However they had not supplied required capacity liquid oxygen pump necessary in terms of volume as well as pressure. However they were confident to supply liquid oxygen pump. They were therefore asked to manufacture the pump and test it, in their workshop, at the exact operating conditions, including capacity, temperature and pressure to be encountered in the plant before delivering the same. M/s. Linde agreed to the same.

The ammonia plant offered by M/s. Linde included following processes and units.

(1) Gasification and Carbon extraction section with high pressure gasification (85 kg per cm^2) utilizing RFO from Gujarat Refinery as feed stock: Texaco process
(2) Air separation unit with liquid oxygen pump operating at 100 kg cm^2: Linde process.
(3) Sulphur resistance CO shift catalyst for conversion
(4) Single stage selective rectisol wash for removal Carbon dioxide and Hydrogen sulfide.
(5) Liquid Nitrogen wash: Proprietary technology of M/S Linde.
(6) Ammonia Synthesis (Halder Topsoe technology)
(7) Sulfur Recovery (Clause plant by shell)

On the 25th anniversary of GNFC, according to the Vice President of Texaco Mr. Falsetti "this was the largest Gasifier in the world for the manufacture of fertilizer and the first- ever Texaco Gasifier to use liquid oxygen". Mr. U. Wege Managing Director of M/S Linde AG stated "Constituting a technological innovation in the fertilizer industry, this plant attracted world wide notice".

Agreements with above parties were signed by GSFC between 18th and 25th March 1976. KFW (A German Government Financial

Institution) had agreed to provide loans of D.M. 85 million to meet foreign currency requirements of these facilities.

Selection of Urea Technology

Three tenders were received for urea plant 1) Toyo Engineering Corporation Japan 2) Snamprogetti, Italy and 3) Stamicarbon, Netherlands. After detailed discussions on technical and commercial aspects, the tender of Toyo Engineering cooperation was found to be the best. GSFC also had satisfactory experience of operating two urea plants based on technology supplied by Toyo Engineering. The Board of Directors approved the selection and asked the management to approach Government of India for their approval. Lots of follow up was done with the government of India for approval of the selection of the contractor for urea plant but we were not able to make any progress.

After a few months, one day Secretary Fertilizers, Government of India, rang up Mr. M.D. Rajpal, who was at that time Managing Director of GSFC that honorable minister Mr. P.C Shetty would like you to meet him in Delhi. Mr. Rajpal asked me to accompany him. We went to Delhi and met secretary fertilizers who took us to the minister's chamber. The Minister seemed to be in bad mood. After secretary introduced us to the Minister, the minister asked Mr.Rajpal what he knows about the urea technology. Mr. Rajpal stated that Mr. Gami is the technical person and he can reply to the question. Mr. Sethi asked Mr. Rajpal who is the Managing Director? Further he said I am asking you (Mr.Rajpal) the question. Then looking at both of us he said that you do not know any thing about urea technology. I tried to tell him that we were operating two urea plants and we have experience of the technology. Minister said that he was not talking to me. Again he used impolite language implying that we do not know how to select technology. This went on for about ten minutes. Secretary sensing that Minister was getting angry; he suggested that we take leave of the minister.

When we came out of the chamber of the Minister, the Secretary apologized to Mr. Rajpal stating that he did not know that minister had called him for this purpose. If he had known he would not have asked Mr. Rajpal to come to Delhi. He suggested that we should rethink about the selection of the technology. We returned back to Baroda and reported to the Board of directors what happened in Delhi and the suggestion of the secretary, fertilizers. The Board after detailed discussions decided to stick to the original selection and asked us to approach Government of India again. We wrote to the Secretary Fertilizers that the Board of Directors of the company has discussed the matter and has decided to select the same contractor, namely Toyo Engineering Corporation, for Urea plant as applied earlier.

After few days, secretary fertilizers wrote to GSFC stating that the YEN credit from Japan was not available for urea plant and suggested that in view of this, we may select another contractor. We referred the matter again to the Board and the Board decided, in view of non availability of YEN credit for payment in foreign exchange, to select 2nd best contractor, namely Snamprogetti, Italy. We again approached the Government of India with the recommendation for approval of Snamprogetti as urea plant contractor. In few days time we received approval from the Government of India. During the final discussions on the contract, Mr. Quotrochi, representative of Snamprogetti, assured us that he will ensure that GSFC gets the best urea plant. As there was no foreign exchange credit available, from other sources, for Urea plant of Snamprogetti, Government of India released free foreign exchange (U.S. $ 22.3 millions and D.M. 15 million) in spite of shortage. This was surprising, where as Government of India did not want to release free foreign exchange for Toyo Urea plant, they were more than happy to release the same for Snamprogetti Urea plant. Contracts with Snamprogetti were signed in September 1976 six months after signing of Ammonia plant contracts.

Becoming Managing Director

After I became Technical Director, some friends suggested that I should try and become Managing Director (MD). I consulted my friend Lalit Upadhyaya, who was also legal advisor to the company, to find out advantage and disadvantage in becoming Managing Director. He told me that if I want to become MD I will have to be flexible in my approach and do what politicians want in 100% cases. On the other hand if I want to follow professional approach, I can come in conflict with political leader/leaders and in that case I should be prepared to leave at moments notice. Further it will require political influence with the Chief Minister to become Managing Director. I gave a lot of thought and decided it would be worthwhile to become MD and should prepare myself to leave at a moment's notice..

My cousin in Delhi Dr. Vinodrai Gami knew Mr. Ajmera who had very good relationship with Gujarat politicians and especially Chief Minister Mr. Madhavsingh Solanki. I talked to Mr. Ajmera. After talking to the chief minister, he asked me to take appointment of the Chief Minister for meeting. I rang up the Chief Minister for appointment. He gave me an appointment and asked me to meet him at Nadiad, where he had some meeting. When I met him, he said I know you are a good technical man, but you do not know anything about finance. I told him that as far as term loans are concerned, I have very good relationship with financial institutions and in fact no Managing Director in the past had gone to them without me. You can check with financial institutions on this. He said he will think about it and meeting was closed. Government made me Managing Director on 9th. January 1977. Mr. Rajpal, who was then M.D. for 3 years after retirement from Government as additional Chief Secretary, was very much annoyed with me, as he wanted to have further extension. He was given six months extension earlier in July 1976.

After I became Managing Director, Jute mills located near Kolkatta wanted me to visit them, as we were buying jute bags from them since 1967. I was reluctant to go but after repeated request, and specially from our material manager S.K. Mehta I agreed and we (Dr. C.B.Patel, executive Director, S.K.Mehta materials manager and I) made a visit on 5th. February 1978. Next Day Birla Jute mills had arranged lunch and plant visit. While going to the plant in the car, I felt unusual pain in the chest, but it subsided in about 5 minutes.

I suspected I was going through a heart attack as my doctor, Dr. M.B. Chitale Chief Medical Officer of GSFC had told me the symptoms of heart attack few years ago. When we reached the jute mill, we climbed to the first floor to the general manager's (GM) office. After brief introduction the GM said as weather was pleasant he was not running air conditioning. Looking at me he asked me whether I was feeling hot, as I see perspiration on your forehead. On his asking this question, I immediately asked him whether there is a doctor around, as I may be experiencing a heart attack.

He told me to lie down on the floor and he will immediately get the doctor. He said there is a comfortable room with sofa etc on the ground floor and if I like we can go there. I agreed and we went down and I rested on sofa, within five minutes Doctor came and almost immediately I started experiencing severe pain and breathing difficulties. Seeing me doctor was very much worried and wanted to take me to hospital in the city which was one hour drive away. I requested him to wait for few minutes when pain will subside, he was unwilling to wait and we started by two cars, in one car myself, doctor and Mehta and in other car Dr. Patel and GM of Birla Jute mills. I was kept for three weeks in Intensive Care Unit (ICU) and asked to be in hospital and guest house for another month, before I was allowed to return to Vadodara, that too by Rajdhani train accompanied by my doctor and taking one day rest at Delhi. Those days there were no facilities in India for angiography, angioplasty or bypass surgery. The treatment was mainly rest and light exercise such as walk. After that I was absolutely alright, brisk walk every day for half hour kept me healthy for next 10 years. I served GSFC as its Managing Director for a period of more than 5.5 years and left it on 1st. September 1982.

Selection of Site

Coming back to GNFC, Shri. R.B. Amin Director of the company had a vision and had also the dream to develop Dahej as port and bring back prosperity to Bharuch. He had been working on this development since late 1950s. He therefore suggested that new project should be near Dahej / Bharuch. This would help in all round development of the backward area and would help in accelerating the development of port at Dahej in Gujarat. The board unanimously agreed to his suggestion.

The fertilizer project requires large amount of water and access to roads and railways for bringing in feed stock, fuel and for the distribution of the fertilizers. Further high tension electric supply is required. Also a special consideration was required to be given to site as Dahej / Bharuch were on the Earth Quake fault line.

A special team, consisting of D. C.Gami and V. A. Sanghani, was appointed for the selection of the location of site. The team went to Dahej and various areas around Bharuch. Even drinking water was not available between Bharuch and Dahej and proper road also was not laid. Further bringing in railway line and water pipe line required construction of 35 -45 Km rail track and 55-60 KM. water pipe line. This would be too expensive for the size of the proposed project. Dahej therefore was ruled out for the site. Different sites on the bank of Narmada River and out skirts of Bharuch were investigated. As tides were making sweet water of the Narmada salty, up to 20 K.M upstream of Bhaurch, bringing in water was expensive.

Ukai canal was across the bridge over Narmada River. Considering these aspects selection of site near railway and highway and not too far from the possible location of water source was required. Fortunately a site between highway and Chavaj railway station just outside Bharuch city was found to be suitable. Water was drawn from Ankleshwar Distributary of Ukai right bank main canal. As canal is closed two-three months in a year, a storage capacity, in the form of a large Pond, was made. Ukai canal was on the other side of the river. Railway authorities agreed to allow the water pipe line along the railway bridge to take water to the factory and Narmada Nagar. In order to be doubly sure of availability of the water on 24 hour basis whole year round, a second source of water was suggested at 20 KM from Bharuch where, tide water was not affecting the sweet water.

When we now look at the vision and foresight of Mr. R. B. Amin, we can see that the selection of GNFC location at Bharuch and the establishment of GNFC had triggered industrial development not only around Bharuch but also for Dahej. Now there are huge petrochemical and chemical complexes of I.P.C.L. GACL, Essar, Hindalco (Copper and Gold plant) etc and three jetties and Government of Gujarat Port terminal. Dahej is now being developed as major port.

Land Acquisition

Dr. C.B. Patel executive director of G.S.F.C was entrusted the task of the acquisition of the land. Land acquisition was carried out by him with the assistance of Mr. A.K. Modi who was deputy company secretary at that time in GSFC. Some changes were required in the land for arranging proper lay out of the company and the township. The land acquired at village Chavaj was given up and additional land from the villages Zadeswar for township, and Vadadla and Vagusan for plants was acquired. The National high way was passing through the acquired land and was separating the factory from the township. Since there would be lot of traffic in this portion of the highway, it was essential for proper safety that this highway is acquired by the company and government requested to construct a bypass which will go around the company's site. Village people objected to this. Though the government appealed to the villagers, the people from the Vadadla started agitation against the acquisition of the portion of the highway, as that would necessitate villagers to go around longer distance. Mr. A.K. Modi visited area several times and villagers were pacified with amicable solution.

As Bharuch is on the earth quake fault line, it was necessary to ensure that designs of foundations and structures take care of this factor. Dr. Jay Krishna, then vice chancellor of Roorkee University, who was at that time considered as one of the leading world authority on earth quake engineering for design of structures for the earth quake prone areas was requested to provide consultancy service for this. He agreed to provide consultancy services and after investigations, prepared a detailed report which formed the basis of designs for all foundations and structures. As Bharuch soil is black soil, special consideration was also required in the design of foundation. All plant structures have withstood earth quakes since then without even a crack in any structure showing that design basis provided by Dr. Jay Krishna were very sound.

Financing

Project report was prepared in June 1974. As the first oil shock came in December 1973 and consequent price push had not stabilized price of equipment and materials, the cost estimates of Rs. 2700 million were based on prices prevailing prior to the oil shock. Following this, there was substantial increase in the prices of oil and all related products.

For financing of the proposed project, applications were made to KFW, Germany(a Government development bank) for foreign exchange loan and to Industrial Development Bank of India (IDBI) for rupee term loans in June 1974. KFW deputed its team of experts to the company in September 1974.The team wanted to understand company's methods of project planning, cost estimation and general outline for implementation of the project. They also enquired how the company had planned and implemented earlier projects. The KFW team went into the details of the cost estimates of Rs 2700 million for the project and the basis followed in cost estimation. They expressed satisfaction on the methods of estimation and the way the estimates were actually worked out.

The team however, had observed that the cost estimate will go up substantially when prices of equipment and materials would get stabilized with up-ward trend in oil price. After due assessment KFW approved the term loan of DM 85 million. On the other side, IDBI constituted a consortium under its lead, with other financial institutions and banks as members for the appraisal of the project. IDBI in due course approved the cost estimate at 2740 million in 1976.They were however, reluctant to approve the term loan as the total magnitude was very large and further, in their view, with increased cost of raw materials/inputs, ultimate economics and viability of the project was rather uncertain. The present subsidy scheme of the Government of India was not available then and that could also be a reason for their reservation for loan commitment of such a magnitude.

As IDBI approval for term loan was not forthcoming, KFW addressed a communication to the Government of India stating that they will not be able to disburse the loan unless IDBI approved the project and as also the required term loans. The company was also feeling that if first payment was not made in time to the foreign contractors, consequent delays would increase the project cost and project schedule would also be affected. The company realized the gravity of the situation of uncertainty and approached Ministry of Finance, Government of India for their intervention. On due representation, Mr. M. R. Shroff, Additional Secretary in charge of Banking agreed to release free foreign exchange to meet the first down payment, provided the company had necessary rupee funds available with it. The company responded positively to this requirement and accordingly first down payment in foreign exchange was made in April 1976 and this development made it possible to make the contracts effective. At this point, IDBI had not taken any view with regard to approval of the term loans.

In the context of above developments, Mr. M. R. Shroff who was in charge of Banking Department convened a meeting inviting the chairman of IDBI and representatives from other financial institutions to seek their views for the approval of term loans. It was expressed by the institutions that they did not have adequate resources to sanction loans of such a large magnitude. Thereupon, after detailed discussions and consultations, perhaps there was a consensus that Government of India would agree to release additional funds to IDBI and other financial institutions to enable them to approve and provide term loans for the project. Further, to Placket the IDBI on their reservations, it was further understood that the Government of India would issue a letter to IDBI that in the event of failure of GNFC to meet its obligations of repayment of loans and/or accrued interest, the Government would find a way to meet such repayment obligations of GNFC.

The Government of India agreed to support the project since GNFC project was of national importance in making available much needed fertilizers to the farmers, save valuable foreign exchange required for the import of fertilizers and further ensure economic utilization of large quantity of Residual Fuel Oil (RFO) to be produced by nearby Gujarat Refinery, which was otherwise a waste product leading to enormous problems in disposal. Further, any other commercial disposal of such large quantities of RFO was not feasible as in transportation of RFO to retail and consuming points special type of railway wagons and special storage tanks would be required.

After resolving on these various connected issues and on assurances from concerned Government agencies, ultimately IDBI approved the project and sanctioned the term loan of Rs.1134.9 million and thereafter the loan agreement was signed by Mr.M Sivagnanam Managing Director of GNFC on 4th May 1977. During this intervening period, site and other project activities continued uninterrupted and GSFC funded the expenditure, which was of the order of about Rs.350 million, which was later on reimbursed by GNFC. Thus, timely intervention of Banking Department in the Ministry of Finance, Government of India and the initiative of its Secretary Mr. M.R.Shroff could make this giant complex a reality for serving the national cause.

IDBI and other Financial Institutions/Banks started disbursing Rupee loan funds as required for the project in accordance with the terms of the loan agreements and the project proceeded as planned and at no time the project was held up for lack of funds or financial assistance. Foreign exchange loan approved by KFW of DM 85 million was subsequently raised to DM 92 million and disbursements were received in time to meet contractual obligations in foreign exchange.

The firm project cost estimate was prepared in May1979 when all the equipments and materials were ordered. The up-dated firm project estimate worked out to Rs. 4450 million including margin money for working capital of Rs.140 million and pre-operative expenditure of Rs. 1200 million. IDBI formally approved the project estimate and on that basis approved increased term loan of Rs 1975.9 million, after considering the requirement of equity of Rs. 890 million, at 20% of the project cost.

The term loan approved by IDBI was at that time the largest sanctioned by them to any company and in the total financing arrangements. Other 9 financial institutions provided loan of Rs.210 million and consortium of 14 banks agreed to provide term loan of Rs 870 million. Considering the circumstances prevailing then, financial institutions funded interest of the period from 1st January 1980 to 30th June 1981 amounting to Rs.504.1 million.

While approving loans of this magnitude the IDBI and other financial institutions stipulated number of stringent conditions on GNFC including (1)to secure undertakings from Government of Gujarat and GSFC that they would bear any additional cost of overrun for the project beyond Rs.4450 million.(2) right of conversion of 20% of loan into equity (3) shall not declare any dividend if it fails to meet its loan repayment obligations and (4)shall not declare dividend of more than 15% without prior approval.

GNFC floated the public issue of Rs. 436.1 million in May 1981 when there was significant progress on the project implementation/ completion. This public issue was the largest in the country then. Certain unique features of the issue were that Rs. 120 million worth equity were reserved for farmers and Rs. 80 million earmarked for subscription by Non Residence Indians (NRI). GSFC, co-promoter, had a high reputation on the stock market and GSFC was considered to be a blue chip company and even its equity was in command on the market. This helped a lot to the success of public issue of GNFC. GNFC highlighted the exemplary performance of GSFC in its prospectus for public issue in the following words "GSFC has been popular scrip returning about 800% in overall and 58% per annum on an average to its original shareholders." Similarly commending observations about GSFC and its enterprising directors were also made by GNFC in promotional literature and slide shows for the public issue campaign. The success of GNFC public issue was reflected in the response from the subscribers as it was oversubscribed by 2.5 times, a unique feature of the time, and the total number of shareholders was about 488,000 including 120,000 farmers. In the prospectus issued, GNFC had conveyed its confidence on project completion by stating that it will be completed in the middle of 1981.This fact was also a note worthy feature of the public issue."

Project Management

D & R department of GSFC had done all work for conceptualization, for preparing specification, inviting tenders, selection of process licensers and negotiations of contracts, selection of contractors and signing of contracts, selection of site and acquisition of land. When GNFC was incorporated on 10th May, 1976, the Government appointed four directors of GSFC, namely M/S Jaykrishna Harivallabhdas, R.B. Amin. H.K.L Capoor, and M.D. Rajpal as first directors of GNFC. Agreement was signed during 1976 between GNFC and GSFC for proper implementation of the new fertilizer project. Further all contracts were to be assigned to GNFC at appropriate time. As this was the most prestigious project for GSFC with very high financial stake, GSFC appointed a separate project team (NFP Team) consisting of senior executives and officers from various disciplines such as chemical engineering, mechanical engineering, electrical engineering, instrumentation, finance, marketing, legal etc. to carry out the project work initially under the supervision of Managing Director, GSFC and later on under the supervision of GNFC managing director. Ammonia plant contracts became effective on 15th. April 1976 and Urea plant contracts became effective from 15th. November 1976.

During 1976 basic engineering activities were started by all licensors and contractors in their home offices. M/s. Engineers India Ltd. was appointed as detailed engineering consultant for ammonia plant, Project & Development India Ltd (PDIL). a division of Fertilizer Corporation of India for detailed engineering of Urea plant and associated facilities. Tata Consulting Engineers. was appointed consultant for detailed engineering for raw water, DM water, railway siding and other works. They had commenced their work. The detailed soil survey of the site was completed and fencing work and foundation work had started. Letter of Intent for boilers was placed with BHEL. All the plant and machinery required to be imported were cleared for import from Director General of Technical Development (DGTD).

Government of Gujarat appointed Mr.M.Sivagnanam as first Managing Director of GNFC on 15th January, 1977. He was given office at GSFC next to the office of MD GSFC. He started working from this office and arranged to rent out office in Baroda city for the NFP project team which moved to new office. The IDBI started appraisal of the project for which some team members had to go to Mumbai till appraisal was completed by March, 1977 and the project cost was provisionally estimated by IDBI at Rs.2740 million. Team would go to site at Bharuch twice a week and if required more often and also stay at night at Bharuch. At Bharuch the work on compound wall, buildings, soil testing, and work on town ship began immediately. The foundation work for machinery foundation started in July, 1977 and two substations for power with capacity of 1 M.W. each required for construction activity were completed and commissioned in June, 1977. Orders for most imported equipment for Ammonia plant were placed and some shipments had arrived at site. Urea plant engineering had progressed 70%. Most of the imported equipment orders were placed. First shipment was expected to reach site by the end of April 1978. 40% of the engineering of integrated offsite facilities was completed by Tata Consulting engineers. Site construction activities had commenced

As the detail specifications of the equipment materials were being received, enquires for equipments and materials were floated and orders were placed. By the end of 1978 most of the orders for the equipments were placed. It was now possible to work out detailed cost estimate after taking into account the exchange rate fluctuation between D.M. and Rupee, increase in excise duty from 1% to 8% estimated updated revised cost worked out to Rs. 4640 million in 1978.

The high pressure Texaco process was being established for the first time not only in India but also in the world; as a result the back ground information was not available from which fair estimates can be made. The company, therefore had to wait till basic engineering was completed and detailed specifications were prepared before enquiries for the equipment could be floated. Perhaps Mr. Sivagnanam was not able to explain this fully to IDBI, as he was not yet probably confident of the estimates made in 1978 as above by the NFP project team. Further he preferred to go alone to Delhi and IDBI Mumbai instead of taking with him technical persons who visited IDBI separately. M/s. IDBI were getting very anxious as firm project estimate was not yet determined and they were not able to get appropriate clarifications. Uncertainty in the mind of the Managing Director regarding the firm project cost might have caused anxiety in the minds of IDBI executives and may have prompted IDBI, as per rumors, to request the Government of Gujarat to change the Managing Director of GNFC.

Government of Gujarat selected Mr. S.J. Coelho who was at that time Additional Secretary Ministry of Industry Government of India. He had five year term and had completed only one and half years. He was therefore reluctant to come. However Government of Gujarat insisted that he should join GNFC as MD. Mr. Coelho took charge as Managing Director of GNFC on 30th. April, 1979. (it was rumored that Mr. Coelho had requested that he may be made permanent Managing Director and he would resign, as IAS, from Government Service, however this was not accepted by the Government of Gujarat) Immediately he wanted the project office to be shifted to the site and requested GSFC project team also to shift to site at Bhaurch. He also asked all the team members to join GNFC as executives and most of them joined on promotion as compared to their position in GSFC. Those who joined were provided housing at GNFC Township called

Narmada Nagar. Those who did not join stayed at GNFC guest house and returned on week end to the family at Baroda. Those who did not stay at Narmada Nagar did daily up down from Baroda to Bharuch by car. Thus all the top executives in various technical departments as well as finance, legal, secretarial and marketing were headed by the executives from GSFC who were transferred on the rolls of GNFC or who worked as GSFC executives on project team.

During 1979, most of the imported equipment for Ammonia plant had arrived at site. Two thirds of the indigenous equipment had also arrived at site. Heavy equipments were placed on foundation. All the imported equipments for Urea plant were received at site. 60% of the indigenous equipment had also arrived at site. Urea prilling tower was completed (93 meter height). Associated and offsite facilities were progressing well. 132 KV main receiving station was energized on 23-August 1979. Project cost was firmed up to Rs. 4450 million.

During 1980 all imported equipment for Ammonia Plant except one air blower were erected. Pre-commissioning activities had started. For Urea plant all imported and indigenous equipment were erected. Erection of piping, instrumentation and electrical were under progress.

Commissioning of the complex

Commissioning of associated and off site facilities had commenced. Pre commissioning of some sections of Ammonia plant was completed by February 1981. 12 equipment of sulfur recovery unit were delayed. However this did not affect commissioning of Ammonia plant. Commissioning of different units of Ammonia plant had started. Erection of piping, instrumentation and electrical installation were progressing well. It was expected that barring unforeseen circumstances, commissioning of Ammonia and Urea plants will commence in first half of 1981, and commercial production in second half of 1981 however all the plants were commissioned in December 1981 and commercial production started in July, 1982.

Commercial Production

Plant operation started very smoothly, except some teething troubles which are normally encountered in all such projects. The process people absorbed the new ammonia technology, being used in the biggest plant being built for the first time in the world, in short time and both ammonia, urea plants worked very well. In fact the finance position was so good that GNFC started making prepayment of the loans from the first year itself along with normal interest charge. The company extended financial year for 18 months from End December 1981 to 30th June 1983.

During 12 months from July 1982 company produced 4,44,911 MT Urea which can be considered commendable. Company made a cash profit of Rs. 508.1 million and after providing depreciation of Rs. 429.5 million made a net profit of Rs. 78.6 million on the basis of provisional retention price (as notified by Government of India) of Rs. 3351/MT for Urea and Rs.3,999 per MT for Ammonia. It may be recalled that Government of India had introduced retention price scheme for nitrogenous fertilizers from November 1977. Under the Government of India Retention Price policy, fertilizer industry is assured of 12% post tax return on net worth (equity plus reserves), equivalent to 29.36 % pretax at that time, provided plant operates at 80% capacity and achieves prescribed level of efficiency.

Ammonia, urea plants worked very well and operating at more than 100% capacity from the third year which is very commendable. It was great satisfaction for the GSFC, NFP project team and GSFC executives who had joined GNFC. Further the risk taken by GSFC in selecting the process for ammonia for the first time in the world was justified.

All ammonia as per installed capacity was not used in the conversion of Urea and there was 270 MT/ day surplus Ammonia for which GNFC started thinking of diversification and in 1981 initiated discussions with Gujarat Industry Investment Corporation

(GIIC), who had license for Methanol plant. It also engaged PDIL as consultant for the preparation of feasibility report for the manufacture of nitric acid, formic acid and DAP. It also engaged Engineers India Ltd as consultant for captive power generation plant. This policy of GNFC was absolutely opposite of GSFC policy. GSFC relied on internal management to look for new projects, diversification and growth. While GNFC decided to lean on external consultants for the same purpose

The estimated project cost was Rs.4450 million but was completed at cost of Rs. 4277.0 million with savings of Rs.173 million The cost of the same capacity plants which came up subsequently but based on gas or naphtha was much higher as can be seen from the following data in Table 4, even though the gas or naphtha based steam reforming plants should be at least 10% cheaper in capital cost as compared to capital cost of partial oxidation plant using fuel oil as feed stock.

Table 4

Sr.No.	Year commissioning	Company	Feed stock	Capital cost Rs. Million
01	April, 1985	R.C.F, Thal	Gas	4500.0
02	July, 1985	R.C,.F Thal	Naphtha	4500.0
03	April, 1986	Kribhco, Hazira	Gas	4500.0
04	December, 1987	NFL, Vijaipur	Gas	5070.0
05	1988	IFFCO, Aonla	Gas	6470.0
06	November, 1988	Indo Gulf	Gas	7010.0

Thus capital cost of the NFP project worked out to be lower than projects which came up after words which corroborated with the opinion expressed by me at the time of approval of the project to the board of directors of the GSFC that the future projects would be more expensive, as at that time GSFC board was very much worried about profitability of project due to high capital cost. GSFC is a founder promoter of GNFC; however after production started GNFC did not officially consult GSFC in important matters such as investment, diversification, expansion etc, even though it is a joint promoter with 25% equity. It is virtually acting as a Government Company. My only regret is that, the position of GSFC is reduced from being a co-promoter to that of a mere share holder.

⌘ ⌘ ⌘

Chapter 6
Other fertilizer related projects/
topics at GSFC

Purge Gas Recovery

In the operation of the Ammonia plants, large quantities of inert gases get accumulated in the synthesis loop. It therefore becomes necessary to purge them out from the system. These are purged out and flared through chimney. Along with inert gas, large quantities of synthesis gas also get purged out. This was an economical loss. As soon as the process for the recovery of the synthesis gas from the purge gas got developed abroad, GSFC decided to establish purge gas recovery system in 1975. The technical discussions on this revealed that it would be possible also to recover pure argon liquid as well as pure methane along with synthesis gas with only marginal additional cost. However the market for argon was very small about 0.14 Million cubic meter per year where as the production from the proposed plant would be 2.9 million cubic meter per year. Since the argon was very important with high potential for growth especially for fabrication for stainless steel and alloy steel equipment and argon was very expensive and in short supply in the country, the company decided to go ahead with the project at a cost of about Rs.100 million with the production of liquid Argon and Methane along with the recovery of synthesis gas. On the completion of the project economics of ammonia plant improved with the recovery of synthesis gas thereby reducing the requirement of feed stock. Further it gave additional income to the company on the sale of argon. Since the cost of production of argon for the company was very low, the company reduced the price of argon substantially so as to stimulate the growth of argon consumption in the country through development of new uses as well as make it easy for all the fabricators of stainless steel and alloy steel equipment with the easy availability of the argon.

Oxo Syngas

During 1980 Indu Nissan Oxo Chemical Industries ltd. requested GSFC to manufacture special synthesis gas for use as raw material for Oxo Alcohol which they were planning to manufacture for the first time in the country. GSFC accepted the request and signed a bilateral agreement, in 1980, to supply Oxo Syngas. GSFC set up a special facility at a cost of about Rs.100 million. The capacity of the plant was 8.5 million M^3 / year with special quality of syngas as agreed to between the parties.

Company had taken a loan of Rs. 70 million from banks for medium term. As company was producing this from Methane it was not required to obtain special license for this as it was considered to be covered under license capacity for the production of Methane. The production started in the beginning of 1982.

There was small controversy on this. Mr. Narendra Bhuva, the promoter of Indu Nissan, requested me to be the chairman of this new company. I was Managing Director of GSFC since January, 1977 when I informed the board that Mr. Narendra Bhuva wanted me to be the chairman of his company, Mr.H. K.L Capoor who was Chief

Secretary of the Government of Gujarat and director of GSFC stated that I must take permission from the State Government for this. I told him that since I was not a government officer and became Managing Director of GSFC as its nominee, I did not require permission of the Government and I can decide this issue on my own, but I thought it is better through the GSFC board. Mr. Capoor stated that Mr. Bhuva may take advantage of me. I told him that since I get my bread and butter from GSFC why don't you think that I may take advantage of Mr. Narendra Bhuva? Especially as GSFC is a much bigger company.

I do not think Mr. Capooor and Mr. Shivgnanam who was Secretary Iindustries Government of Gujarat and director of GSFC liked this. They took the copy of the agreement between GSFC and Indu Nissan to study to find out in what manner I have tried to help Indu Nissan. They could not find anything for which they could blame me. In fact agreement was more favorable to GSFC than to Indu Nissan. However since then both of them were trying to remove me as MD. Oxo Syngas plant worked well and supplied gas to Indu Nissan till Oxo Alcohol plant was operating.

Leaving GSFC

Shri H.K.L. Capoor retired as Chief Secretary of the Government of Gujarat and Mr. Sivagnanam became Chief Secretary. In May 1982 he rang me up saying that the Chief Minister wanted to see me. Can I come and meet him first and then we both will go to the Chief Minister. When I met Mr. Sivagnanam in his office he told me that Chief Minister Mr. Madhavsinh Solanki wants to appoint some one else as Managing Director of GSFC and would like to offer me position in the Government. We discussed various possibilities; his idea was to offer me technical adviser position. Earlier Government had offered some years ago similar position to Mr. J.J.Mehta, a well known technocrat and former chairman of Indian Petrochemicals Corporation Limited (IPCL). I have a feeling that he was not very happy as IAS officers would create problems. I was therefore not interested. After long discussions we could not come to any conclusion, we then went to the Chief Minister. He asked me why not accept position in Government, I told him that, to my mind, in the Government there was nothing equivalent or better position than that of the Managing Director, GSFC.

Since he had appointed me as Managing Director and now that he wants to appoint some one else, I do not mind stepping down and leave GSFC. He asked me what I will do. I told him I will be able to manage myself. He then said he would like the new person to get acquainted with the company operations by working with me for a period of three months before I leave. I said O.K. He then told me that I must ask for something. I told him to provide full pension benefit to me and life time access to GSFC library. This is how I left GSFC. News papers however made big headlines out of this, as Government, in their wisdom, stated in a press statement that I was not keeping well and was sick and therefore I was leaving. I had a heart attack four years ago and I was working as any other fit person. When news papers continued to write, Mr. Jayakrishna our Chairman told me that Chief Minister had desired that I should make a statement to press clarifying my position. I told him I will not do so as Government made a false statement that I was sick. He did not press me further and the matter died in due course.

Coastal DAP Plant

As stated earlier, the Government of India had decided not to give license for nitrogenous fertilizer plant in Gujarat. They were on the other hand very much interested in giving license for DAP at Gujarat Coast, as DAP requires import of Rock Phosphate and Sulphur or Phosphoric Acid. Further Gujarat location can serve Northern and central India as DAP can not be produced economically there. On application made by GSFC in 1981, Government of India issued letter of Intent for DAP plant with a capacity of 326,000 MT/year at Coastal location. GOI preference for location was Porbandar. The estimated cost of the project was Rs. 900 million, excluding the cost for jetty and port development. Porbandar was not a good location as there were always law and order problems. GSFC found Sikka as better location which Government of India approved. After establishment of GSFC DAP Plant, there was very big industrial Development of this region of Saurshtra as Reliance and Essar set up their refineries ringing in investment of thousands of million Rupees..

Joint Sector power generation plant

Gujarat was experiencing shortage of power as (1) demand was higher than generating capacity and (2) during erratic monsoon, power demand for agriculture would shoot up and Government would cut power to industry to provide the same to agriculture. Company was, therefore, experiencing constraints on account of power cuts and resultant interruption in production. Further GEB power cost was also increasing very fast. An idea was therefore developed in 1982 to establish a power plant under joint ownership of large corporations so that large power plant can be built to produce power for all participating corporations at lower capital and operating costs.

The generated power can be shared by all participants. This required formation of a new Company, separate location, availability of gas for power production, change in law to enable consortium of companies to produce power and use it among themselves and permission of GEB to wheel power from generating station to various consumers. Idea was to involve GSFC, Heavy Water plant authorities, GNFC, Petrofils etc. This took several years. A new Company in the name of "Gujarat Industries Power Company ltd. was formed by the Government of Gujarat in June 1985 after all above formalities were completed. GSFC contributed Rs 160 million in equity of the new company for a 36 Mega watt (M.W.) share of power out of 245 M.W. capacity of the power plant. However project was considerably delayed and power generation started only from 15th January 1995.

Captive power plants

As Joint sector power generation was getting delayed and company also needed large quantum of steam which at that time was being produced using expensive fuel, the company decided to establish captive power plants using Naphtha and gas as fuel for cogeneration of steam and power in three phases, first phase was completed in March 1989, second in March 1990 and third from December 1993 to January 1995.

Birth of Southern Petrochemical Industry Corporation Ltd (SPIC)

Earlier I had mentioned that Government of Madras (now Tamilnadu) had approached chairman GSFC for advice on setting up similar plant in Madras (now Chennai). Following up of this, in early 1969 Mr. M.A. Chidambaram, one of the biggest industrialists of south India, visited GSFC. Mr. Srivasta told me to take him around the plants and explain him details about GSFC working, its management etc. After the plant visit and discussions were completed, Mr. Srivasta had lunch with Mr. Chidambaram. Normally he would invite me for lunch but this time he did not. Afterwards I came to know the reason for the same, as he was negotiating with Mr. Chidambaram how he can be involved in establishing the new company

In June 1969 I was on vacation and touring south with my family. When I was in Madras (now Chennai) the secretary department of Industries Government of Tamilnadu rang me up and requested me whether I can meet him. (I was surprised how he knew about my whereabouts. Perhaps Mr. Srivatsa might have informed him.) I met the Secretary and had one hour discussions as he was interested in knowing how the Government can go about establishing a Fertilizer plant similar in concept to that of GSFC. After detailed discussions he asked me what is the most important criteria to make the plant successful. I told him that the Government should not interfere with the management of the company and allow the professional management to manage it. This will require sacrifice from the government as even though they would have financial stake/ control and legal powers to interfere in the management of the company, they will have to remain aloof from the management. If they do so new company would be successful.

In July 1969 Mr. Srivatsa told me that he was planning to leave GSFC and start fertilizer plant in Chennai with Mr. Chidambaram as main promoter along with Government of Tamilnadu as a joint sector partner. He told me he will be the Vice Chairman and President and asked me to join him, stating that I can get any salary and position I may want. I told him that I came to Gujarat to serve my family and state and therefore would not be able to leave GSFC even though offer was very tempting. He told me in that case he will have to take some of my deputies to the new plant. He took two of the best persons from D&R department and some from production and instrumentation.

This is how SPIC was conceived at GSFC.

Phosphoric Acid Plant De- bottlenecking

From the beginning Phosphoric Acid plant was giving trouble and plant could not be operated at high efficiency and high production levels due to problems in digester, filter, evaporator etc., Problems were mainly due to break down on account of corrosion and choking of filters and various equipments due to imperfect reaction in digester etc, as it was not possible to process quality of rock phosphate on which design was based. Company was receiving rock phosphate from different sources with different impurities which accelerated the problems. Rock phosphate was purchased by Minerals and Materials Trading Corporation (MMTC) by floating tenders and supplying to all fertilizer companies.

Evidently there were basic design defects especially in the design of digester and filtration system. M/s. Chemico, the original process licensor, had gone defunct and other process licensors, when approached, refused to take up the case of correction of design as well as to carry out de- bottlenecking to increase the production capacity.

During 1975 when World Bank representative visited GSFC, I talked to him about the problem of the phosphoric acid plant. He told me that no licensor would agree to take up the work on the plant designed by somebody else who also had supplied the process. Only some private firm or individual experts on the process would agree to do this. On my request he suggested the name of M/S Bearden Potter Corporation which was practically a one man show. I sent them a fax and they replied that they will have to come to GSFC, check the plant and decide on what is required to be done. Only after this they can give proposal. They wanted to be paid for this initial work for making the proposal; I told them that this was not possible. I then again requested World Bank representative to persuade them to make proposal, after visiting and studying the plant without any charge. After persuasion by the World Bank representative, M/s. Bearden Potter agreed.

I then went to Delhi to talk to the advisor fertilizers, Government of India Mr. Venkataraman whom I knew well and discussed with him whether Government of India would approve the engagement of M/s. Bearden Potter Corporation for the de-bottlenecking of Phosphoric Acid plant. He told me that if the representative of the World Bank writes to him recommending his name stating that he is capable of doing the job, he will be able to get approval of the Government for such arrangement. I again wrote to representative of World Bank who was nice enough to write a letter to advisor fertilizers.

After this I put the proposal to our board of directors informing them about the informal discussion I had with adviser Fertilizers and stating that after Bearden potter visits GSFC and prepares preliminary report suggesting steps to be taken, the company will have to accept the consultancy fees he may ask and give the order to him, without inviting proposals from any other party. As the board of directors, and specially Mr. Arvind Lalbhai, our Director, was very keen to improve the phosphoric acid plant capacity, the Board approved the proposal. In fact Mr. Arvind Lalbhai at every accounts meeting used to tell me that Gami you are doing alright, but I am, disappointed with you for phosphoric acid plant performance. Why do you not do something and every time I had to tell him we are looking for a specialized consultant knowledgeable of this process.

We then invited M/s. Bearden Potter Corporation to send representative to GSFC to study the phosphoric acid plant and make the proposal. During the visit, the manner in which he was asking questions and collecting data on various problems and studying the actual operations, we were satisfied that he knew the technology very well as he was also making suggestions on what was required to be done while studying the plant. After going back he sent us a proposal for changing design of the digester, filtration systems and other equipments and indicated his fees for basic and detailed engineering. Equipment had to be ordered by us as per his specifications and also to be paid by the company.

On receipt of his proposal we obtained the approval from our Board of Directors as well as from the Government of India in 1976. IDBI sanctioned a loan from the IDA line of credit to meet the foreign exchange cost. After completion of Basic and detail engineering by Bearden Potter and ordering indigenous and imported equipment and erecting them, production was started in June 1979. Since then plant has been working efficiently at high level consistently and has been producing up to 130% of the capacity. This enabled us to increase the production of DAP as well as that of ammonium sulfate which is produced from co product gypsum.

Ammonia three Plant

Department of Atomic Energy wanted to establish heavy water plant utilizing synthesis gas from both the ammonia plants and approached GSFC in the early part of 1968 for the purpose. While discussing this GSFC asked the question as to what advantage GSFC would get by allowing use of synthesis gas for heavy water. It was stated that the capacity of the ammonia synthesis section would go up. However there was not sufficient synthesis gas capacity to take advantage of this. It was therefore decided to set up ammonia synthesis gas plant at GSFC. On negotiations, Department of Atomic Energy agreed to bear the capital cost of the 50 MT per day synthesis gas plant to be established at GSFC.

As the capacity of the ammonia synthesis would go up to 100 MT per day. GSFC wanted synthesis gas plant with capacity 100 MT per day and after negotiations GSFC agreed to bear the additional capital cost to raise the capacity to 100 MT per day. GSFC had the responsibility of operating the Ammonia three plant, supply utilities, and market Ammonia while Department of Atomic Energy would arrange to supply natural/Associated gas as feed stock for the plant. There were complicated formulas, for determining cost, quantity of Ammonia produced and sold by GSFC and proportion of share of profit. This plant worked well and contributed substantially to the profit of both GSFC and the Department of Atomic Energy through sale of additional ammonia produced.

Heavy Water Plant

Process for the production of heavy water at Nangal in Punjab was a unique one as it depended on availability of very cheap power (1.35 Paisa/unit). It was therefore not possible to use this process at any other place in India. Department of Atomic Energy (DAE) therefore undertook research to develop independent process for the production of heavy water. Since DAE required a number of heavy water plants to meet the need for the production of nuclear power, they were also searching for the process for heavy water. French had developed Ammonia-Hydrogen exchange process on pilot plant, and they were in touch with DAE.

Dr. Vikram Sarabhai, who was Chairman of Atomic energy commission and director of GSFC from its inception, had suggested at the GSFC board meeting during 1968 that Department of Atomic Energy (DAE) would be interested in setting up heavy water plant at GSFC site to utilize synthesis gas from both the GSFC ammonia plants. After extracting deuterium from the synthesis gas, the same would be returned to GSFC for conversion to ammonia.

In September 1968, GSFC deputed Mr. B. Bandyopadhyay, who had long experience of Ammonia plant to the ICI steam reforming operating symposium at Brussels Belgium. Mr. Tradurouder of M/S Sulzer Brothers, Switzerland contacted him and asked him whether he knows if heavy water plant is established and integrated with Ammonia plant, efficiency and capacity of Ammonia plant will increase. When Bandyopadhya said he was not aware, he said that if he is interested he can show him such a plant in France. Apparently the purpose of M/S Sulzer brothers to show heavy water plant was to impress upon GSFC that it is advantageous to integrate heavy water and ammonia plants at their Vadodara complex.

He took him by car to the heavy water plant in Mazingarbe in France where they stayed two days. Plant manager told him that heavy water pant can be integrated with Ammonia plant without disturbing normal operation of the Ammonia plant even when heavy water plant is operating or shut down due to any maintenance or any other problems, and further efficiency and synthesis capacity of ammonia plant will improve. After this visit Bandyopadhya decided to check with two experts on Ammonia (1) Mr. Nielson of Halder Topsoe in Denmark who said that if impurities from synthesis gas are removed, Ammonia conversion efficiency could increase by 2-3% but he had no experience, and (2) Dr. Tosseli of M/s Ammonia Cassale in Italy, who said he was not aware of this. On return to India he talked to Mr. Srivtsa Managing Director of GSFC, who arranged a meeting with DAE in Mumbai to apprise them of what information Bandyopadhyay had brought.

The discussions between representatives of DAE and GSFC consumed lot of time first to understand the implication of the proposal and then to thrash out various, technical, financial and commercial points. In the mean time Mr. Srivatsa resigned and left GSFC in August 1969 to establish SPIC. The discussions continued with Mr. Heredia, who joined GSFC as MD in August 1969. GSFC wanted to know the advantage GSFC could get if such a proposal is accepted. DAE representative stated that the capacity of ammonia plants would increase from 950 to 1000-1050 MT per day. Further energy consumption per MT Ammonia would go down or remain same and quality of ammonia also would be same. As brought out in earlier paragraphs on Ammonia three, as a result of these negotiations, synthesis gas plant of 100 MT/day was built to give advantage to GSFC and DAE.

The main question to resolve was to determine the loss of synthesis gas during processing in the heavy water plant. As the gas is conveyed at high pressure of 650 Kg / cm^2 and returned at almost the same pressure, it was not possible to measure gas quantity accurately going from GSFC to heavy water and returned, as the accuracy of meters will be much less than the likely loss of synthesis gas. After protracted negotiations it was finally agreed in the meeting when Chairman Atomic Energy Commission and Chairman G.S.F.C were present, that notional loss of 1 MT/day would be considered and GSFC would be compensated for the same by DAE.

Elaborate formulas were worked out for determining the cost of supplying various utilities to heavy water plant, cost and share of the production at Ammonia-3 plant and share of profit on sale of ammonia. The heavy water plant was commissioned in 1979 and worked smoothly except for two years when it was shut down to repair the damage caused by the fire. When French Collaborators were conducting guarantee test run they found that refrigeration capacity was not adequate to meet the production guarantee. They calculated that it will be possible to compensate this by injecting liquid ammonia to the separation tower to provide additional cooling. The French designed and fabricated the elbow in France for connection and on restarting the plant, immediately the elbow gave way, due to wrong design and selection of material of construction of the elbow, resulting in a big fire damaging the structure and entire quantity of synthesis gas vented into the atmosphere. The plant remained shut down for a period of two years to carry out the repairs before it could be restarted. Since then plant had worked smoothly till the ammonia two plant of GSFC was shut down in 2000, thereby agreement between GSFC and DAE came to an end as per the terms of the agreement.

Arbitration

In 1984, GSFC found that actual synthesis gas loss was much higher than notional loss allowed in the agreement. After negotiations they made agreement for the new quantity of the loss of Synthesis gas from the date of starting up of the heavy water plant in 1979, subject to approval of DAE. DAE, after consulting ministries of fertilizers and chemicals and finance, did not approve the same. However GSFC did not agree and this became dispute number 1. Later on Fertilizer Industry Coordination Committee (FICC), on recognizing the establishment of captive power generation capacity by GSFC, revised retention price of GSFC and made a very large claim of refunds from GSFC. GSFC in turn asked DAE to share the cost of this, which DAE refused stating that earlier GSFC must have made higher claims for electricity charges. This became dispute number 2. Both tried to resolve these disputes for years, but could not resolve as time passed by, disputed amount rose to a large sum of money nearly Rs. 270 million. Managing director GSFC and Chairman Heavy Water Board decided in a meeting in December 2000 to submit the dispute to a sole arbitrator as provided in the agreement and both suggested my name as sole arbitrator. They both wrote to me to be the sole arbitrator.

I was not sure whether I can adjudicate this dispute as I had worked for both. I therefore consulted former chief Justice of Gujarat Justice Diwan and asked his advice. He suggested that I should write facts to both parties, stating that as I had worked for both parties, I could be considered as interested party. They should reconfirm if they still want me to be sole arbitrator. They not only reconfirmed to me in writing but chairman heavy water board and Managing Director GSFC came to my residence to tell me that they had full confidence in me. They would only like that the award should be a reasoned award.

There after I accepted the assignment. It was the toughest job I had undertaken mainly because it involved not only two disputing parties but also Ministry of Finance, Ministry of Fertilizers and Chemicals of the Government of India. Further the executives of both GSFC and Heavy Water Board were very loyal to their respective organizations. It was therefore almost impossible to make them agree even to their wrong assumptions on the case being argued by them. Though it was a tough assignment, I was happy when I declared my award in November 2003 for 2 reasons (1) knowledge that executives of my old organizations had displayed deep loyalty to their respective organizations and (2) both parties accepted the award in Toto without even asking any clarifications.

⌘ ⌘ ⌘

Chapter 7
Diversification and Growth

New projects for the production of (1) caprolactam, (2) nylon chips, (3) melamine, (4) liquid Argon and (5) MEK Oxime were selected as per the Strategy of Growth as out lined in the chapter "Innovations in the Management". Project details for caprolactam, nylon chips and melamine are given in the following sections. Project details for liquid Argon is given under Purge Gas Recovery and that for MEK Oxime is given under Product research.

GSFC started planning and applying for letter of intent (LOI) for expansion of ammonia and urea plants and diversification for projects such as caprolactam even before the first phase fertilizer complex went into operation. The company called new projects as diversification, though in reality, they were all related to fertilizer operations. New projects either drew the raw materials, or the intermediates or products from one or more of the fertilizer group of the plants or they produced as co- product fertilizer or downstream projects to make value added products. For example all raw materials, except benzene, for the caprolactam were obtained from intermediates of ammonia plants and Sulfuric acid, sulfur dioxide and oleum plants and produced as co product ammonium sulfate fertilizer. Purge gas recovery plant used purge gases from ammonia plants as raw material and produced synthesis gas as raw material for ammonia and caprolactam and new products argon and methane. The melamine plant consumed urea fertilizer as raw material and produced ammonia as co-product which can be utilized for caprolactam and other fertilizers. Oxo syngas produced from methane, the co-product of liquid Argon, is used as raw material to produce oxo alchohol manufactured by Indu Nissan oxo chemicals Ltd. The nylon chips and nylon compounds were value added products using caprolactam as raw material. MEK oxime a new product, the technology of which was developed in research centre, was produced from HX which was an intermediate of the Caprolactam plant.

Some of the raw materials required for diversification projects were produced in more than one plant. Technical integration of all plants was done through crisscross pipe lines, controls and some additional equipment to provide flexibility in operations of different plants. For example synthesis gas required for caprolactam plant is produced in three ammonia plants and purge gas recovery plant. The second raw material ammonia can be provided from three ammonia plants as well as melamine plant and third raw material Sulfur dioxide and oleum can be provided from three different plants namely Sulfuric acid, sulfur dioxide and oleum plants. Returned synthesis gas from heavy water plant can produce additional quantity of ammonia. This integration helped during power shortage; power failure and any plant break downs in any plant to shift production so as to maximize total production/profit in the company under the circumstances. As the profitability of each product is different at different times, this provided the opportunity to maximize profitability of the company by increasing production of a product which improved profitability or decreasing production of the product which has lower profitability. A techno economic model was prepared which is revised from time to time depending upon change in profitability of individual product. This way operating personnel can maximize profitability by making appropriate selection of the products to be produced at a given time.

In his book "Corporate Strategy", (1965) Igor Ansoff provides a rational model by which strategic and planning decisions can be made. Ansoff looks at strategic, administrative and operating decisions. This model concentrates on corporate expansion and diversification rather than strategic planning as a whole. The model is highly prescriptive and advocates heavy reliance on analysis. GSFC however used simple analysis for planning of its diversification. This was all right during secured time as was prevailing during the seventies. Ansoff is recognised as a godfather of corporate strategy even today.

Alfred Chandler in his book "Strategy and Structure" (1962) defines strategy as the determination of the long term goals and objectives of an enterprise, and the adoption of courses of action and the allocation of resources necessary for carrying out these goals. He argues that a firm's structure is dictated by its chosen strategy – unless structure follows strategy, inefficiency results. Strategy and structures are inextricably intertwined. Chandler's point was that newer challenges give rise to new structures. GSFC selected products with long term goals, as all these products, except caprolactam, are growing at reasonably fast pace even after twenty five years from the date of starting production of each product, show that strategy for selection of products was appropriate. Organizational structure was tuned to the selection and the requirement of the new product and plant.

According to Gary Hamel by 1990 strategy had become discredited. All too often 'vision' was ego masquerading as foresight; planning was formulaic, instrumentalist and largely a waste of time in a world of discontinuous change; 'strategic investments were those which lost millions, if not billions of dollars. Discontinuous change as experienced by the world since the last few years may be the cause of slow growth of the market for caprolactam. At the time of planning for caprolactam, the frequent change in duty structure by Government and the impact of better usefulness of polyester fiber was not visualized; as a result, growth driver for caprolactam, which was originally Nylon Yarn, Saris during 70s and 80s, is now mainly engineering plastic nylon 6 and tire cord, as nylon yarn growth from 1990 is very low.

Gary Hamel and C.K. Prahalad, in their book "Competing for the Future" (1994) believe strategy has tied itself into a straitjacket of narrow, and narrowing, perspectives'. "Among the people who work on strategy in organizations and the theorists, a huge portion, perhaps 95 percent, are economists and engineers who share a mechanistic view of strategy. Where are the theologists, the anthropologists to give broader and fresher insight?" "While strategy is a process of learning and discovery, it is not looked upon as a learning process and this represents a huge blind spot".

Hamel and Prahalad observe, "For all the research and books on the subject there remains no theory on strategy creation. Strategy emerges and the real problem, executives perceive, is not creating strategy but in implementing it". GSFC did encounter lots of problems in implementing its strategy but it could overcome these problems and implement complete diversification and expansion programs as per original strategy. Kenichi Ohmae in his book "The borderless world (1990) defines strategy as 'creating sustaining values for the customer far better than those of competitors'. GSFC can claim that it has created sustaining values for all its customers through their products including fertilizers, through special marketing services, developing new products and rendering technical advice.

Caprolactam

While government of India gave industrial license for the first phase of the fertilizer plants to GSFC, it had stipulated that the company should not convert all ammonia into fertilizers but keep annually 20,000 M.T of ammonia free to make available for sale to future acrylonitrile plant to be established by Indian Petrochemicals Corporation Ltd.(IPCL) and caprolactam plant to be established by Private Sector Company.

Once the contract for fertilizer plants became effective and work commenced in 1966, I started to investigate to find out who is likely to be purchasing ammonia (I did this though it was not my responsibility but because there was no marketing department at that time. Further without sale of ammonia, profitability of the company would be affected). I went to Delhi for the purpose as that time IPCL had main office in Delhi and met Mr.Krishnan who was the technical chief. He told me that it will take several years before the acrylonitrile plant will come up, as it was part of the "Naphha cracker Complex". They were first going ahead with setting up DMT plant first. I found from DGTD that there were 13 companies who had applied for letter of intent (LOI) for establishing caprolactam plant with a capacity of 50 M.T / day. However no LOI was issued to any party. I got the names and addresses of these companies. All the companies were producing either Nylon yarn from caprolactam or in textile production and were interested in back ward integration by establishing caprolactam project.

I wrote to each of these companies to find out how much ammonia they will need and the likely date when they would purchase ammonia. Response of each of them was prompt, however they did not supply information asked by me, but requested letter from GSFC that GSFC would supply required quantity of ammonia to them. They also came visiting us. When I discussed with them the quantity of ammonia required and the likely month and year they would purchase ammonia, their answer was that they were not in a position to reply as LOI was not given to them. When I asked them to give time from the date LOI is issued to them they were not in a position to give even this. They did not have project manager for caprolactam plant nor any technical person who had studied caprolactam process. On enquiry they stated that their suppliers of caprolactam would provide them technology as their promoters had very good relationship with them. And once LOI is received by them they will be able to obtain information from their suppliers.

I asked Mr. Sheikh Mohmad who was my deputy to find out from the library the process/processes for the production of caprolactam as well as the names of major manufacturers of the caprolactam in the World. He had to look at libraries in Baroda and Ahmedabad to find the necessary information. When he prepared the report we found that the caprolactam, besides ammonia and benzene, required a host of other chemicals such as oleum and gases such as sulfur dioxide, carbon dioxide, hydrogen, Nitrogen etc. It is not possible to transport gases economically over long distances. Since none of the applicants for the caprolactam had plants anywhere near the above gaseous raw materials and had no production capacity of manufacturing the same, it would be very uneconomical and difficult, if not impossible to produce caprolactam by them as producing such raw materials in the quantities required would not be economical. They were also far away from the source of Benzene which is hazardous to transport by road tankers in very large quantities.

We therefore prepared a note for the board of directors stating that none of the 13 applicants for caprolactam would be in a position to establish caprolactam plant for various technical and economical reasons and that if the Company wants to dispose of additional ammonia, the company itself should produce caprolactam. Note further stated that only Gujarati Refinery, Fertilizers and Chemicals, Travancore (FACT) and GSFC were capable of setting up an economical caprolactam plant. Fact established caprolactam plant in 1986. Further ammonium sulfate fertilizer is produced as co product for which non Fertilizer Company would require to set up special department for marketing of Ammonium Sulfate, and therefore the fertilizer company should produce caprolactam. The board felt that this was too much of diversification and 13 applicants were very sound and influential and therefore GSFC should not go into the production of caprolactam. And further there was little chance for GSFC to get LOI. On my plea board finally agreed that company may apply for LOI.

Securing Letter of Intent (LOI) for Caprolactam

Normally after the Board meeting there is a lunch for the directors and I was always invited for the same. After this meeting Mr. Satarawala, who was our director and who was secretary industries, Government of Gujarat, asked me to go with him in his car to the guest house for lunch. In the car he asked me whether I can convince Secretary to the Government of India about the caprolactam proposal, as he had studied my note and had a feeling that, with proper convincing arguments, the Government of India can be persuaded to give LOI to GSFC. He told me that Mr. B.B. Lal ICS, who was industries secretary in the Government of India, has to be convinced and whether I feel confident of convincing him. I told him that I will be able to convince him, provided he has open mind. He told me that Mr. Lal is very intelligent and shrewd and difficult to convince but we can try. He told me to send application for LOI and send him a copy. He will ring up Mr. B.B Lal, 15 days after he receives the copy for an appointment. He said he will take me to Delhi with him to meet Mr. Lal but I will have to do all the talking.

At Delhi after introduction Mr. Lal told me that young man, 13 of the large and influential companies had applied for LOI and you are the 14th so there is little chance for GSFC to get the LOI. I explained to him the reasons why other companies can not set up caprolactam plant as the financial resource and influence were not the only requirements; there are a number of technical requirements such as producing economically various raw materials except benzene and ammonia. Further transportation of Benzene by tanker is hazardous. Caprolactam produces ammonium sulfate fertilizer as co product which has to be marketed for which these companies do not have any expertise. Further technical expertise required for the management of the caprolactam plant is quite different from what they now have. Considering these aspects I was confident that they will not be able to set up caprolactam plant. I suggested that LOI may be issued to all 14 and I say with confidence that only GSFC will be able to implement the same. He told me that it is not possible to give LOI to 14.

I further explained to him that no where in the world a textile company is producing caprolactam for the reasons given by me as above. He got interested and asked me where in other parts of the world caprolactam plants are located and who are producing the same. I showed him the list of caprolactam producers in the world which showed that caprolactam was either produced by Fertilizer Companies or highly integrated petrochemical and chemical companies. It seemed he was convinced by this argument. He then said that GSFC does not have funds to set up this plant. On this Mr. Satarawala stated that if required, Government of Gujarat would provide the funds to GSFC to set up the caprolactam plant. He asked whether Mr. Satrawala can give this in writing to him. Mr. Satrawala replied that he will be able to send him such a letter. After that the meeting was closed. When we came out Mr.Satarawala congratulated me and told me that Mr. Lal was convinced and GSFC should shortly receive LOI. Government of India were also keen that caprolactam plant should come up as fast as possible as Government of India was spending lot of foreign exchange for import of the same.

Negotiations and Selection of Contractor

LOI for caprolactam was received by GSFC in November 1966. Development division of GSFC undertook preparation of feasibility report on the marketability and profitability of caprolactam. A detailed feasibility report analyzing all available processes was prepared in April, 1967. When Chairman and Managing Director of GSFC visited Japan, they brought some basic information on processes and some idea of capital cost and consumptions. This helped in making the report more practical. The report revealed that existing capacity for the manufacture of nylon in India was about 7000 MT / Year which was likely to increase to 13000 MT / Y by the middle of 1971 and to 21000 MT / Y by 1974-75. The report concluded that it would be feasible and profitable to establish a 50 MT/ day capacity caprolactam plant at GSFC. The report was submitted along with a note to the board of directors for their approval. The Board of Directors approved the same.

As there were no consultants, the specifications were prepared departmentally inviting tenders for license, know how, basic engineering, supply of imported equipments, supervision of erection and commissioning of plant. Tender documents ran into 800 pages.

Bidders appreciated the documents which provided clearer scope and specifications. Eight parties from Europe, USA and Japan submitted the tenders. Scrutiny of the tenders, studying of different processes submitted by various bidders (each bidder had a different process) and technical discussions took long time. Further the plant visits of the bidders were made as a result of visits several technical modifications were discussed and incorporated, and accordingly specifications were modified. After bringing all on more or less equal technical footing, negotiations for the commercial aspects were started with three bidders, after eliminating others for either not giving satisfactory technical information or not having enough operating experience on the process recommended by them. We found that, though technically each process was different, commercially the three were practically very close. We therefore decided to give details of all the three bidders to the board and leave it to the board to make the final selection. As there was tremendous competition among all, we decided not to give names of each party but instead give them alphabetic names like A,B & C. The detailed note was circulated well in advance to the Project committee and the Board.

When the meeting of the project committee was held to discuss these tenders, Mr H.M Patel, our director, was very angry and asked me, if I do not trust the directors and why we have not given the names of the companies. I explained to him that representatives of all companies were very vigorously following up. Since we have to make at least 15 copies of the note, we were afraid that it may leak from any of our office. We know that directors keep everything confidential and there is no question of any doubt. After this explanation, Mr. H. M. Patel asked me to give the names of A, B & C companies. After the discussions started, first on technical matter and I was asked whether we had any preference from technical point of view. I told them that technically all are very good and each is experienced in the process offered by them, and therefore there was no specific preference.

When it came to financial aspects, Mr. Arvind Mafatlal who was our director stated that the cost estimates and the total amount to be paid to the contractor seemed to be very high thereby project may become unviable. I explained to him that we have negotiated to our best ability to reduce the price to the minimum. Mr. Arvind Mafatlal stated that you have done your best . He then stated that now let the board itself negotiate to see how much further we can reduce the price. This suggestion was accepted by the board and the board decided that we should send telex to all three parties to send fully authorized technical and commercial delegation to negotiate all aspects of the tender with the board of directors of GSFC. The board further stated that, in order to make them very serious to reduce the price, the telex should also mention that board will take immediate decision at the end of the board meeting and issue LOI to the selected party.

The telex was sent to all the three parties giving them date and place of the GSFC Board meeting in Ahmedabad. They immediately responded and stated that their fully authorized delegation will arrive on the date to discuss and negotiate all technical as well as commercial aspects.

At the board meeting held for the purpose, Shri. JayKrishna, chairman suggested that Shri Arvindbhai may conduct the proceedings as it was his suggestion to call the parties for negotiations. Arvindbhai stated that we will call each party one by one and ask them, after discussions are over, to wait outside board room till board took final decision. He then asked M/s. BASF representatives to be called in first. He informed them that the company was satisfied with their technical proposal, however felt that there was scope for reduction in price and he asked them to give their views. Representatives of BASF stated that they have had detailed negotiations with the management and provided the minimum price, as a result there was no scope for further reduction in the price and regretted that they can not offer any further reduction. Arvindbbhai thanked them and asked them to wait outside and ask the second party, M/s. Hitachi Ltd. to be called in. After introduction and informing them about the technical aspects of the tender, he asked them to suggest reduction in the price. M/s. Hitachi Ltd. stated that they had already offered the minimum price and regret that they were not able to reduce price further. Arvindbhai thanked them and asked them to wait. He then called the third party M/s. Stamicarbon. He asked them the same question and M/s. Stamicarbon stated that they regret they were not in a position to offer any further reduction in the price.

The Board of Directors was surprised at the above outcome. Arvindbhai still insisted that the price was very high. After some thinking, he suggested that the Board may ask them to increase the capacity of the plant, maintaining the same price. His suggestion was that 20% increase in capacity that is from 50 MT/day to 60 MT / day should be adequate. I told Board that this would make position of the technical team very difficult, as we had fixed up capacity of all equipment including total lump sum price and with increase in Plant capacity, capacity of most equipment will have to be revised, and it would be very difficult for us to judge the required increase in capacity of each equipment. Arvindbhai said this is your problem and not the problem of the board and the technical team should be able to manage it. The board accepted the suggestion where by parties were again called in one by one. M/s. BASF stated that they were not in a position to increase the capacity of the plant even by 1 MT/ day at the price given by them. M/s. Hitachi Ltd. stated that they could increase the capacity from 50 MT/ day to 60 MT/day provided LOI was given to them immediately. Avindbhai stated that since we are negotiating with all three parties and still one party has to be called in, he therefore requested Hitachi ltd. to maintain his offer till the end of the board meeting. M/S Hitachi Ltd. agreed. He requested them to wait outside

He called M/s. Stamicarbon. They stated that they never anticipated such negotiations of asking for increasing capacity of the plant without increasing the price. They therefore needed to consult their head office and would require time till next day morning 11 o' clock. Arvindbhai told them to wait outside and he will inform whether the board can grant additional time. He then called M/s. Hitachi and requested them to extend the time till the end of the board meeting next day as one party had requested for additional time. M/S Hitachi ltd. agreed. Arvindbhai asked them to wait and called Stamicarbon and told them that they must give their answer by next day morning by 11 a.m. After that the meeting was adjourned till next day.

When the board of Directors met next day M/s. Stamicarbon were called in. They stated that they can increase the capacity to 55 MT / day and would require 3 days more time for various calculations to decide whether they can increase the capacity to 60 MT / day. Board stated that it was not possible to give further time as all other parties have given their answers and board also had informed them that the final decision will be taken by the end of the board meeting. Arvindbhai asked Stamicarbon to wait outside and called Hitachi Ltd. He asked whether Hitachi Ltd. can immediately give letter specifying the capacity at 60 MT/day without changing any other conditions including commercial terms, price but change guarantees for 60 MT/ day capacity plant. M/s Hitachi Ltd. agreed and provided the letter confirming the discussion in the board meeting. This was accepted and board decided to give letter of intent to Hitachi Ltd. for 60 MT/ day caprolactam plant. Accordingly the LOI was issued to M/S Hitachi Ltd. The meeting was then adjourned.

After three days M/s. Stamicarbon informed GSFC that they can supply the plant with capacity of 60 MT/day with the same price. I consulted our Chairman; he told me that it is now not possible to accept their offer as LOI was already issued and told me to inform them accordingly. I thereafter informed M/s Stamicarbom that it was not possible to accept their revised offer now, as they were probably aware that the GSFC Board had issued LOI at the end of the Board Meeting..

M/S Hitachi Ltd. invited us to come to Japan for new negotiations for the revised capacity of the plant. I consulted Chairman who first thought that he, myself and three or four technical executives should go to Japan for a period of three days for discussions. I told him that three days were not enough it may take as long as 10 days as it will be very difficult negotiations as capacity of each equipment will have to be studied and revised. We went to Japan and started the discussions. There were prolonged discussions for many days lasting for more than 12 hours. They were accepting revision of capacity for equipment which was to be procured from India. However for imported equipment they were reluctant and we had to go in lot of technical details before deciding whether capacity is to be revised and to what extent. The way discussions were going I had a feeling that M/s Hitachi Ltd. were probably not making their customary profit. My earlier experience was that they were not so rigid on negotiations. After discussions we finalized the negotiations and agreement was signed in July, 1968.

Obtaining release of Foreign Exchange

We submitted the application to the Government of India for approval of the contract and release of foreign exchange. The Government of India approved the contract in February, 1969 and initiated discussions for release of yen credit with Japanese government. Our earlier experience with Japanese contractor was that they would start discussions with their government for release of yen credit as soon as agreements were signed. In this case we were therefore following up with Hitachi Ltd. to find out the progress they had made for getting release of yen credit. We were also visiting Government of India to enquire about the progress. Government was also requesting Japanese Government for expeditious decision. Approval was getting delayed from Japanese side, an almost a year passed by without getting approval of the Yen credit. As Government of India was very keen to start the caprolactam plant, the ministry of finance included release of yen credit for caprolactam plant as top priority in the list of discussions which Prime Minister Indira Gandhi was to have with Japanese Government in her ensuing visit in July/ August 1969.

When the Prime Minister went to Japan, she found that Japanese government was reluctant to provided yen credit for caprolactam project. However they were willing to give same or larger amount for Jetty at Goa for transport of Iron ore. This was accepted by the prime minister and when she returned back to India, she informed the finance ministry that yen credit for caprolactam project will not be available. Finance ministry informed GSFC of the same and asked GSFC to negotiate with other bidders. At that time Mr. Srivatsa had resigned as Managing Director and Mr. Heredia was appointed as new managing director.

Securing Confidence of the New Managing Director

One week after Mr. Heredia joined as Managing Director in August 1969, he telephoned me and asked me if I was doing anything urgent, when I told him nothing urgent, he asked me to come and join him for a cup of coffee. I had known him earlier as he was director of the company from the beginning. When I reached his office, after usual greetings he asked me whether I know when he took charge as Managing Director, when I told him a week ago, he asked me then why I have not called on him. I told him that I thought he would be busy getting acquainted with the Company and I did not have anything urgent for which I had to see him. He then told me all executives had called on him except my self, he then asked me whether I have any complaints against any executive or would I like to tell him about any executive. I told him that I did not have any complaints and do not have any thing special which I would like to tell him about any executives. He told me that, however there are complaints against you. I told him, if so, he must investigate. He asked me whether I want to know what are the complaints,

I told him no. After that he told me that he is getting acquainted with plants and processes. He opened his desk drawer and showed me all operating manuals of the plants. Before becoming Secretary for Industries, he had gone to U.K. and had visited new ammonia plant of M/S ICI and had done extensive visits in Europe, on behalf of the Government of Gujarat, to study fertilizer industry there. Otherwise also he was very studious, pains taking and well read. He told me he may need my assistance to understand processes. He further said that he would like to visit plants every day, I told him I will be happy to take him around, he said he did not want to bother me but would take one of my deputy. I asked him who he would like to take, he said Lashkar Singh. He then told me that we should take coffee every week; I told him yes, he may give me ring whenever he is free. After that we met p regularly, nothing special happened except discussions on plants.

After some weeks, one day he told me he is going to test me. He said suppose I am driving myself and noticed a friend's wife standing on the road waiting for a bus and going in the same direction as I was going, what would I do? I told him that I would stop the car and offer her a lift. He then asked where I would ask her to sit in the back seat or in the front seat. I told him that since I was driving and there was no body else, I would open the front door and ask her to sit in the front seat. He immediately said you have failed the test. (Just for information. He was Home Secretary in Government of Gujarat, before becoming industry secretary. He therefore had a police mind too and believed in strict discipline and enforcing the same. I asked him how I have failed; he told me that people will talk about you and the lady. I told him I do not agree, especially as I give her ride only occasionally. He advised me that I should not give lift to a lady. I said I do not agree when it comes to friend's wife. After that he developed good trust in me and became, good friends.

Once he told me he does not think our general manager (GM) (works) is knowledgeable, and he is thinking of giving him three months notice to find another job. He then asked me why I was covering him in the daily production meetings. I told him that he was not able to properly explain events happening in the plant to other managers and further former Managing Director had asked me to help him in the matter. After he gave him notice and GM (works) left, Mr. Heredia asked me whether I would take care of his duties. When I said yes, he gave me two designations, one GM development and another GM works. After few days he asked me how much additional salary I want. I told that I will not ask and he should decide that. After some time he also made me executive Director Operations. Mr. Heredia very strongly believed in discipline and honesty. He used to keep track of all officers, managers and executives through security department. GSFC did not have a vigilance department. He did remove one general manager and few managers and officers for corruption.

Searching for the new contractor

Now coming back to Caprolactam, He called me for discussions on the issue and we decided it will be best to go to Delhi to find out how to proceed further and the type of the credit which would be available for the project. We then went to Delhi to meet finance ministry to find out how to proceed further. We were told that it was not necessary to invite fresh tenders but we can negotiate with the parties who had already tendered. Further ministry stated that the Government would be able to allocate U.K and or French credit for the project and we should find out the company/companies which could utilize these credits. As foreign exchange position in the country was very tight, the government could not release free foreign exchange even though caprolactam was top priority project.

We decided to contact M/s. BASF and M/s. Stamicarbon to find out their interest in doing the project with U.K. or French credit. M/s. BASF stated that they were not in a position to utilize either of the credits. M/s. Stamicarbon invited us for discussions at their head quarter at Gellen, Netherland, as they felt they can utilize the U.K credit. We went to them in September 1969. As M/s. Stamicarbon had in their tender incorporated basic engineering and supply of equipment by Continental Engineering U.K. they invited them to participate in the negotiations, as they could utilize the U.K. credit.

When we met, M/s. Stamicarbon stated that as most of the credit would be utilized by Continental Engineering he would ask them to indicate implications of utilizing U.K. credit on the project. Instead of explaining to us about the implication of the use of credit, they expressed doubt as to whether we know anything about caprolactam project and whether we have ability to undertake the project. Representatives further stated that this was very sophisticated project and they are not sure whether GSFC can do the same. I told them that they had already come to India and we had discussed various technical details and they had made their final offer also. Therefore it is no use talking about our ability and would suggest they may indicate the new prices and any other matter connected with utilization of U.K. credit for the project. They however went on the same line in his derogatory style when I informed him that we have not come here for this if you are not interested in the project please say so. After some further arguments managing director of Stamicarbon stated that we are not making any progress and it is best that we close the meeting. After the meeting he apologized to Mr. Heredia for the behavior of the representatives of Continental Engineering and stated that he never expected such behavior from them. If he had known this, he would not have invited us for the meeting. My feeling was that Continental Engineering was purposefully using derogatory language to pressurize us, as he might have thought that we had probably no other alternatives. Further it was possible that, rejection of their belated letter offering to increase the capacity of caprolactam plant to 60 MT/day, might be weighing on their minds. In business matter such considerations should not be given importance.

We returned to hotel. Mr. Heredia was very much depressed and worried and stated that caprolactam project was now doomed. I suggested that let us go to my room and we can discuss various other possible alternatives for the project. He stated that let us have a drink first and then discuss. He was so let down by the events of the day that he suggested that we should dig two graves at caprolactam site of GSFC and put an inscription that here lie two men who wanted to establish caprolactam plant at GSFC. I tried to cheer him up by saying that there are always alternative possibilities and we will be able to do the caprolactam project.

While we were discussing different possibilities of utilizing World Bank or other credits, the telephone rang. I picked up the phone and heard a voice which sounded familiar. The voice said I think Mr. Gami you are in difficulty. I then recognized the voice of Mr.Mueller the commercial director of M/s Inventa who had come to Vadodara a few times for discussions and negotiations as Inventa were supplying know how to Hitachi through M/s Ube, who was partner of Hitachi in this project. I asked him how he knew we were here in this hotel. He said that he was keeping track of us since he came to know that Japanese government was not offering yen credit for the project. He stated that he can put up a package utilizing French credit for the project and invited us to their head office in Chur, Switzerland and said he will receive us at the Zurich airport. I asked him to hold on and talked to Mr. Heredia and asked him whether we should accept his invitation. Mr. Heredia asked me whether I think he can really help. I told him that I cannot be sure but he is very shrewd and capable person and in any case we do not lose anything by going there and meeting him. Mr. Heredia agreed, I told Mr. Mueller that we will come to Zurich next day and will inform him about the flight when reservation is done.

Mr. Mueller received us at Zurich airport and while driving to Chur, he explained that he had arranged meeting next day with M/s Technip of France who can utilize the French Credit and Technipetrol of Italy who had engineered caprolactam plant, with annual capacity of 20,000 MT, based on Inventa knowhow in Spain. He said he can arrange visit to the plant. Technip and Techniperol are working together on a number of projects and they have ongoing relationship.

Next day morning we had meeting with representatives of M/s. Technip, Technipetrol and Inventa. As Inventa had the copies of the original contracts signed with M/s Hitachi Ltd. The basis of different contracts was explained and the scope of the work including supplying of equipments was determined. They said they would work out the cost and will come to Vadodara with proposal for discussions and negotiations.

We completed contract negotiations after they came to India and after detailed discussions. The scope of the revised contracts confirmed in all respect to the latest policy of the Government of India of maximizing engineering to be done in India (this was for the first time that detail engineering was done in India. In earlier projects engineering was done abroad) as well as maximizing indigenous procurement and materials. To meet these requirements, GSFC divided the project into two parts, 1) Main Plants 2) Auxiliary plants and other facilities. GSFC took upon itself the responsibility for auxiliary plants and for coordination of the project. Accordingly three agreements, relating to the (1) main plants for "technical know how and basic engineering with M/s. Inventa of Switzerland, (2) front end engineering with M/s. Technipetrol of Italy, and (3) supply of equipment required to be imported with M/s. Technip of France, were prepared. Fourth agreement for detailed engineering to be performed in India was signed with M/s. Engineers India Ltd., Delhi (A Government of India undertaking).

This enabled GSFC to maintain practically the same foreign exchange cost as visualized in the earlier contract, in spite of the fact that European prices are normally higher than the Japanese prices and that during the two years that had elapsed since entering the first contract in July, 1968 considerable escalation in European prices had taken place. GSFC itself decided to undertake procurement of equipment and materials in India, civil works, erection and commissioning of main plants, obtaining, wherever required, expert advice from Inventa, Technip, Technipetrol and Engineers India Ltd. GSFC also undertook complete responsibility for engineering, supply and erection in respect of auxiliary plants and off sites.

While negotiations were nearing completion, Marubani Ida of Japan informed chairman of GSFC that in the ensuing aid India consortium meeting to be held in Paris on 27th/28th may 1970, Japanese Government will propose providing yen credit for the caprolactam project. They requested chairman not to sign agreement with other parties. Chairman of GSFC informed them that he will ask GSFC to wait and not to sign agreement with other parties. However if the Japanese Government does not offer YEN credit for the project in the meeting to be held on 27/ 28th May, 1970, GSFC will not wait further. As Japanese Government did not make any offer of the YEN credit in the said meeting, Chairman asked GSFC management to go ahead with other contracts and the LOI was issued to above parties on 7th of June, 1970 and contracts were signed on 23rd. June 1970.

Obtaining Government Approval

Government of India approved all contracts / agreements and also approved financial arrangements in February, 1971. M/s. ICICI provided loan of US $ 4 million (Rs. 30 million) to meet requirement for payment of knowhow fees to M/s. Inventa. This way we could make the contract, for knowhow and basic engineering with Inventa effective. Government of India released foreign exchange (French credit) in installments first 60% in March 1971,, next 25% in May 1972 and balance 15% in December 1972. Total foreign exchange, for the project for knowhow, basic engineering and imported equipment was Rs. 120 million. M/s. Inventa completed basic engineering and M/s. Technip front end engineering by December, 1971. M/s. EIL started detailed engineering in May, 1971. GSFC entered into agreements for auxiliary plants namely sulphur dioxide, oleum and steam generation with Indian companies and contracts were awarded in 1971. Procurement of equipment in India as well as abroad commenced in late 1971.

During 1972 the GSFC carried out further market survey, this indicated that present demand for caprolactam is 11,200 MT / year which is likely to increase 29,000 MT / year in 1974 and further to 55,000 MT in 1976, if the program of expansion visualized by licensed Nylon spinners is realized. This included the requirement of yarn, staple fiber and tire cord but did not include engineering plastics. At that time there were four companies producing Nylon yarn in India.

Additional Foreign Exchange

After completion of the basic and front end engineering, M/s. Inventa informed that they would like to make certain changes and would like to come to Vadodara for discussions. While we were doing procurement of indigenous equipment, we found that certain special steel plates were not available in India and will have to be imported and also some equipment may have to be imported. M/s. Inventa suggested during the discussions that they would like to change material of construction for HX plant from special plastic to titanium as the special plastics would not be available in India and will give rise to shut down due to corrosion and therefore they think titanium metal, even though very expensive, would be more suitable as it will provide smoother operations without shut down due to corrosion. They also proposed to change purification system from distillation to melt crystallization.

Melt crystallization was the latest development, at that time, in chemical engineering for providing highly pure materials and through this system the purity of 99.999% can be achieved. M/s. Inventa had carried out pilot plant work specifically for the purification of caprolactam; which work was just completed and suggested that we should incorporate the same. They suggested that if required, technical person can visit Inventa, which was done and I had seen the operation of the melt crystallization pilot plant at Chur. This was for the first time in the world that such a purification system was adopted for caprolactam and adopting it was a risky decision, but justified on the ground that better purity product could be manufactured.

After detailed discussions they indicated additional cost for all these. I requested them to provide the details of the original estimates of the old systems of HX and purification and give a new estimate of the new proposed system. We wanted to ensure that they do not make any additional profit on account of changes. They did not agree to show the books of accounts giving the details of cost but assured that they do not make any additional profit. The discussions went on for more than a day, however since they were not agreeing to our request, Mr. Heredia suggested that we may accept their assurance that they are not making any additional profit and negotiate the increased price. After negotiations for few days we arrived at net additional price required to be paid and accordingly additional supplementary agreement was signed.

After this Mr. Heredia and I went to Delhi and discussed with Mr. Loveraj Kumar advisor Petrochemicals, Government of India. We explained to him the reasons why agreement had to be modified and changes for equipments etc. He understood and told us not to worry as he will get it approved. After some days we received the approval of the Government of India.

We had appointed Engineers India Ltd (EIL) to carry out detailed engineering. In order to ensure that no time is lost in communication, we had arranged the fixed time telephone call everyday between Technipetrol and EIL so that either party can discuss any pending issues requiring clarifications.

For sulfur dioxide oleum plant we had invited tender from Indian parties. After discussions and negotiations M/s. Larsen & Toubro Limited (L&T) approached Mr. Heredia stating that they are keenly interested in the project and are prepared, if required to reduce the price further to get the contract. In fact they were already lowest, knowing their keen interest Mr. Heredia asked me to indicate the reduction required. I told him that it will be difficult for us, as this is a turn key contract and we do not have means to quickly estimate the cost. The best thing is to ask EIL to make estimates and after receiving their estimates we can indicate the reduction in price required. After receipt of information from EIL we indicated the price which L & T accepted and the contract was given to them.

The delay in release of foreign exchange did have some effect on project schedule. We could, however start basic and front end engineering, as ICICI had provided loan in free foreign exchange. According to the requirement of the government, about 70% of the total equipment was procured indigenously. Unfortunately indigenous manufacturers could not adhere to the delivery schedule agreed to by them. There have been severe shortages of power and raw materials such as steel and cement in the country during that year. To avoid delay the company decided to manufacture 30 large alloy steel heat exchangers in their own workshop.

Commissioning and production

The erection work was completed in 1973 and plant was commissioned on 4th April 1974 by the senior most employee of the company Mr. R. S Barot in the presence of various dignitaries. This was unique way of commissioning the project. The plant commissioning was quite smooth except minor problems which are normally faced during commissioning of such complex project. Regular marketing of the product started from August 1974

Financial Management

The cost of the project was estimated at Rs. 360 million. The following table 5 gives the data on net worth (equity plus reserves), loans drawn/repaid, assets created and dividend paid from the year 1970-71 to 1974-75 to convey the important financial aspects of the company.

Table 5

Rs.million

At the Year end 31st. March	Equity + Reserve	Loans	Total finance	Cash & bank Balance	Gross fixed assets	Dividend paid in the year
1970-71	193.033	399.213	592.246	56.405	598.767	13.583
1971-72	273.760	367.824	641.584	72.515	662.578	17.183
1972-73	374.927	340.821	715.748	49.727	820.039	20.782
1973-74	410.25	284.632	694.657	22.959	965.306	18.983
1974-75	561.663	222.412	784.075	81.533	990.557	13.585

Source of Data: Annual Reports and Balance Sheets of GSFC

The equity of the company till 1973-74 was Rs. 119.225 million which increased with the issue of bonus shares of 1 for 3 equity shares held (3:1) to Rs. 149.9 million in 1974-75.The above Table shows that due to large amount of internal generations, accumulated reserves and surplus reached to an impressive amount of Rs.411.7 million by March 1975.This was more than the project cost. In that situation, there was no compulsion to resort to additional borrowings for execution of the project. The company practically relied on its own resources to execute the project, a very creditable feature in the company's march for development and growth. The available resources even made it possible for the company to repay certain loans with the result that loan borrowings decreased from Rs.399.2 million in 1970-71 to Rs.222.4 million in 1974-75, which was the period for project execution. The Company with the execution of this project substantially increased its gross block of fixed assets from Rs.508.7 million to Rs.990.5 million.

Major plant problems

The production gradually increased and reached 80% level in 30 months time which was considered very good those days, especially considering that this was new technology and the plant was being set up for the first time in the country. There were few problems; one was the breakdown of the aluminum piston rod of large air compressor which was supplied by Ingersoll Rand, Germany. This caused shutdown of the entire plant. The first time they said that the alignment of compressor may not be right and therefore piston cracked. They insisted on payment before supplying the spare by air but agreed that if it was their fault they would refund the money. The second piston also failed when they stated that it must be the foundation, they sent their expert to check. The expert found that alignment and foundations were correct. In the mean time pistons were failing and pistons were replaced seven times. Mean time we were paying for each spare which was being air freighted.

As the problem was not getting solved, GSFC took initiative to find out the reasons of cracking of the piston and the piston rod holding glands. Micro structure of the cracked and damaged piston rod was studied. The grain structure of the casting was found coarse where as it should have been fine. This was perhaps due to uneven and varying thicknesses at the circular hole for gland fittings. Further thicknesses were less than the thickness of the wall of the cylinder. This anomaly may have resulted in uneven cooling rate at different dimensions of the piston during heat treatment cycle of the piston. All data and photographs were sent to Ingersol Rand, who after sending their representative to India, finally agreed that there was a fault in design and heat treatment of such large aluminum piston. They had for the first time manufactured such large aluminum piston. They had not informed us about this earlier. This is how a number of Multi National Companies make guinea pig of the developing countries and take them for a ride. They refunded the money for all the spares. However they did not compensate the company for the loss of production. The company had minimized the loss by running the compressor with cracked piston at 50% capacity as explained bellow.

In fact when this problem came up, I was abroad, Mr. Bandyopadhya who was G.M. Development informed Managing Director that this could cause fire or explosion in cyclohexanone reactor, and advised Managing Director that it would be safer to shut down the plant. Accordingly plant was shut down. When I returned I asked for the reasons for plant shutdown and asked whether they had thoroughly checked the condition of the piston. I asked them to restart the compressor, in my presence with all concerned executives, without any load, and see what happens. At no load compressor worked smoothly. We then increased the load in the increment of 10% and simultaneously measuring the vibrations. In this manner we could safely increase the capacity to 50%. However at higher capacity vibration would increase. This enabled us to operate the plant at 50% capacity, thus minimizing loss to the company. For safety, we had kept twenty-four hour vigil by posting an operator only for this compressor.

The Second problem was concerned with vibrating conveyor used for transfer of melt slurry from the first crystallization stage to the top of the second stage. The vibrating conveyor would simultaneously cool and lift the material. This was repaired by our workshop people. However the conveyor continued to give problem and new conveyor was ordered and replaced in 1979. M/s. Inventa and we were looking at solving the problem on permanent basis, finally it was found that it will be possible to replace vibrating conveyor by a slurry pump and a heat exchanger. Inventa dispatched the slurry pump; however it would not function properly. Our engineering people modified the design and obtained the indigenous pump which is working satisfactorily.

The third problem was with respect to cyclohexanone reactor. In fact there was no problem except the fear that, by any chance if composition of the air and cyclohexanone mixture falls within the explosive limit, there would be fire or explosion. There were controls to ensure that this does not happen. However the fear was always there. Just before we commissioned the plant, there was a big explosion at caprolactam plant, at Flixboro, U.K. killing a number of people including all persons in the control room and damaging hundreds of houses in nearby villages. Though the reason for the same was different, it had a terrific psychological effect on operating personnel. Therefore as soon as company found that safer reactor design is developed by Polish company for their Cyclopol process, The Company decided to replace the reactor with safer reactor.

In the mean time original 316Ti clad reactor had developed bulging and was to be replaced. In view of increasing demand of cyclohexanone, an opportunity was availed to increase the capacity of cyclohexanone plant, while replacing reactor on adopting more safe technology. Since M/s Cora Engineering, successor of M/s Inventa, was having the license of Polish Technology (cyclopol Process), we held discussions with them and appointed them as consultants. They increased the capacity of cyclohexanone plant by 25% by (1) replacing Oxidation Reactor by reactor design of Polish technology with 316Ti as material of construction instead of original 316Ti clad steel for better safety and longer life, (2) introducing S.S. Sulzer packing in couple of columns and (3) replacing larger-size dehydrogenation reactor using S.S.Vessel in place of Cu-lined of original supply which was damaged beyond repair. GSFC-technical/design department introduced a small column to recover some more cyclohexanone from waste stream to increase the capacity further, thus ultimately reaching 30% additional capacity for cyclohexanone plant from January 1988.

Politics by customers: Marketing of Caprolactam

Our main problems were with the customers, as one of them was deprived of establishing caprolactam plant. There was a cartel of nylon producers and it was known as "nylon lobby". They were always trying to find fault with the company. First of all they stated that quality was not right and complained to the Government of India. When we told the Government in a tripartite meeting that the company had informed all the consumers about the quality which company will produce before signing contracts, and if they had any comments they should write to the company. However no reply was received in spite of the reminders and we are producing as per the specifications given by us. We also arranged a meeting of chemists of all consumers to discuss the quality. It was found that everybody had different methods of analysis depending upon from whom they were importing caprolactam, as there were no international standards for quality and its analysis. In this meeting the method of analysis was standardized and everybody agreed to use the same method. Subsequently they had no problem on quality after using standard testing method.

After some time the consumers stated that now requirement of quality of caprolactum has become stricter and they would like to have better quality. We asked them to give us the specifications of the quality they want and we will improve at that level and also requested them to send the samples of the quality received by them from their foreign suppliers. The company instituted quality improvement program by engaging M/s Cora Engineering-successor- of M/s Inventa in 1982, as they had an access to other technology. They added Heat soaking Unit after rearrangement reactor and Cat Ion Exchange Unit after Lactam-distillation, but prior to final stage of melt crystallization. Thus we reached high quality, equal or better than International, and marginally higher production of caprolactam to serve also the export market.

After the problem of quality was solved they started lobbying with the government and arranged to get reduction in excise duty on sale of caprolactam from 50% advalorem to 25% effective from March 1976.. Further caprolactam was placed under open general license (OGL). Government of India also placed nylon yarn under OGL. Customer virtually stopped buying caprolactam from GSFC since imported caprolactam became cheaper, and the consumers made commitment through state trading corporation for large quantities of imported caprolactam. This resulted in accumulation of stock of caprolactam to a level of 6 months of production which further increased by February, 1978 to 75% of the capacity. The Government of India, after examining the cost aspects of caprolactam, had suggested in December, 1975 to the company to keep the caprolactam price as determined by the government at least for a period of three years ending December, 1978. In spite of this, as a first step company had to reduce the price substantially and simultaneously representations were made to the Government for reviewing the policy of allowing caprolactam under OGL The off take continued to be lower and stocks accumulated further. We took up the matter with the Government, that they should regulate import keeping in view the availability of indigenous caprolactam. Government from 1979 started regulating the import of caprolactum. As a result company disposed of all stock as well as new production. Government however increased the price of Benzene, the main raw material, with retrospective effect. Company requested the Government to withdraw the stipulation regarding retrospective increase.

Company however was required to reduce the price of caprolactam from time to time for above reasons. Further consumers were able to manipulate with Government to arrange reduction in import duty with effect from 23rd April 1980 and increase in excise duty. This resulted in practically no sale during May and September 1980. Price was further reduced to encourage consumers to buy indigenous caprolactam, even though it reduced profitability of GSFC substantially. Unfortunately at about the same time government revised the price of the raw materials, specially benzene, naphtha and fuel oil which had adverse effect on the cost of production. Company approached Government explaining that revised duty structure has resulted in our caprolactam becoming more expensive than imported and as consequence the off take of caprolactam was considerably low. In fact there was no sale of caprolactam during the first two months of 1981 also. Company had to drastically reduce the price and offer special discounts and extended credits to the customers. The government finally decided to restrict the imports, and allow import after considering the availability of indigenous caprolactam.

Caprolactam Expansion

Those days the question of expansion verses grass root plant was debated in the country. The Government of India had decided that the expansion of fertilizer plants, where feasible, should be encouraged instead of setting up grass root plants. Similar consideration would also hold good for caprolactam also. It is known fact that if proper thought is given for expansion at the time of finalizing initial layout of the plant, it is possible to make the expansion at a given location more attractive than grass root plant of even higher capacity. When GSFC decided to set up caprolactam plant, it decided to incorporate space in the layout for its expansion to ensure that plant remains economically viable in future to offset the economics of future larger capacity plant and to take care of growing requirement of the basic material.

As that time nylon capacity was growing fast. After one year of successful operation, GSFC decided to apply to the Government of India for doubling the capacity of its 20,000 MT / year caprolactam plant. A number of visits were made to follow up with the Government; however there was no positive response. In 1975 we decided to check the market. The Table 6 shows data projected by the nylon industry for the production of nylon filament yarn; tire cord, staple fiber and the estimates for nylon molding powder for the years 1975 to 1977.

Table 6

Product	Year MT 1975	Year MT 1976	Year MT 1977	Licensed capacity MT
Nylon Filament Yarn	13,380	15,312	16,020	20,310
Nylon Tire cord	4,032	5,414	6,239	11,910
Nylon Staple	174	-	-	1,200
Nylon Molding powder	500	550	650	4,500
Requirement of caprolactam	19,894	23,404	25,200	41,712

Considering the above data the company decided to do feasibility study of expansion of caprolactam. As by that time Company had experience of successful operation, its operating personnel could identify the bottle necks. By removing such bottle necks, it would have been possible to increase the capacity of caprolactam production by at least about 20%. If expansion and de-bottlenecking are combined together, it would be possible to establish a total capacity of 50,000 MT/Y of caprolactam at the same site.

If total capacity of 50,000 MT/Y is established in this manner, it would be far more economical in capital as well as operating cost than a grass root plant of 50,000 or even 70,000 MT/Y capacity. The company had advantage that first 20,000 MT/Y caprolactam plant was set up at price prevailing prior to 1973 oil crises. Subsequent to this due to inflation, the cost of setting up chemical plant including caprolactam had gone up substantially. The economic study indicated that the 50,000 MT/Y plant with total integration with existing plant would cost additional Rs.870 million plus Rs. 360 million for existing plant, a total of Rs. 1230 million. The cost of grass root 50,000 MT/Y caprolactam plant would have worked out, at that time, to Rs.1650 million.

From the data of the above table, it was inferred that it would take another 2-3 years before caprolactam consumption would reach 40,000 MT during which period expansion of existing plant can be completed. If however one thinks of 50,000 MT / year grass root plant, the total production of caprolactam would increase to 70,000 MT which would take another 5 years for the consumption to match the new caprolactam plant capacity.. It was therefore most economical to set up total capacity of 50,000 MT/Y, including existing capacity caprolactam plant.

The company was following up with Government of India; finally, in 1980 Government of India gave LOI for expansion by 25%. Since this was not economical company followed up with the Government to allow doubling the capacity. Finally in 1985 Government gave LOI for expanding the plant by another 30,000 M.T making total capacity of 50,000 MT/Y. In the mean time government had set up a committee to determine the economic size for various petrochemical plants and committee recommended that economic size of the caprolactam plant should be 100,000 MT/Y. Company accordingly applied for 100,000 MT to be set up in two phases each of 50,000 MT capacities. The Government of India gave the LOI for the same.

Nylon Chips

On the application made by the company, Government of India had issued letter of intent (LOI) on 26 May, 1971 for establishing manufacturing facilities for 3,320 MT per year of Nylon Chips for filament yarn and 1000 MT / year of Nylon chips for molding. The company had finalized arrangement for license, know how, design and engineering, supply of imported equipment and advisory services for 3,320 MT/yr for Filament Yarn grade chips and 2000 MT / year of engineering plastic grade chips including compounded chips with M/s Inventa of Switzerland and had issued LOI to them on 3rd October, 1973. The company had sent application to the Government of India for the approval of agreements with M/s. Inventa. The Government of

India did not respond, even after several follow up. This was perhaps due to the fact that Government of India had issued a LOI for filament Yarn to GIIC. The company sent revised application for manufacture of 4000 MT/Y of engineering plastic grade chips and molding powder.

At that time industrial application of Nylon chips was growing fast in USA and Japan especially for use in the production of automobile components, gears, non-lubricated parts and substitute for metallic components. Therefore there was great potential of increasing consumption of Nylon chips (engineering plastic). In 1975 the production of Nylon Chips in India was carried out by two small companies and an estimate of their production was 500 MT/Y and was not growing due to import restrictions. We had therefore tough time to explain to the Government of India the need for such large capacity plant. After a lot of explanation specifically that availability of nylon chips, for application for engineering plastic, would help industrial development by substitution of metallic components for various applications as described above. This would reduce the cost of the same and improve the quality and finish. The company also explained to the Government that the company would establish application development centre to increase the demand of the product. It would not only render technical service on application of the chips but also develop different grades of chips for Indian market and also develop knowhow for making different components from these new grades.

In 1975 the Government of India, without approving the agreement with Inventa, asked the company whether company would be agreeable to reduce the capacity of the plant to 2000 MT/Y instead of 4000 MT/Y. Company considered this, since company wanted to have both continuous operation as well as batch operations for different grades of chips, company found that it was necessary to have a minimum 10 MT/day continuous plant and 5 MT/ day batch plant. It was therefore not possible to accommodate this with 2000 MT/Y plant. The company explained this in detailed to the Government and the Government of India finally issued LOI for 4000 MT/Y plant in the end of 1975 and approved the agreement with M/s Inventa in

1976. The foreign exchange requirement for the project was Swiss franc 11.1 million and for this ICICI was approached to provide the term loan.

The basic engineering of the plant was completed by M/s. Inventa by the end of 1977. In the mean time Government of India had cleared the equipment required to be imported. Civil works for the projects started in 1978 and was completed by 1979 when erection of the equipment started. The plant was completed in October, 1981. The production in 1st year was 241 MT (for 5 months). The second year 822 MT(only 20% of the capacity due to limitation of the demand), the application development centre developed different grades as well as provided technical services and organized seminars so as to increase the market of the product. The new entrepreneurs took about two years to set up the plant for new products/components after which the growth of the nylon chips market was good and within 5 years production as well as market demand reached 7500 MT / year. The plant could produce at 180% capacity level. A new line was set up so that in course of time the production can be increased to 14000 MT/Y.

Melamine

When GSFC employees were going to Japan for training they found that Melamine kitchen wares were available very cheap and each one was bringing a dinner set from Japan. This prompted us to study Melamine and its application. We found that it had a number of industrial applications such as laminates, paints, furniture and electricals, besides kitchen wares and house hold items. The potential consumption for domestic applications was considerable which could be realized fast with the help of application development centre.

The study indicated that it is produced from urea as basic raw material and produces co-product ammonia which is an intermediate in the fertilizers. This fitted well with our strategy for growth. We therefore, decided to make market study which indicated very low consumption on account of restrictions on import. However when the industries were contacted they indicated very high potential of the product especially for laminates if produced indigenously. Company therefore made application in 1972 for LOI for 5000 MT/Y melamine plant. The government of India's view was that there is not much of import of melamine and further as melamine consumes urea which is an essential fertilizer and in short supply they would not like to encourage this industry and did not give LOI. We further pursued Government of India specially indicating the impact on the industrial growth and specially by making available better products and further that urea consumed in the melamine was a very small fraction of 1%. Further it provides some quantity of ammonia as co product. It is therefore worthwhile for the growth of the industry, and to provide more beautiful furniture for homes, to set up melamine plant. The government of India finally gave LOI for 5000 MT/Y melamine plant during '74-'75.

After inviting tenders from various process licensors from Europe and Japan, the company after due discussion and negotiations selected Voest Alpine of Austria as the main contractor for the melamine plant for supply of know-how, basic engineering and supply of imported equipment. Simon Carves of India were selected to carry out detailed engineering of the plant. A team of engineers was sent to Voest Alpine for engineering conference to determine various parameters of the designs of the plant.

Clearance from the Director General of Technical Development (DGTD) for import of the equipment and machinery got delayed and could be obtained only during 1977. Company applied to ICICI for term loan in foreign exchange. Government of India was very slow in releasing the foreign exchange and ultimately foreign exchange was released in 1980 when civil engineering work started. Civil engineering and structural work were completed during 1981 when Mechanical, Electrical and Instrumentation work started and was completed by March, 1982. Production of Melamine started in

November, 1982. Total cost of the project was Rs. 180 million with foreign exchange component of Rs. 60 million.

The plant started smoothly. Occasionally problems on quality were encountered, as some dark specs were coming in the product. This was solved. The main limitation was marketing. Application development centre helped substantially by providing technical guidance for production of different products from melamine to promote its use. The production during 1st year was only 822 MT (20% of the capacity), due to limitation of the market.It increased to 115% capacity of the plant within 4 years. Immediately (1986) company applied for LOI for capacity of 10000 MT/Y to make a total capacity of 15,000 MT/Y.

Financial Management

The company had made applications for letters of intent for various projects of interest between the years 1971 and 1975.However, due to delays in receiving requisite clearances of proposed projects by government agencies, it so happened that those projects got bunched up for implementation when the clearances were actually received. To meet this unforeseen situation and to deal effectively on each project for planned execution, a separate project department was established. D&R department, however, continued its role to conceptualize the projects, select technologies and finalize contracts. Project department would then step in to organize and implement each project till commissioning of the plants and commencement of the production and then hand over to operating department. All these projects were completed during the period 1979-1982.The years 1975-78 were in the circumstances a blank period with no major project activities and therefore there was no growth in terms of new products, creation of new assets etc.

During the period 1977-79, the company embarked upon external investment in equity of other important companies in which the company had direct or indirect interests. Such external equity investment helped in promotion of new corporate enterprises in Gujarat and in this manner the company also contributed to industrial growth in Gujarat. The external investment was of Rs. 150 million in equity of GNFC in 1977, which was subsequently increased to Rs. 225 million in 1979, Rs. 1 million in HDFC, Rs. 15 million in Gujarat Alkali and Chemicals Ltd (GACL) and Rs.18 million in Polymer Corporation of Gujarat Ltd. (PCGL). There was a proposal for active participation in the management of Gujarat Alkali and Chemicals Limited (GACL), however, it was subsequently considered expedient to extend general assistance only. The external equity investment in all these companies was for a substantial amount of Rs.259 million. PCGL which was a State Govt. sponsored undertaking, merged with GSFC from 1st January 1983 and the company saw to its economical revival and made that operating division a viable unit. PCGL, as a separate company, had huge accumulated losses and other unabsorbed charges, and GSFC could see a way to take care of these accumulated losses and unabsorbed amounts in its own tax liability net work, in accordance with the relevant provisions of the Income-tax Act. The financial management played an effective role in successful merger of PCGL with GSFC.

A unique financial feature of the company was that in spite of the substantial investment in a number of its own projects and investment in the equity of other companies of interest aggregating to Rs.833.402 million, there was comparatively little increase in the borrowings by about Rs.82.5 million. This happy situation could be brought about through generation of funds from operations etc. The Table 7 outlines this impressive financial outlook of the company. Another bright feature of the period was that during the same period the company paid a total dividend of Rs. 234.1 million and thereby rewarded the shareholders in a handsome manner.

Table 7

Rs. million

AT the Year End	Equity + Reserve	Loans	Total finance	Cash& Bank Balance	Gross fixed assets	Dividend Paid in the year
1977	786.288	135.042	921.330	200.670	1041.70	29.181
1978	806.115	127.714	933.829	175.674	1054.03	29.181
1979	856.910	144.197	1001.107	205.755	1082.43	29.181
1980	887.831	329.507	1217.338	49.104	1211.402	35.194
1981	957.551	395.559	1353.110	84.301	1421.504	35.194
1982	1095.433	327.126	1422.559	119.555	1625.625	38.390
1983	1293.478	337.420	1630.898	320.705	1644.400	38.390

Source of DATA: GSFC annual reports and balance sheets

The company had been paying dividend from 3rd year of operations by making modest beginning of 8% and gradually increasing to 24% in the year 1983. The company had also issued on three occasions bonus shares, first in 1974-75, then in 1979 and again in 1983. The company's distinct performance was also brought out in the prospectus issued by GNFC in connection with its mega public issue by stating that the "GSFC had provided return totaling to 800% on the initial investment and average return of 58% to its original equity subscribers. Thus the company had rewarded its shareholders substantially and added to that appreciation in equity share value was equally significant.

Marketing of Industrial Products

Ted Levitt published his article 'Marketing myopia' in 1960 wherein he argues that the central preoccupation of corporations should be with satisfying customers rather than simply producing goods. In his book 'Innovation in Marketing' (1962) he says Management must think of itself not as producing products but as providing customer-creating value satisfaction.

He argues that "companies must broaden their view of the nature of their business. Giving examples, he says railroad in USA, in sixties, got into trouble because they assumed themselves to be in the railroad business rather than in transportation business". Recent success of turning around Indian Railways by Mr. Lalu Prasad Yadav, the Railway Minister, can be attributed to his conviction that railways were in transportation business and he should reduce the cost of transportation of goods and he took policy measures to do it. Similarly film industry in USA failed to respond to the growth of television in the sixties because it regarded itself as being in the business of making movies rather than providing entertainment. GSFC did not fall into this trap as it considered itself to be in the business of increasing (1) food production and (2) industrial development by providing first special services, training, demonstration etc, to farmers-its customers, and teaching them how to increase food production. For industrial products development, its second objective, it first satisfied its customers but did not confine itself to the customers of its products but created new products, thereby creating new customers for its primary customers, thereby giving fillip to the growth of customers, their products and industrial development.

Levitt writes there is no such thing as a growth industry. Growth is not a matter of being in a particular industry, but in being perceptive enough to spot where future growth may lie. Levitt says history is filled with companies which fall into 'undetected decay' usually for a number of reasons. These insights have proved themselves depressingly accurate. In GSFC we had to ensure that the company is able to spot the growth. To ensure this we selected products carefully with good growth potential and were successful in such selections, and took special measures to see that market will definitely grow by providing special customer service, through development of new products, training of new entrepreneurs, etc through Application Development Centre. The table 8 shows quantitative market growth during first twenty five years for major industrial products of GSFC.

Table 8

Product	Units	second Yr.	26th Yr.	Total Growth %
Caprolactam:	Metric T.	10,653	65,051	610
Liquid Argon*	1000NM3	456	27,590	6000
Eng. Plastics: (Nylon 6 chips)	Metric T.	716	7975	1100
Melamine:	Metric T.	1110	15423	1380
MEK Oxime:	Metric T.	34	2699	3900

Liquid Argon plant was shut down in 2000, as Ammonia-2 plant was scrapped as per condition of the Government of India for grant of license for Ammonia-4 plant. It was restarted in 2006. Value wise growth of each of the above products will be very much higher as unit prices of products were increasing over the years. Growth rate of caprolactam was rather low. This can be explained from the following.

Phillip Kotler in his book "Marketing Management: Analysis, Planning, Implementation and Control"(1967) regards marketing as the essence of business and more. He writes 'good companies will meet needs; great companies will create markets. Market leadership is gained by envisioning new products, services, life styles and ways to raise living standards. GSFC created new markets through developments of its downstream products as can be seen from the following paragraphs. "There is a vast difference between companies that offer me too products and those that create new product and service value not even imagined by the marketplace. Ultimately marketing at its best is about value creation and raising the world's living standards."

For example Caprolactam, Nylon engineering plastic chips, melamine, liquid Argon, MEK Oxime were new products, being produced for the first time in the country by GSFC. All these products enjoyed market leadership and achieved very good growth, as can be seen from the above table, by creating value added products with the help of the Application Development Center. It not only developed/ produced new downstream products but helped entrepreneurs by rendering technical assistance to enable them to manufacture these products. Details can be seen in respective sections. GSFC could achieve this growth by creating demand, and customer-creating value satisfaction. Added value products were provided through engineering plastic for Automobile, Railways, Textile Defense and other industries. All these are customers' customers created by GSFC.

Downstream products of Melamine provided, besides products for industrial sectors, beautiful products for every house even in villages. This has created new life styles in every home through the imaginative uses (beautiful furniture, cup boards, crockery etc) of melamine laminates. GSFC is still the only producer of melamine in the country though its market has grown many times (13.8 times) during last twenty five years. Market of caprolactam, however could not grow as fast, as GSFC failed to recognize that polyester with its better properties would eat into textile market of caprolactam and change in duty structure by Government of India which made polyester more economical. GSFC could not have produced polyester chips or DMT/TPA as it would not integrate with other plants. Liquid Argon provided new uses such as for the production of steel. Such new uses of GSFC products were not imagined at the time of establishing these products. Details of the development of market for each product are given in following paragraphs.

Ammonia

GSFC was the first one to start marketing of Ammonia on large scale. Ammonia is hazardous as well as obnoxious, and fatal in case of very large exposure. Therefore small leakage can cause panic. Further at the room temperature it is in gas form and requires to be kept under pressure to maintain it in liquid form. GSFC developed design and got fabricated special tankers, for the first time in the country, which can carry up to 5 MT of ammonia in liquid form for large bulk consumers. GSFC also filled ammonia in 200 kg cylinders for small consumers. Dedicated tankers were supplied directly to large consumers as well as to big distributors who would fill ammonia from the tankers into the cylinders to meet the requirement of the nearby customers. GSFC has several distributors and stockiest. GSFC has been marketing large quantity of ammonia 70 MT per day throughout India.

Ammonia is used for the production of large number of chemicals such as Methyl Amines, Mono Ethyl Amine, Pharmaceuticals, soda ash, nitric acid, sodium nitrite, cyanides, amides, extraction of copper from ores etc. It is also used in food, beverages, leather industries etc and as a refrigerant in cold storages and small chemical plants. The uses of ammonia are quite versatile and without large availability of the ammonia, products such as caprolactam, acrylonitrile, melamine, sodium nitrite, amines etc could not have been produced. The growth of market of ammonia for products, other than those of GSFC, can be judged from the fact that initial sale of about 100 MT/Y (Rs.0.15 million per year) in the first year increased to more than 50,000 MT/Y (Rs. 600 million) in a span of 30 years by GSFC alone. In the same period consumption of ammonia grew only 5 times for the production of fertilizer, caprolactam and melamine at GSFC. It is seen that the growth of market of Ammonia for other industrial products is very high.

Technical grade Urea

When GSFC set up the fertilizer plant, there was no subsidy but government was controlling distribution and indicating maximum price at which individual product can be sold to farmers. Since there are large uses of the urea for manufacture of various dyes, chemicals, pharmaceuticals etc, GSFC thought of making special grade of urea for this purpose. GSFC established capacity of 3200 MT/Y technical grade urea. However customers chose to use fertilizer grade urea as it was cheaper, even though it was illegal to do so. As a result very little quantity of technical grade urea could be sold.

Sulfuric Acid and Oleum

Sulfuric Acid is not only used in practically all chemicals and pharmaceutical products but also for manufacture of Rayon, in steel industry, refrigeration, textile etc. Oleum is used in dyes and other chemicals. The high growth of the market can be judged from the fact that GSFC market for sulfuric Acid was less than Rs. one million in the first year which grew to Rs.100 million per year in 20 years.

The main problems in marketing were unsteady sales due to uncertain availability of byproduct Sulfuric acid. When this is available price goes down sharply. Further there are also merchant manufacturers of Sulfuric acid. They are single product company and sell by product steam to neighboring companies. As a result they have to sell Sulfuric acid to keep their plant running. This also affects the price of the product.

Caprolactam

GSFC started producing caprolactam in 1974. It was at that time only producer of caprolactam and remained only producer for next 15 years till Fertilizes and Chemicals Travancore Limited (FACT) started producing it. Marketing therefore had to shoulder responsibility of convincing customers for buying domestic product against imported one and also pushing the growth of the market. In the beginning main users were nylon filament yarn manufacturers who manufactured in small quantities however they were highly profitable and had developed clout with the government as they grew and they were also organized as cartel.

Though GSFC had excellent relationship with all the customers of the other products, in case of caprolactam it was not so because the customers wanted to control the prices. Company had much smaller problems with the plant operations but very big problems with the customers. First they complained against quality. A meeting of chemists of all the companies was organized it was found that all chemists had different method of testing in absence of international standard on quality and testing. The method of testing was standardized and every one was requested to use the standard testing method. After which the complaints stopped.

We used to call meeting of all customers every quarter and determine the quantity to be supplied to each customer on the basis of their forecasted production. Idea was to ensure that each customer got product propionate to his production, as total demand was more than GSFC capacity. After failing to get benefit on complaints on quality, they tried their influence with the government and succeeded in changing from year to year excise duty, import duty, putting the product under OGL etc. As they were managing this by lobbying with the Government they would know in advance the change coming and they would either stop buying the product or buy large quantities. This continued for three years 1977-1980. As a result company had to offer lot of discounts, special credits and even then had to shutdown plants two – three months in a year due to high stock. Even though the total demand of the caprolactam was much more than GSFC capacity to produce. At one time GSFC had stock of seven months of production. It took long time, three years in fact, to convince the government to regulate imports on the basis of availability of indigenous production so that import is minimized. Government finally agreed to regulate this in 1981 after which marketing of this product had become smoother.

The demand of caprolactam was increasing and GSFC applied in 1975 for doubling the production capacity of the caprolactam. However Nylon lobby manipulated so that the doubling capacity license is delayed. This went on for more than 10 year and only in 1985 expansion license was given by the government and Nylon lobby merrily continued to import caprolactam till then.

Engineering Plastics – Nylon Chips

Foreseeing the potential future demand, GSFC established a 4000 MT/Y Nylon Chips plant though the demand of the product in the country at that time was hardly 500-600 MT/Y. There were few small producers. To accelerate the growth of the market GSFC established application development centre to develop new grades and new uses and also developed technology for producing new products from new grades and imparting knowledge of the same to the customers. It took some time to convince the entrepreneurs, after providing technical services and advices, and induce them to set up plants for further manufacture of new products.

Nylon Chips produced by GSFC is marketed under the trade name 'Gujlon' The application development centre developed 11 grades of injection molding type and two grades of extrusion type products. These were important engineering plastics raw materials used for engineering application and techno commercial application for various industrial sectors, as a substitute of metal parts being used in textile, automotive, automobile, railway, electronics, electrical, home appliance, medical, packaging, defense, hardware, non lubricated components of the machinery etc. These components can be produced in any color and can be transparent or translucent. As a result a large number of components say about 32 for automobiles, 22 for engineering usage, 38 for electrical and electronic equipment, 29 for textile machinery etc. were developed through GSFC's assistance and manufactured by a number of new and existing manufacturers.

A number of products are produced from extrusion grade nylon. Such as 1) tubing which are resistance to most chemicals, oils and hydrocarbons. As a result they are used to convey refrigerant in automotive air conditioning system. 2) Rods which are used to make different components as this can be machined and cut etc as per the design. 3) Films : The multi layer films can be produced which are used in packaging of both solid and liquid products such as meat, fish, snacks, spices, jam, vegetable, dry fruits, and liquids such as edible oils, motor oil etc. These packages can also be printed. The packaging can be also done under vacuum which keep all above products under very fresh condition. The mono nylon filament yarn is produced from the chip which is mainly used for making fish nets. This is one of the largest uses of GSFC Gujlon. The sale of Gujlon was only 68 MT in the first year and increased to 4000 MT in the 5th year and is continuing to grow at high rate reaching production of 14,000MT/yr.

Melamine

GSFC was the first in India to manufacture melamine with the capacity of 5000 MT/Y. Demand of this at that time was hardly 100 MT/Y due to import restriction and lack of knowledge of its use. Before melamine production started laminates were made with phenol formaldehyde resins. GSFC's Melamine is sold in the trade name of Gujlamine from which melamine formaldehyde (MF) resins and MF molding powder are manufactured by others for which application development centre provides guidance and technical services. MF resins are made in several grades from melamine. There are specific grades for different uses such as flooring, furniture body, fire retardant material, product with aluminum core etc. From the resins two grades of laminates are produced 1) Decorative laminates which have found hundreds of uses in house hold even in small villages, as they can be produced in any color and can also be produced with various designs such as wood pattern, flowers, etc

2) Industrial grades which are a class of industrial insulating materials. These have versatile combination of electrical, mechanical and chemical properties and are used in various electrical and electronics components. Gujlamine is also used in the manufacture of medium density fiber board (MDFB). This can be carved and machined like wood. It is resistant to moisture and has uniform strength and can be finished as desire. MDFB is used as ceiling panels, flooring, railway car interiors etc. There are two grades for use as interior or for exterior use such as for doors, windows, hoardings, sports score boards etc. The application development center has done an excellent job in promoting market of Melamine as its use grew from 96 MT in the first year to 5000 MT in five years and the use is growing at more than 12%/year. To day it is 15,000 MT/Y. As a result of this a number of small and

medium scale manufacturers have been established. After 25 years of the production, GSFC is still the only manufacturer of the Melamine in the country though growth is very high.

Liquid Argon

Here again GSFC put up a very big production capacity plant, twenty times the existing consumption. Till GSFC started production it was produced in small quantities by industrial gas manufacturers as co product of oxygen and nitrogen. The Argon at that time was very expensive, had small impurities of oxygen and was in short supply for use in fabrication industries, specifically for welding of SS, aluminum and alloy steel. Argon produced by GSFC has purity of 99.999%

The Application development center developed newer uses of argon and also started supplying in cryogenic tankers, for the first time in the county, as argon is liquid at minus 185.6°C. The same cryogenic containers used for liquid nitrogen can be used for this. Argon is used in large quantities in the manufacture of stainless steel (A.O.D process), in metal refinery especially for copper, titanium and zirconium, for brazing and soldering specially for low temperature application. GSFC also fills argon in cylinders at high pressure in the same manner as filling of nitrogen cylinders. There are hundreds of small users; practically every small fabrication shop in the country uses argon in cylinders. The consumption of the argon in the first year was $133,000$ M^3 which rose to more than 1 million M^3 in fifth year and still capacity utilization was low as annual capacity was 2.9 million M^3. The plant was shut down in 2000 as a result of scrapping of Ammonia-2 plant and was restarted in 2005-6. Consumption of GSFC argon in 2007 was 3.1 million M^3.

Methane Gas

This is a co product of the argon from the purge gases of the ammonia plants. It is 99.999% pure. It was used as feed stock for Oxo Syngas till Oxo Alcohol plant operated. After this it is used as feed stock for Ammonia plant.

Oxo Syngas.

This was specially produced at the request of M/s. Indu Nissan Oxo Chemical Company Ltd. Who wanted to establish plant next door to GSFC and who was interested in using this for manufacture of Oxo Alcohol, which was basic raw material for plasticizers for PVC industries and was the first and only plant in the country for many years till it was shut down. The capacity of the plant was 8.5 Million M^3 per year. It was supplied through pipeline from GSFC to Indu Nissan.

MEK Oxime

The process of this was developed by D&R laboratory utilizing hydroxyl amine sulfate, an intermediate of caprolactam, as a raw material. This was scaled up to pilot plant and then 100 MT/Y commercial plant was built in 1982. The quality was very good and accepted internationally and consumption grew from 100 MT/Y to 3000 MT/Y of which 90% was exported earning valuable foreign exchange. It is marketed in 190 Kg zinc galvanized mild steel drums. This is also supplied in 25 Kg HDPE carboys for small consumers. Its main use is as additives for paint, varnish and printing ink industries. GSFC is the only producer of MEK Oxime.

Cylohexanone

It is an intermediate in the production of caprolactam and GSFC had provided initially additional capacity of 2000 MT/Y of cyclohexanone, which was later on increased to 5000 MT/Y to be made available to the market. Besides its use in the production of caprolactam and adipic acid, an intermediate in the production of Nylon 66, it is used as solvent and thinners for lacquers, vinyl chloride resins and co polymers. It is an excellent solvent for pesticides such as DDT and other pesticides and insecticides. It is marketed in 200 Lt. Mild steel drums.

⌘ ⌘ ⌘

Chapter 8
Development and Research

At GSFC we called it Development and Research and not Research and Development, because our objective was to develop the company first and then to carry out research. Development included expansion and growth of the company through new projects as well as by de-bottlenecking. Research included engineering research for development of import substitutes. Research was also carried out to reduce cost, increase efficiency, and develop new processes and new products.

a. Engineering Research

Indigenous Development

The company had initially procured spares estimated to last for 3 years. After company went into operation and started consuming spares, it found, after floating purchase enquiries, that the imported spares were very expensive. Therefore import substitution cell was established. Cell had engineers with good experience on mechanical engineering and fabrication and other technology. The cell, consisting of 5 engineers, started studying various important and expensive spares and preparing drawings. The group started studying the drawings of the spares and checking the material and developing the designs, many times it was necessary to test materials to find out the exact composition. At a time two or three engineering companies were contacted to discuss the possibilities of developing individual spares and components. To encourage the company to develop spares, GSFC was offering to meet all costs of development and to purchase spares from the party once they are developed. Several meetings and trials had to be done before individual spare part could be developed. In this manner hundreds of spares were developed.

Foreign suppliers would not provide material specifications, manufacturing technologies, testing standards, chemical and physical properties, hardness, required heat treatment, dimensional tolerances and drawings of any spares or components. It was found necessary to develop all these, if company wanted to procure spares / components from the country or produce the same by itself. The damaged spares / components were taken up for study to determine the above properties which were studied along with representatives of other engineering and fabrication companies. Also drawings for each spare were developed.

The Government of India was also interested in developing Indian industry. It formed "Technical Development Committee" (TDC) with fertilizer Industry and Refineries which were recently nationalized. Each company was made a member of the committee. Each company would nominate a member to the committee who will attend all the meetings which were held quarterly at different places depending upon the invitation from any company. GSFC had become member and had nominated its representative as member to this committee. Several sub committees of the TDC were also formed depending upon the expertise required for the different types of spares / components. Efforts made by each company, problems encountered and success achieved in developing spares and components would be discussed in detail in each meeting and technical information shared with all members.

Liaison was also maintained with other fertilizer plants to take advantage and give advantage to others on any improvements achieved by any unit. Fertilizer Association of India (FAI), with membership from all fertilizer companies, had various committees for technical, R&D, pollution, marketing, training etc. I was chairman of some of these committees during 1977-1982. Committees would meet at different fertilizer factories to discuss with the executives of the host fertilizer company and to get to know on the first hand realities on the ground situation. This also provided lot of information and helped to solve our problems. Arrangements were made so that one company can borrow from any other company, catalysts, spares, chemicals etc. FAI had high standards and only Managing Director of a fertilizer company can become the director of FAI, of course through election.. I was elected as Vice chairman of FAI for 1980 and Chairman for 1981-82

Fabrication of spares and equipment

The above brought in awareness of necessity of improving and maintaining excellent quality, and understanding different codes (AWS, TEMA, BIS, JIS, DIN, etc) and correlating the same with ISI / ISO codes. This also helped in improving foundry practices, forging, precision machining facilities, heat treatment, and elevated temperature testing etc in the country. GSFC had established a work shop to carry out maintenance work. It was headed by an experienced engineer who would cooperate with the import substitution cell to provide any assistance / advice required. Workshop developed a number of technologies and many spares were manufactured utilizing these and other available technologies.

In this manner various spares / components were developed. This included 1) forged carbon and alloy steel components for different equipment operating up to as high a pressure as 650 Kg/cm^2 2) Aluminum alloy forged gaskets for ammonia converter operating at 650 Kg/cm^2 3) Forged shafts for pumps and compressors, 4) Spares and components made of materials such as alloy steel of different grades, zirconium, Inconnel, Alloys such as H.K-40, H.K-9, etc and 5) Special high pressure alloy steel gasket materials, required for different types of equipment, were developed and produced in the company and also by third parties as indicated above.

The value of import substituted spares and components increased from Rs.one million/yr in 1970 to Rs.20 million/yr in 1995. Overall cost of import substituted spares was only one fourth of the corresponding cost of imported spares. In some cases as cited in example 1 and 2 above, cost differentials were as much as 20 times.

These activities lead to establishment of drawing office, corrosion cell, inspection cell, which included instruments such as 1) Ultrasonic sound "crack detention machine" 2) magnetic particle testing instrument,3) vibration analyzer (help of outside party was taken where required) 4) Non destructive testing facilities. For radio active isotope devises outside help was sought.

For large components and repairs of large equipments it became necessary to enlarge workshop and install new equipment as and when required for such work. The workshop after detailed study suggested the equipment required. This included 1) Face lathe 2) Horizontal boring machine 3) Universal Milling machine 4) Bending machine to bend plate up to 25 mm. thickness. 5) Lapping machines 6) Hydraulic press 7) Dynamic balancing machine and 8) Valves testing and reconditioning facilities. The honing machine was designed and fabricated in the workshop. This was used for matting surfaces with the liners of the cylinders of the compressors. Similarly TIG welding technique to achieve 100% x-ray quality joints was developed and technicians (Remember all the persons who did work were fresh technicians ITIs as well as diploma holders trained in training centre), further trained in workshop and trained by suppliers of various specialized instruments as listed above.

Foreign suppliers would manufacture spares / components as per their own countries codes and standards such as ANCC, SNCT, DIN, API, ASTM, AWS, BIS etc. These were coordinated with electrode manufactures in India as per IS code after checking physical and chemical properties and prepared list of equivalent ISI code electrodes. At that time this information was not available with electrode manufacturers in India and GSFC had shared this information with them.

With the above facilities workshop carried out maintenance work on equipment. Some of the major equipment repaired included 1) Carbon Dioxide regenerator for ammonia No. 2 plant, 2) Air preheater for ammonia 1 plant. 3) Titanium lined urea reactor 4) Tires on DAP drier 5) Graphite coolers 6) Phosphoric acid digester 7) Vertical vibrating conveyor in Caprolactam plant 8) aluminum piston for air conditioning compressor 9) Cyclohexane oxidizer 10) Titanium Heat exchanger etc.

Apart from looking after repairs maintenance of the plant, the work shop manufactured 33 heat exchangers and other equipments with various material of construction such as alloy steel, stainless steel 316 L and 316 TI , Titanium and special alloy with 5 CR ½ Mo. Material. These were fabricated for the caprolactam and oxosyn gas plants. Company could also fabricate other equipment such as towers, columns etc required for chemical, fertilizer and petrochemical plants. M/S Engineers India Limited (EIL) found workmanship, quality and the delivery period within which GSFC fabricated equipment was as good as that of the best company in the country. EIL was very keen to place orders of equipment for third parties. As this would involve various aspects of taxation, it was necessary to build separate facilities outside the company.

Establishing engineering company

It was estimated that there was substantial demand for equipment for chemical, petrochemical and fertilizer plants; and company was capable of making such equipment. Company would make good profit if separate company is established for the purpose. A project report was prepared to start Fabrication Company, with a capacity to fabricate 2,500 MT of equipment/year, on the basis of experience developed by the company. Estimated investment was Rs. 107 million, sales at 50% capacity of Rs. 84 million at the end of fifth year, it would make profit from the second year. The report was placed before the Board of Directors for approval. The Board felt that this was a very different kind of diversification from the chemical company, which GSFC is, and further it will require different type of marketing, management and other expertise. Considering these factors they did not approve establishment of a separate company. It is also likely that directors' opinion was influenced by the fact that similar facilities owned by some of the directors were not giving desired results. This could be weighing on their minds when the Directors took this decision. Real thing was that we could not convince the board that GSFC had special expertise which was needed for manufacture of sophisticated equipment for chemical, fertilizer and petrochemical plants.

Besides indigenous development of spares and components following additional activities were done.

(1) Development of alternate sources, such as competitors from other countries, for supply of spares and components and equipment.
(2) Reclamation of costly components, such as damaged pistons, Nitride rods; large size cylinder liners, special valves etc, were done by necessary modifications depending upon the requirement such as ceramic coating, surface treatment etc. depending upon the type of the component.
(3) Developing indigenous manufacturers to replace imported equipments such as specialized pumps, turbines etc.
(4) Inspection facilities were provided to other fertilizer plants

On all these activities not only GSFC helped a number of fertilizer companies, but a number of other companies in Petrochemical field. GSFC also helped a number of engineering and fabrication companies.

Consultancy Services

State fertilizer manufacturing corporation (SFMC) of Ceylon approached the company in 1968 for consultancy on setting up fertilizer plant in Ceylon. The company provided consultancy for determining the capacity of the Ammonia, Urea plant, preparation of project report, preparing detailed specifications, inviting tenders, and selection of foreign process licensers, and foreign contractors. SFMC wanted further participation by GSFC for planning and execution of the project however it was not possible for GSFC in view of its own commitments.

EID Perry approached GSFC to provide consultancy service for improvement of the operation of their Ammonium Sulfate plant. GSFC was successfully operating its Ammonium Sulfate Plant based on byproduct Gypsum. GSFC had sent delegation for several months to advise and incorporate modifications in their plant so as to operate it more efficiently.

Savings in Energy, water and raw materials

A number of schemes had been planned and implemented with above objective at a total cost of Rs. 130 million till 1982. This included modifications of plant operations, installation of booster compressors, installation of more efficient pumps, elimination/ modification of electric motor operations, change of reciprocating compressors to centrifugal ones, installation of additional heat exchangers, flash steam and condensate recovery, minimizing and recycling of liquid effluents etc. Following savings were achieved at 1981 prices.

Savings of 4 million gallons of water/day
Reduction in power consumption by Rs. 24.5 million/year
Reduction in consumption of Rock phosphate by 4%/year
Recovery of ammonia, Urea and DAP worth Rs. 5.5 million/year from liquid effluents. This reduced the pollutants in effluent by 20%

b. Process Research

Corrosion & Materials Lab

There were a number of problems in various plants due to corrosion. This was caused by water, process fluids such as Carbamate solution, sulfuric acid, Phosphoric Acid, different intermediate compounds etc. To solve this problem, I thought it will be best to establish corrosion cell to study cause of corrosion as well as to find right materials to withstand specific corrosion problems. Dr. G.H. Thanki had Doctorate in Chemistry with specialization on corrosion and corrosion inhibition. I thought he will be the best person to start corrosion & Materials Lab and was appointed to head the same. I explained to him that corrosion is a big problem in practically all plants. It is therefore necessary to do research to solve this problem.

He started going round the plants and talking to plant personnel to know the specific areas of the problems and set up a laboratory to test various materials to find suitable material by comparing corrosion rates of different materials in the fluids causing corrosion problems. As problems started getting solved one by one, he received more encouragement from the plant personnel and they started telling him of the new problems. He started developing lab furher by establishing more sophisticated equipment, such as(1) specially designed glass vessels, including induced draft cooling towers as per BIS and ASTM standards requirements for evaluation of various materials, (2) wide field metallograph with monitor and all accessories, including insitu metallographic system to evaluate effect of hot gases and fluids up to 1300 C temperature, (3) equipment and machines for wafer cutting, surface preparation including ultrasonic cleaner, etching(electrochemical system) for material failure studies, etc, and started doing research on different materials to establish economic materials to fight specific corrosion. He established test racks in various locations in plants to evaluate atmospheric corrosion. He also established online corrosion monitoring instrumentation in all cooling towers and both caprolactam plants. This was for the first time such a system was established in Southern Asia. He started getting enquiries and work from European countries to solve specific problems or to determine corrosion resistance of their materials in different corrosive environment. This earned foreign exchange for the company which made us very happy. He would come to me and report to me about the new developments he was undertaking.

Biofertilizers

The company undertook to develop different biofertilizers processes. At first process for Rhyzobium was developed. This was formulated using lignite as inert material and packing it in small packing of 250 gms. A small plant was set up to manufacture the same and started supplying to the farmers. The shelf life of bio fertilizer is only 6 months; therefore great care was necessary not only in manufacturing but also in logistics, of supply, storage and application of biofertilizers. Special training had to be imparted, first to the agronomist of Farm Information Center, and then to the farmers. Other biofertilizers azetobactor, azospirrilum were developed. These biofertilizers extract nitrogen from air and make it available to the plants. A packet of biofertilizer (250gms) is sufficient to extract 15-25 kg of nitrogen per hector. Because of this additional availability of nitrogen the crop production increases. The main precaution to be taken is to ensure that biofertilizer is active and as per standard specification. The company had also developed Phosphate solubilizing culture which would convert unavailable phosphate in the soil to the available form of phosphate which can be absorbed by the plant. The production of biofertilizer started in a small manner and reached to 700 M.T per year, sufficient for nearly 3 Million hectors of the farm.

Production of biofertilizers has become very important, practically all fertilizer companies and a number of private companies are producing and marketing the same. Biofertilizers improve soil fertility,, productivity and provide complementary service to Urea and DAP, thereby help reduce fertilizer subsidy.

Neem coated Urea

GSFC was among the first one to start in 1970s research on the use of neem coating on Urea. After several experiments it was established through farm research that Neem Coated Urea gives at least 10% higher yield. GSFC developed small devise where by farmer can himself do the coating of Neem oil on Urea. Demonstrations were done in farmers' fields to show how this can be done and how it improved the yield. However farmers did not use the method as probably they were finding it time consuming to make Neem Oil from the Neem seeds available on the trees in the villages and mixing them with Urea. Therefore farmers did not adopt it. At that time, process for making Neem coated urea in situ in Urea plant was not available.

Noting that this is very valuable, Indian Institute of Agriculture Research started developing the process in 1994 to make Neem coated Urea at the Urea plant. After successful trial in several plants, two fertilizer manufacturers started production of Neem coated Urea after the Government of India made an Fertilizer Control Order (FCO) for the same in 2004. Today nearly one million tons of neem coated urea is produced and marketed, though Government at that time did not even reimburse the additional cost of production and both manufacturers had to sell it at normal Urea price. Large numbers of farmers, who are using neem coated Urea, are experiencing ten percent increase in production of food grain. In July 2008, the Government of India has modified Fertilizer Control Order. This will permit Neem Coated Urea manufacturers to charge 5% more than the control price of Urea. This will now encourage more urea manufacturers to convert their Urea plant to produce neem coated urea. This will reduce subsidy to the extent additional neem coated urea is produced and consumed by the farmers.

Reformer Tubes

These tubes are very expensive, at that time nearly U.S. $ 2000/ tube. There are more than 200 tubes in a reformer. Further if tube is weak at any place along the length, at those temperatures, it can rupture and can give rise to fire and/or explosion. Thus risk was very high on changing over to indigenous material. Two companies namely 1) Uni Abex and 2) Nitin Casting had started manufacture of centrifugal cast alloys components. They approached GSFC for specifications of Reformer Tubes to enable them to develop the same. After some time they could develop the special alloy as well as cast the centrifugal tube as per the requirement and specification of the original imported reformer tube. We tested one in laboratory for strength, composition etc.

Setting up pilot plant for testing this tube is very expensive, and further testing of reformer tube in the plant is a risky affair, if it develops hot spot there can be a fire, explosion and possible destruction of tube and perhaps reformer if the tube is not nipped and isolated in time. We decided to take the risk and change one reformer tube for a period of six months with 24 hour continuous observation, when this was found to be operating satisfactorily, we changed 5 tubes and tested them in the same manner. On satisfactory results, we then invited tenders for the supply of reformer tubes from these two parties and the reformer tubes of Uni Abex were selected and installed and have worked satisfactorily since 1975 with the normal life as experienced with the imported tubes. Thus GSFC was the first one to install indigenous reformer tubes in the country. Subsequently all the fertilizer factories changed over to indigenous tubes for their gas or Naphtha based ammonia plants.

Primary Reformer Catalyst

In order to indigenize imported catalyst, GSFC and other companies were requesting ICI, who had a world monopoly on the Naphtha reforming catalyst to start manufacturing the same in India as a number of plants were coming up based on ICI reforming process. While ICI did not take interest for several years, M/s United catalyst of USA started discussions with GSFC and requesting GSFC help in commercial development of the catalyst. We asked them to start catalyst production in India as they were manufacturing other catalysts for ammonia plant. They established an Indian Company and set up the plant in Nandesari, Gujarat and developed the process for Naphtha reforming catalyst in laboratory and tested the catalyst for various properties and then they approached GSFC whether it can try this out. Changing over to indigenous catalyst was very risky as, if catalyst does not work, one does not get same quality reformed gas and entire quantity of feed stock goes to waste and further no Ammonia could be produced, in addition to risk of hazards, fire etc as prevailing conditions are very high temperatures produced by gas firing and medium pressure inside the tubes.

Since establishment of pilot plant to test such catalyst is quite expensive, after several testing of catalyst, from May 1978, for its properties and strength in the laboratory, we decided to take risk and charge the catalyst in one of the reformer tubes and keep observation on 24 hour basis. After the successful operation of one tube for about 6 months we decided to load 5 tubes with this catalyst and after successful operation of 5 tubes we decided to change the catalyst in September 1980 for the entire reformer of the first Ammonia plant. Catalyst in second Ammonia plant was changed in May 1981. The catalyst worked very well. GSFC was the first one to use indigenous catalyst in the country. Subsequently other fertilizer companies started using indigenous catalyst.

Seeing the success of the competitor, M/s. ICI made application to the government of India for license to manufacture reformer catalyst. Since Government and industry were asking them earlier to start manufacturing but they did not do it, Government of India appointed a committee to make recommendation as to whether ICI should be given the license. The Government of India nominated me as Chairman of the committee to recommend whether ICI should be given license. The committee had several discussions and deliberations especially on the subject of motive of ICI to now come forward to manufacture. The committee thought that their new interest in manufacture perhaps could be to eliminate the competitor using their financial strength and thereby putting the industry again at their mercy. Considering this aspect the committee recommended to the Government not to give license to ICI for manufacture of reformer catalyst.

Cyclohexane Catalyst

The government of India nominated me as a member of the executive committee of the Regional Research Laboratory, Hyderabad. RRL were interested in developing catalyst which were imported. I suggested to them to develop catalyst for Cyclohexane which is produced by Hydrogenation of Benzene. Both are highly hazardous. They developed, jointly with GSFC, the catalyst in the laboratory and asked us to try out in the plant. The catalyst was produced in small pilot plant. After testing the catalyst for the chemical, physical properties and strength we decided to use the same in the adiabatic reactor of the Cyclohexane plant in place of imported catalyst. The catalyst worked satisfactorily till the reactor developed cracks due to overheating, identical reactor was replaced by reactor designed by design department in May 1987. Since it was techno-economically advantageous to import catalyst, GSFC preferred to import it from Germany.

c. Product Research.

Styrene acrylonitrile Resin (SAN)

As company had applied for letter of intent for manufacture of Styrene and Polystyrene, Company took up development work for development of process for SAN. After laboratory development, pilot plant was made. After successful operation of the pilot plant and testing of properties of the product, company decided in 1981 to set up 1 MT per day plant for demonstration and marketing of SAN. Marketing had started, quality was acceptable, but cost was high. The company decided not to proceed further on the commercialization of the SAN as with out any raw material produced in house by the company the production of SAN would not be economically attractive.

M.E.K. Oxime

One day our chief chemist Mr. M.D Patel approached me and stated that it will be possible for him to develop process in the laboratory for M.E.K Oxime from HX being produced by us as intermediate in the caprolactam plant. I told him to go ahead. When he completed the laboratory development with commercially accepted quality of MEK Oxime, we decided to go ahead with pilot plant to produce 50 Kg/d and test market the product. When it was found that there is a good demand, we decided to set up 1 MT/d plant which was gradually increased to 3 MT per day. Capacity at present is 10MT/day. M.E.K Oxime is marketed in India and nearly 90% of the production is being exported earning foreign exchange to the company.

Application Development Centre (ADC)

As GSFC started construction of Nylon Chips plant, the market study revealed that total market in India was about 500 MT as against the proposed plant capacity of 4000 MT/Y. It further revealed that there would be a great demand for specially compounded Nylon chips. We therefore decided to set up an application development centre, at a cost of Rs. 6 million, which would develop different grades compounded Nylon chips, produce the same in ADC and develop application of such compounds for manufacture of different components. The potential customers would be invited to application development centre to show them the advantage of manufacturing different components from the various grades of compounded nylon chips. With the help of development centre, the market for Nylon chips for industrial application could be developed substantially requiring expansion of the Nylon chips plant which was expanded from 4000 MT to 15000 MT/Y in due course of time. Similarly ADC helped in the development of melamine based products to increase substantially the growth of melamine.

⌘ ⌘ ⌘

Chapter 9
Lost Opportunities

GSFC, during these years, had lots of opportunities to do many more projects. I described below some of the projects for which GSFC lost opportunities.

Gas based ammonia urea plant

In 1975 GSFC made application for obtaining letter of intent for 1350 MT/ day ammonia 1800 MT/day urea plant based on gas, as large quantity of gas was discovered and Government of India were planning to install gas pipe line from Hazira in Gujarat to U.P. After several visits to Delhi and follow up on the project, when we did not receive LOI, I met secretary fertilizers to request him for the clearance of the project. He told me that Government has taken basic decision not to license any more ammonia urea plants in Gujarat as two additional plants in cooperative sectors at Hazira and Kalol are licensed. He further told me that since GSFC has a good record he would be happy to give license to GSFC, if GSFC agrees to establish a plant in Uttar Pradesh (UP) at any location of its choice, as at that time consumption of fertilizers in UP was very high. In fact it was the highest fertilizer consuming State in India and it still is. There was no fertilizer plant established there. It was therefore virgin territory where government wanted to establish about four plants.

I reported the matter to the board of directors and stated that it would be economically attractive for the company to establish fertilizer plant in UP. Immediately Mr. H.K.L. Capoor, who was the Chief Secretary of the Government of Gujarat and Director of the company, reacted asking me, whether I wanted to lose my job by recommending investment outside the State. I told him that the investment to be made by the company in UP will be quite small as compared to the amount of loans which will be available from the financial institutions and the cash generation will be very high. This can be invested in Gujarat. Thereby there will be more additional funds available for investment in Gujarat compared to what GSFC would invest in plant in UP. However he did not buy the argument and asked me to follow up with the government to get license for a plant in Gujarat. I told the board that Government has decided not to grant license for nitrogenous fertilizers in Gujarat. However they would grant license for phosphatic or complex fertilizer plants in view of the favorable location as there is large coast line making it easier to import raw materials which are required for complex fertilizers. This way the company lost the genuine opportunity to establish one more nitrogenous fertilizer plant and becoming very large fertilizer manufacturer. Further there would have been more opportunities. In fact fertilizer plant in U.P. would have made more money as is being done by fertilizer plants which came up there later. Thinking now, I believe if I had talked to the Chief Minister I might have been able to convince him.

Second hand Ammonia Plant

With oil prices going up, the price of Naphtha was rising very high after 1979. One of the Japanese company decided to close down one of their 1350 MT/ day Naphtha based ammonia plant. We thought it was a good opportunity to acquire this plant and reinstall it at GSFC. The board of directors approved the idea and a team was sent to Japan to inspect the plant and discuss with the owner. It was a very interesting and profitable proposal, as later on GSFC spent more than Rs. 8000 million for same capacity new Ammonia plant. News, about proposal for buying second hand plant spread in Gujarat like wild fire and news papers started writing that somebody in GSFC was trying to make money by getting a second hand plant. In view of such rumors the board decided to let go the idea. Thus wrong rumors deprived the company of installing a good ammonia plant at low cost.

Acquisition of Phosphoric Acid Plant

In 1980 the phosphoric acid price had gone down and its demand in USA had come down. M/s Amax Chemical Corporation of USA, one of the largest producers of Phosphoric acid in U.S.A., decided to sell or find an investor for joint ownership of their 190,000 MT/Y phosphoric acid plant in Florida, USA. Phosphoric acid was being imported in India and is one of the most important raw material for DAP and complex fertilizer plants. As sufficient rock phosphate is not available in the country, both rock phosphate and phosphoric acid are being imported. Considering this, I had started the correspondence with them to find the details about the plant and their proposal for either sale or joint venture in the plant. They supplied information about the plant and stated that they were interested in participation by a foreign company to whom they will give 49% equity in a new company to be formed in which they will keep 51% equity and the new company will jointly own the above plant.

They would also supply 50% of phosphoric acid at cost of production and the other 50% at cost plus price to be determined mutually. However before further discussions could be carried out, I left GSFC. My successor did not follow up and therefore the opportunity was lost. Since last few years Government of India is encouraging such joint ventures. Three phosphoric acid plants and two Ammonia- Urea plants are already established abroad as joint ventures. Similar capacity phosphoric plant was established at Jordan at the cost of U.S.$170 million in 1997. In 2007 M/s Iffco had made a proposal to establish 500,000 MT annual capacity phosphoric acid plant in joint venture in Jordan with total investment of U.S. $380 million. Such joint ventures provide phosphoric acid and Urea to the country at much cheaper price than the prevailing international price at the time of import.

One year after I had started my consultancy I convinced Managing Director of a large house in 1983 to take interest in the proposal. He was interested and therefore further details were worked out. M/S Amax Corporation had estimated investment of US$ 32-36 million for acquiring 49% equity. They also provided formula for calculating cost of production for 50% of the production and sale price for the balance 50% with a minimum and maximum limit to the cost of production and sale. Price of raw material, rock phosphate, which they would supply from their own mine was also specified with an upper limit at international price at the time of purchase. The Indian company had accounts with a very large reputed foreign bank that had originally supported the idea and had promised to give the requisite term loan for the purpose. However when details were worked out, company's profitability had started going down and therefore foreign bank backed out on their promise of giving term loan.

Styrene, Polystyrene, ABS & San plants

GSFC had made application to the Government of India for the letter of intent for the above. Kilachand and Bangur Groups had also applied. On follow up with Government of India, they favored GSFC and gave letter of intent to the company in early 1973. The company sent out enquires to world renowned licensors and contractors and after the receipt of the tenders and negotiations, M/s. Badger Ltd. of U.K. were selected as contactors for supply of knowhow , basic engineering and imported equipment with fixed lump sum price, with the provision of adjustments in the price in case any equipment is not required to be imported as it could be available in India or any equipment which as per agreement was to be procured from India but not available in India and has to be imported. Otherwise price was fixed without any escalation. The contract was signed in August 1973 and the price and terms & conditions were valid till 31st March, 1974. We made application for the approval of the contract to the Government of India.

As Kilachand and Bangur groups did not get the letter of intent, they were very much interested in seeing that Government of India does not approve the contract between GSFC and Badgers. They managed to ensure delay in approval in spite of a number of visits by us and discussions with various officials from lowest to highest and specifically explaining to them, (after the second oil price rise in December 1973) that if contract is not approved by 31st. March 1974, there will be a huge escalation as prices of materials and equipment were rising fast. As on 31st March 1974 contract was not yet approved by the Government of India, M/s. Badger sent us telex stating that the contract was no more valid as per agreement, new negotiations for higher prices are required, in view of increase in oil price which in turn is increasing the prices of equipment and material. Unfortunately it was not until 23rd. May 1974 that Government of India informed the company that they were prepared to approve the agreement provided certain modifications were carried out. In spite of vigorous follow up by the company in the matter, the Government's final approval of the agreement was given only on 22nd. January 1975.

The British Capital Loan authorities had not yet completed appraisal of the project and consequently the foreign credit arrangement still remained to be approved. During the intervening period, M/s Badger Limited asked for an increase in design and engineering fees to the extent of 80%, higher than that stipulated in the agreement, and an escalation to the extent of 100% in the lump sum price of imported equipment.. These increases were so steep that company had to take decision to make a fresh appraisal of the project. As a result of the reappraisal of the project, the board came to the conclusion that project was no longer viable In view of this the company decided not to proceed further with the project. Negative attitude adopted by Kilachand and Bangur groups also hurt them as they did not get the project either. As a result ultimately an MNC was the main beneficiary.

Engineering Company

Board of Director did not approve the establishment of an engineering company to manufacture chemical/petrochemical plant equipment. Probably we could not convince the board about the special expertise the company had developed in the field. With the financial strength of GSFC and the expertise developed as a result of plant operations, maintenance, and major repairs carried out on sophisticated equipment an also in house fabrication (manufacture) of large number of equipment with sophisticated materials of construction, it would have grown into a very large profitable company, as a number of medium size similar companies have grown. It could have become as big as GSFC.

⌘ ⌘ ⌘

Chapter 10
Environmental Control

From fertilizer and petrochemical plants, there can be gaseous, liquid or solid effluents which can cause pollution. When GSFC started production of first phase of fertilizers, there were no laws in India and also there were no strict laws abroad, especially for fertilizer industry. When I was in U.S.A. during 1948 to 1954, we could go swimming in the Lake Michigan, which was one of the largest sweet water lakes in the World. But after about 10 years there were boards on Lake shore that no swimming was allowed. Lake was polluted by that time. It took many years and lots of money to clean it up.

Gaseous Pollution

At the time of signing of contract for the first phase of fertilizer group of plants in 1964, there were no pollution control laws in India and not even in advance countries. Even then company had provided ammonia absorption system to absorb sulfur dioxide from vent gases of sulfuric acid plant. This was the latest system available, at that time, in the world for the Sulfuric acid plant. More than 90% of sulfur dioxide gas, which would otherwise escape to atmosphere along with vent gases, would be absorbed by ammonia and produce ammonium bisulfite a chemical product which can be commercially marketed. In normal cases this helped and there were no pollution problem, however during the monsoon or when the atmospheric temperature dips, or sudden shutdown of the plant due to power failure or for any other reasons the sulfur dioxide, escaping from the chimney, being heavier than air comes down to ground level and depending upon the wind velocity affects some farms in the wind direction. To minimize this company increased the height of the chimney to 165 Ft.

Company simultaneously also formed a committee of the agronomists of the company and farmers representatives of the areas. The committee would meet and visit the site of any farmer who had made complaint regarding damage to his crops. The committee will examine the damage and discuss the cause of damage. If the committee finds the damage was on account of Sulfur dioxide gas, committee would make the assessment of the damage and recommend compensation which will be paid to the farmers. Generally decisions of the committee would be unanimous and the farmers were reasonably satisfied.

Company later on improved the ammonia absorption system and incorporated latest DCDA system in new Sulfuric acid plants as well as sulfur dioxide and oleum, plants. There were no other gaseous pollutants.

Liquid Effluents

The liquid effluents produced from the plants, especially phosphoric acid plant, were collected in two separate ponds one for gypsum and second for chalk. The clear liquid would be pumped out along with liquid effluent from the other plants to pond at Bajwa village from which it would flow through natural kans (nature's way to drain excess water from locked areas to the river/sea to minimize flooding). After a year, once three elephants from the circus, while drinking water from Bajwa pond, died. News paper took it up as a big story blaming GSFC for the incident. As soon as the company heard about this incident, the company officers went to site and requested circus authorities to allow the company to take blood samples from the elephants to know the cause of death. Unfortunately circus fellow would not allow. Except this incident, there were no other cases where animal or human being was affected by the pond water. Even then company decided to construct a pipe line to send the effluent directly from the company premises to the natural kans, bypassing the Bajwa pond. Separate Liquid effluent treatment plants for treating effluent from each plant were also established.

When the above incident took place I wrote to M/s. ICI, U.K to find out what they were doing for the effluent treatment. I was surprised to receive reply that they were not doing any effluent treatment at that time and were discharging the effluent to the river. While investigating laws for pollution in USA, I found that effluent guidelines and standards for fertilizer industry in USA were published in December 1973 by the Environmental Protection Agency (EPA) (full six years after GSFC plant was established). Of these (standards) those which could be achieved using "Best practical control technology currently available" should be established by July 1978 and those which could be achieved utilizing "Best available technology economically achievable" should be established by July 1983. Thus ten years period was given to industries in USA to implement the law in two phases. In India laws are enacted and industries are asked to implement the laws with immediate effect.

Effluent Channel project

As Vadodara is far away from the sea, there were always problems for discharging effluents after treatment not only for GSFC but also for Gujarat refinery, IPCL and other plants in the surrounding areas, as the treated effluents could only be discharged on land and in the Mini river bed where a number of villages are located down stream on the Mahi and Mini rivers.

There are wells in villages as well as on the river banks. The question therefore arose whether quality of water in such wells would be affected by the discharge of effluent in Mahi and Mini rivers. NEERI (National Environmental Engineering Research Institute) was therefore appointed as consultant by the Government of Gujarat to prepare report on whether this would be the best manner for discharge of effluents or some alternatives could be found out. NEERI submitted its report in 1974. Deliberations of these recommendations lead to the new concept that individual companies may pre-treat their effluent to a prescribed, more liberal standard and then discharge it through a common effluent channel to the sea.

The Government of Gujarat appointed a committee to find out feasibility of establishing an effluent channel for collection of effluents from all industries and discharging the same to the sea. I was one of the members nominated by the Government of Gujarat. M/s. NEERI were also appointed as consultant to advice on the design of the system. It was thought by the government that all industries should contribute to the cost of such effluent channel, proportionate to the quantity of the effluent each one was discharging. Data was therefore required to be collected from each unit to know the quantity of the effluent they were discharging at that time and the quantity which they were likely to discharge after 5 years. This was for the purpose of deciding the capacity of the effluent channel.

M/s. IPCL and Gujarat Refinery were reluctant to join. Their argument was that they have spent lot of money on liquid effluent treatment and their treated effluents are good for use in farming. Unless they join the capacity of the channel will not be large enough to be economical. It was therefore necessary to convince them to join the project. The Gujarat Government formed a committee of which I was a member to convince various industries to join as a member of the effluent channel project. Several meetings were held with Refinery as well as IPCL. However their main point was that they have already spent large amount and their treated effluents are very good. The following arguments convinced all major participants to agree to the project and contribute to the cost.

1. Treated effluents are not potable. Since they flow in river bed which is dry for many months they are bound to affect, through underground seepage, quality of the water of the wells of the surrounding villages. This could create political and labor problems for the industry.
2. Effluents are generated 24 hours/day, but farmers do not use them for 24 hours. Quantities of effluent are very large and adequate land was not available to store the same.
3. Occasional/accidental problems in plants could create hazardous situation and discharged effluents at that time may not be meeting requirement of the standards.
4. Standards for discharge of effluents to Effluent channel are more liberal as compared to standards for inland water discharge. This would reduce the cost of treatment to the industries and also to individual companies.

They were convinced on the basis of above arguments that it is advisable to discharge the effluents to the sea rather than on the land. On this basis they agreed to become member and provided information on the present quantity of effluent and the quantity they would be discharging after five years, and to pay the proportionate cost of establishing effluent channel. Information from other members was already received. It was decided to set up 32 million gallons / day design capacity effluent channel with peak capacity of 48 million gallons/day though quantity at that time was 13 million gallons/day.

After discussions with engineering experts on the design, it was decided to have "U" shaped brick masonry covered with RCC slab with a width of 2 meters and depth of also 2 meters. It was also decided that maintenance road parallel to the channel will be constructed. This has now become a nice public road connecting various villages and industries. The site survey also revealed that it will be possible to have gravity flow for the effluents. As per NEERI it was necessary to have treatment facility at the end of the channel before discharging into the sea. They provided the design for the same as well as design of diffuser to discharge effluent water in the sea so that it is properly mixed with sea water. The cost of the channel was estimated at Rs.130 million and was completed in 1981.

The channel has become a very good blessing to the industries. This was the first channel in the country for the purpose of discharging the effluents to the sea. This further led to the design and construction of similar channels at Ankleshwar, and Vapi . Further in order to ensure that small scale industries would pre-treat effluent to the minimum level, three centralized effluent treatment facilities to treat effluent from small and medium scale industries, at Vadodara, Ankleshwar and Vapi were also visualized and established. The participating industries paid proportionate capital as well as operating cost.

Solid Effluent

The ammonia plant had a vetrocoke purification system which annually produced some sludge containing arsenic. There will be about 25 drums of such sludge in a year. This was packed in SS drums which were covered with concrete. These drums were then discharged in the sea, as per the permission given by GPCB and as per the design and details provided by NEERI. Later on process was changed to eliminate generation of such sludge.

The phosphoric acid plant produced co-product gypsum which contains fluoride salts. This was normally used in the production of ammonium sulfate fertilizer and any surplus available was sold to farmers at nominal cost. The byproduct gypsum is a very good soil conditioner and also supplies sulfur which is basic nutrient, as soil at present is deficient in sulfur. The ammonium sulfate produces chalk as by product.

After discussions with ACC, they agreed to make trial use of chalk along with their natural lime stone as the raw material for manufacture of cement. They started using this as raw material along with lime stone in the Sevalia plant and continued to use it till the Sevalia plant was shut down. After the Sevalia plant was shut down the chalk is getting accumulated and is collected as heap (hill). This started giving dust nuisance when chalk dried up and when there was high wind. To get over this problem a two meter soil layer was spread on the heap and trees were grown. This then became a nice green hill and prevented any dust flying off.

Company also had received proposal from a private party who claimed that they had developed a process for manufacture of Eco friendly masonry cement from the by-product chalk from Ammonium Sulfate plant. Their estimate for a demonstration project was Rs. 150 million in 1994. They wanted GSFC science foundation to support and participate in the development. However GSFC did not find this viable as a result proposal was dropped. It is worthwhile, for GSFC, to develop process for making masonry cement from this.

The DAP plant when at high level of production emits dust in the atmosphere to solve this problem a de-dusting system was provided so that no dust would spread in the surrounding area.

⌘ ⌘ ⌘

Chapter 11
Political environment

Government or non Government Company

The Government of Gujarat decided to keep only 49% shares in GSFC and rest to be offered to the public. This, therefore, was neither a Government company nor a private sector company, but created a new ownership structure for the company, which later on became known as joint sector. This created lot of political controversies in Gujarat. Back ground and details of these are given bellow.

Central government included fertilizers in schedule B of the industrial policy resolution of 1956. This being the area in which "the state will generally take initiative in establishing new undertakings but in which private enterprise is also expected to supplement the effort of the state. Till 1966 all nitrogenous fertilizer companies were in public sector (Government owned).

Government of Gujarat in their draft five year plan (1960) stated that annual food production in Gujarat was 2.2 million MT and consumption was 4.0 million MT The techno economic survey (TESG) conducted by national council of applied research (NCAER) stated that the food production in Gujarat was 2.0 million MT but consumption was 3.0 million MT It further noticed that "controversy had arisen in the state regarding the emphasis on food self sufficiency as the primary object of the agricultural policy". The TESG argued that "the state would be ill advised to insist on food self sufficiency "because the deficiency is of such large magnitude that in order to reduce it significantly, a major reorientation of cropping pattern would be necessary. TESG however strongly recommended the establishment of fertilizer plant of significant capacity in Gujarat as part of 3rd five year plan with expansion in 4th five year plan period.

Government of Gujarat had taken decision not to keep GSFC as Government Company as early as end of 1961. However it is not known how or whether such basic decision was explicitly conveyed to the assembly. Mr. Sanat Mehta labor leader of Vadodara stated that the GSFC was to be in the State Public Sector and then ministry had changed this later. Original article of association of GSFC provided as audit provision "that so long as government of Gujarat hold at least 25% of the shares of GSFC it may require audit by the C AG giving the control over the company. Industrialist directors were opposed to this, as in their opinion this would bring bureaucratic approach in the management of the company rather than desired businesslike approach. The article was modified in 1963 as "so long as company is a Government Company within the meaning of section 617 of the companies act, a CAG audit would in any event be obligatory. This means Government should have at least 51% shares to order CAG audit.

Even though there was ample legal and financial base to exert very tight state control over GSFC, the government of Gujarat refrained from exercising such control. This was termed "self-denying ordinance" and provided management full freedom to operate and no decision of the board of directors was referred to the Government. (The Government of Gujarat had more than 50 % shares, in fact

100%, till the public issue was made and fully subscribed by 1967, thus GSFC was Government Company till then.)

Articles of Association clearly stated that the Government of Gujarat will have 49% equity in GSFC; some persistent critics of GSFC insist that the GSFC was to be in the State's public sector and that minority role was accepted later. One critic contended that the question of loans was "the sound economic reason" offered by the Government whose true motive was to deprive the assembly the right to scrutinize closely the affairs of the company. This was the main contention of all political leaders, they wanted GSFC to be Government Company so that Assembly can debate GSFC affairs and CAG can scrutinize GSFC accounts. There were many political controversies on the subject. These are dealt with in detail in the following paragraphs..

Marketing Controversies

During 1960's the government of India felt that to increase the production of the fertilizers, it was necessary to invite greater participation of private sector. The Government of India appointed committee on fertilizer headed by Mr. Sivaraman in 1965. Sivaraman committee and others expressed doubts whether cooperatives were organizationally, financially and temperamentally adequate for the task of marketing the higher quantum of contemplated fertilizer output through aggressive salesmanship which would develop demand, not merely satisfy existing demand. According to them greater reliance was needed on business minded marketers – either manufacturer's own net work depots or established private distributors.

Till 1966-67 in Gujarat the Gujarat State Cooperative Marketing Society (GSCMS) was sole distributors of the fertilizers provided by the central Government. It was therefore natural that they would like to market and distribute GSFC fertilizers on exclusive basis. As many political leaders were associated with cooperatives, they had also support from them. Agricultural Minister Thakkorbhai Desai and his deputy Mr. Madhavalal Shah wanted that GSFC should give exclusive distributorship of its fertilizers to apex cooperative society. Most leading congress party men preferred such course. GSCMS made clear its preference for continuation of exclusive marketing arrangement, it has enjoyed so far. GSFC on its part took pains to complement the cooperatives as a splendid vehicle for distribution of fertilizers.

GSCMS did have an extensive arrangement and considerable expertise and substantial credit was available through them for the purchase of agricultural inputs. However GSFC wanted to have own depots as suggested by Sivaraman Committee and as per the announcement made by GSFC in its public issue. After a lot of discussions GSCMS agreed that they had some weak areas. It was finally agreed that cooperatives would be given distribution rights where they were functioning effectively,and a net work of GSFC's own depots, limited in number and supplementary to the cooperatives, where latter were weak or non existence. In the first instance GSFC opened 29 depots which were later on called farm information centers manned by agronomist. However most of sales were done through the cooperatives.

At Annual General Meeting (AGM) in 1968 after the start of the production, GSFC chairman stated that the company has already started marketing of Fertilizers through cooperatives and company would establish its own depots shortly. Just after the AGM the Baroda district purchase and sales federation demanded that GSFC be obliged to market its output exclusively through GSCMS in order to avoid exploitation of agriculturalist.

During the consideration of GSFC annual report in the state assembly during 1968 outcry was made for 1) poor judgment in the matter of inviting global tenders for caprolactam plant 2) Personal gains by directors and others 3) Neglect of agriculturalist interest and 4) high commission 10% paid by GSFC to GSCMS for distribution of fertilizers. Mr. Jaswant Mehta, minister defended GSFC decision on marketing as well as on payment of 10% commission to cooperatives on the ground that GSCMS absorbed all transportation charges and sold fertilizers at the same price at all points within the state.

The GSFC increased the prices of all fertilizers including DAP in March 1971. Especially price increased in DAP created political storm. The critics stated that decision was not taken with the consent of the State. This gave fodder to various news papers such as Western Times, Times of India, Gujarat Samachar etc, especially as GSFC had declared 12% dividend. Further criticism was that GSFC was profiteering and was inhibiting promotion of progressive agricultural practices by unwarranted price increases. Most consumers considered GSFC as a Government Company and therefore they should get fertilizers at lower prices. Gujarat Samachar published editorial under article "unjustified price rise in fertilizer" stating that fertilizer should be provided at the cheaper, even at subsidized cost. In his view this was the main aim of the GSFC from the beginning. (At that time subsidy on fertilizers was not introduced by Central Government, however Government was specifying maximum price for Urea.) Same editor demanded "deeper and all embracing probe" of GSFC operations. One correspondent wanted sale of DAP through GSFC depots and eliminate the cooperatives and their commission on the ground that DAP sold by itself

The situation got aggravated as GSFC Chairman resigned to fight Lok Sabha election in 1971 on old congress party ticket and the political environment was not stable due to split in congress and instability of the congress. Mr. Jayakrishna lost the election and was reinstated as chairman. Various cooperative organizations, former ministers, prominent politicians, panchayat protested against the price rise and unwarranted exploitation of the farmers of Gujarat on the eve of monsoon.

Fears were expressed that increase in price of DAP would encourage farmers to switch to cash crop from food grain to the detriment of the state's food supply. It seems most of the criticism came from progressive farmers who were already producing cash crops, especially from Saurashtra, where DAP is used for peanut, a cash crop. Jaswant Mehta former minister, in a press conference, demanded a commission of enquiry into the affairs of the GSFC and demanded Government talk to the company to rescind the price rise by a fixed date. New congress leaders, especially Chimanbhai Patel, Chhabildas Mehta and Jaswant Mehta made charges of mismanagement and receipt of kickbacks by directors. Jaswant Mehta had also tabled adjournment motion on the issue. Further criticism was that on one side GSFC had protested to the Government of India against 10% increase in excise duty, on the other hand it itself was increasing price of fertilizers.

Agricultural minister, Mr. Jaydeep Sinh Baria, supported GSFC decision. The motion was withdrawn when Government gave assurance for taking action. Jaydeep Singh Baria however mentioned that GSFC was an autonomous company and that no directive could be issued and no dead line for action can be given. He however acknowledged the extent and depth of the feeling on the issue and assured the house that virtually every one hoped for a reconciliation of price increase and said that Government, on their own were already working in this direction. Discussions were held at the instance of the Government in April and early May and the price increase was reduced by 50% in a decision announced on 12th May 1971 just before the collapse of the Government and imposition of the president rule. This made critics of the company all the more determined to convert GSFC into Government Company to whom orders can be given.

Mr. Chimanbhai Patel in a series octures forcefully stated that the state should assume 51% control of the GSFC, arguing that it was a mistake to have allowed it to become a private sector company in the first place. He further argued that closer control would lead to improved working and finance and consequently there could be both lower prices and better profitability. Further public lending institutions are now allowed to give loans to the public sector and with Government guarantees; there would be no difficulties in getting loans. According to him closer legislative scrutiny in general produces greater social responsibility without reducing profitability.

With the elected government gone, the agitation was directed towards the Governor, Shriman Narayan who being Gandhian it was thought, would be more vulnerable to the kind of arguments critics were advancing. As the public protests continued Jaswant Mehta wrote to the Governor that all chairmen of all Government sponsored corporation should resign as they were political appointee of earlier government. Dr. Jivaraj Mehta, former chief minister and guiding sprit behind the creation of GSFC stated that he favored the present pattern as it amply protected the public interest. He warned against killing the goose that lays the golden eggs.

GSFC directors voluntarily agreed, during 1971, to place annual report / statement of accounts before the Gujarat assembly but not before the committee on public undertaking. Governor suggested that an agriculturalist might be appointed / elected on the board of the company at some time in future. In the governor's view these moves coupled with already ample power in the hands of the government should nullify any demands for formal take over.

The compromise effected by the governor on the reduction in the price of the DAP was not liked by new government which came in power in later half of 1972. It is understood the new government had obtained agreement of the Government of India for conversion of GSFC to public sector. The major critics of GSFC Mr. Chimanbhai Patel became Chief Minister and Sanat Mehta Finance Minister in the Gujarat Government. There was considerable anxiety about the shape of things to come, especially whether the Government would convert GSFC into Government Company by acquiring additional shares to make 51% equity in the hands of the Government. And also the effect this would have on the working of GSFC. Finally new government did not convert GSFC into the Government Company. It seems, and it is my guess, that financial institutions had used their influence with the Government to maintain status quo, that means not to convert the company into Government Company.

While these political discussions were going on, the management of the company operated as usual without any thought as to what changes politicians may make to GSFC constitution. Fortunately for GSFC no such apprehensions became reality.

In June 1980 Government of India increased the price of Urea and DAP substantially. As these were subsidized prices, company must increase the price to get full subsidy. At that time I was Managing Director. I started receiving calls from Industries Department Government of Gujarat that GSFC should not increase the price of DAP. I informed them that if Company does not increase price it would lose money, so I can not agree not to increase the price of DAP. Afterwards I got a call from the Minister of Industries for the same thing, when I told the minister that we can not keep the same price, as company will lose substantial amount. He told me that this is an order that you should not increase price. I told him that as Managing Director it is my duty not to do anything which would result in company losing money. He then told me that he can fire me for this defiance, I told him I know that and if he wants to he can fire me today. He then cooled down and asked me how to achieve Government objective. I told him that he can talk to our chairman as well as to the Chief Secretary to bring up the subject in the Board meeting. He asked me whether I will support if they bring up the matter in the Board. I told him that I will not say anything, but if they ask my opinion I will have to tell that company would lose Rs. 36 million/year if we do not increase the price. I will abide by the decision of the Board if it decides not to increase the price.

In the next Board meeting Chairman stated that Government desires that company should not increase the price of DAP. He looked at the directors, since most of the directors were not aware of the increase in the price announced by the Government of India, they did not react. However Mr. H.M. Patel asked me the implication. I replied that if the company does not increase the price of DAP, it would lose annually Rs. 36 million. Further the same problem may come up in future, at that time losses may be much more. Mr. H.M.Patel asked me why should we lose money if we do not increase the price, I explained that DAP was under subsidy and the company would get subsidy equivalent to the difference in the cost of production as calculated by Government formula and the notified subsidy price for the farmer. If we sell at a price lower than notified subsidy price, we will be reimbursed at the lower price we sell and not at the notified subsidy price. In other words we will get lesser amount of subsidy: that is by the amount of subsidy price increase by the Government of India multiplied by the MT of annual sale. This worked out to Rs.36 million/year on our production/sale base of 90,000 MT DAP. Mr. H.M.Patel immediately said that in that case we must increase the price to the level notified by the Government of India. All directors, except Government Directors agreed.

Chairman then stated that since opinion is divided we may constitute a committee to go into more details and the committee may decide. He suggested committee of two persons Mr. Tribhuvandasbhai Patel, our director and chairman of Amul and renowned political and farmer leader and me. Directors agreed to the same. After the meeting Mr. Tribhuvandabhai told me that he will organize some meetings with GSCMS and Agriculture Department, Government of Gujarat and will inform me the date, time and place when I should join him. He first organized the meeting with the Chairman of GSCMS and asked them to sell DAP to farmers without increase in price, though GSFC would supply at revised higher price. At first chairman of GSCMS said that he will lose lot of money. Tribhuanasbhai told him that up till now they have made lots of money out of GSFC so it is now their turn to sacrifice. After lot of discussions GSCMS chairman agreed to bear 50% of the difference in the price.

Tribhuvandasbhai then arranged meeting with Agriculture Department Government of Gujarat. In the beginning they insisted that GSFC should not increase the price. Tribhuvandasbhai explained that if GSFC does not increase the price it will lose substantial amount and the Government of India will get benefit of lower amount of subsidy to be paid to GSFC, but Government of Gujarat will not gain anything. On the other hand if GSFC increases price it will not lose money and the money thus saved could be used in the investment when

Gujarat will get benefit of this. After lot of arguments Government agreed to bear remaining 50% of the difference in the price. In this manner GSFC did not have to lose money, but at the same time farmers got cheaper DAP. GSFC board was very happy with the outcome.

Labor Union

GSFC had decided to try as far as possible to exclude outside trade union organizers from the company's work force. This was informally explained to workers that no non employee of the company may head the GSFC union unless 75% of the work force voted for him. There was always a company union. This angered Mr. Sanat Mehta who was labor leader in Vadodara, controlling several unions in various companies. In his view GSFC being a de facto Government company should strive to be "model employer" which includes free exposure to labor organizers. This was often cited as a concrete example of industrialist / government collusion to the detriment of the "socialist pattern of society" to which congress party was committed. This was the major reason for the personal attacks on GSFC by Mr. Sanat Mehta. He could not convince GSFC workers to elect him their labor leader.

Caprolactam: Alleged bungling in Global Tendering

LOI for caprolactam was received in November 1966; GSFC had invited global tenders and awarded contracts to M/s. Hitachi Ltd. Japan, in July, 1968. (For details see under Diversification, Caprolactam) The government of India had approved the agreement (but the public did not know about this) However the Government of India could not release foreign exchange for a long time as discussions were going on between the Governments of Japan and India for the Yen credit. Since this was delaying the project, there were lot of speculations and political discussions alleging bungling in inviting tenders for caprolactam by GSFC without knowing the availability of foreign credit. To clarify the position chairman of GSFC made following statement at AGM of June, 1973.

"At this stage I feel it is my duty to make reference to some canards that have appeared in the press very recently about the project, because they gave rather a misleading view of the project and its progress." Caprolactam project was for the first time thought of in the year of 1966. There upon, your company invited global tenders for the project in July, 1967. In all 8 tenders were received from different parts of the world. At no time the Government of the India had notified any particular country or any particular credit for the project. After careful consideration of the tenders received, your company selected M/s. Hitachi Ltd., Japan as a contractor for the caprolactam project and the contract was signed with them on 1st July, 1968. The government of India approved the contract in February, 1969. Thereafter in spite of several efforts both by the Government of India and your company spread over a period of about a year, the Government of Japan did not approve allotment of Japanese credit for the project. In the result, the contract with M/s. Hitachi Ltd had to be abandoned."

"Thereafter in consultation with the Government of India, your company entered into negotiations with European parties for the project in February, 1970. The negotiations for the project with M/s Inventa of Switzerland and M/s. Technip of France were concluded in May, 1970, and LOI were issued to them on 8th June, 1970. Contracts with said party were signed on 22nd June, 1970. The government of India approved the same contracts by March, 1971. The foreign exchange required for the imported equipment was released by the government of India in 3 installments namely 60% in March, 1971, 25% in May, 1972 and 15% in December, 1972. This delay in release of foreign exchange naturally affected the project schedule."

"According to our country's policy, we placed orders for about 70 percent of equipment required with indigenous manufacturers, but unfortunately, they have not been able to adhere to delivery schedule agreed to by them. For some of the delay, there were reasons for which they had no control. Then, there have been severe shortages of power and raw materials such as steel and cement in the country during the past year. Nevertheless, we now expect that by about the end of December, 1973, or soon thereafter, the erection of the plant would be completed. Even so you will observe that the project will be completed within 33 months from the first release of the foreign exchange by the Government of India, and 28 months from the date the foundation stone was laid. Such complex and complicated project is being set up for the first time in India and I make bold to say that judged by any standards, what we shall have done will come to be regarded as a major achievement by your company. And this has been made possible only because of the advance planning undertaken by your company and vigilance with which the project has been pursued to overcome numerous difficulties which your company has had to face. This is why I have been distressed by the uncharitable comments in the press. What we have done and hope to do should be a matter of pride for all of us."

Conversion of Naphtha to Gas

When we applied for expansion project in 1966 we were told that no gas was available and new ammonia plant was to be based on Naphtha as feed stock. However in 1968 when plant was under construction GSFC was informed that no indigenous Naphtha was available and GSFC should change over to Gas as feed stock from Naphtha. However anticipated gas was not available and therefore plant after completion did not have to change to gas as feed tock and has been operating on naphtha as feed stock. Originally available indigenous Naphtha was process naphtha, which ICI was reluctant to use. Fortunately, however, when plant was commissioned straight run naphtha was available.

The rapid development of Bombay High gas field indicated that by 1979 a large quantity of Gas, (estimated at fourteen million M^3/day), would be available. GSFC by that time had three ammonia plants, ammonia one was operating on mixture of Naphtha and Gas, ammonia two was operating only on Naphtha and ammonia three on Gas. If ammonia two is converted to utilize gas in place of Naphtha, it would save annually at (1979) international price of Naphtha (US$ 200/ MT) US $ 27 million/yr (About Rs. 230 million) in foreign exchange. Against this the investment required for ammonia two to convert from naphtha to Gas as feed stock would hardly be Rs.40 million. The country therefore, had tremendous advantages in changing over the feed stock of ammonia plant 2 of GSFC from naphtha to Gas..

At that time naphtha was supplied at price of Rs. 600/ MT for the manufacture of fertilizers whereas if it is exported it would earn to the country foreign exchange @Rs. 1700/MT this means not only country gains foreign exchange but also make profit of Rs.1100/ MT over its use as feed stock in the fertilizer plant. It was for these reasons government of India at that time was not encouraging new fertilizer plants based on naphtha as feed stock. The fertilizer subsidy during 1979 was expected to cost exchequer Rs.4500 million as per the budget. Any gain by reducing the cost of production of fertilizer, directly or indirectly would reduce subsidy, and would provide above stated advantages to the country.

Babubhai Patel who was chief Mister at that time was calling Managing Directors of various state corporations every three months to discuss with them about the respective companies problems. In one such meeting during 1979 I informed the Chief Minister about the Gas being flared by ONGC and possibility of using the same by GSFC and thereby saving foreign exchange to Government of India and reducing the Fertilizer subsidy, reducing cost for GSFC and increasing the ONGC profit by sale of gas instead of flaring it. He took interest and told me that he will arrange a meeting with Mr. Bahuguna who was at that time the Petroleum Minister, Governnment of India to discuss the proposal. He arranged the meeting with Mr.Bahuguna and asked me to join him and attend the meeting.

During the meeting Chief Minister explained to Mr. Bahuguna various advantages the Government of India, ONGC and GSFC can gain by converting feed stock of ammonia two plant from naphtha to gas. Mr. Bahuguna stated that surplus gas was not available as all gas was already allocated. When we told him that even if gas was made available to GSFC for interim period till the allocated companies are ready to use the Gas, there would be a lot of savings to all concerned. Further GSFC was ready to go back to the use of Naphtha at short notice of few days as GSFC stores Naphtha for use in its ammonia one plant. However Mr. Bahuguna told Chief Minister no gas was available even for interim period. I told CM in Gujarati that minister was lying as the companies to whom gas is allocated will take several years to complete their plants and be in a position to utilize gas. We all know that large quantity of gas was being flared and it continued to be flared for many years. However CM told me in Gujarati that we can not say this to the Minister. In spite of various arguments Mr. Bahuguna would not agree to allocate any gas even for interim period and meeting was closed.

I was wondering why minister was lying so bluntly, was it because he did not want Gujarat to get any advantage? Most people in Gujarat felt at that time that the Government of India was against Gujarat. The truth was that it was not that Gujarat would get advantage but Government of India, ONGC & GSFC. Government of India would have got advantage of Rs. 380 million per year (Rs.230 million in foreign exchange and Rs.150 million in the export), ONGC at least Rs. 100 million/year and GSFC would have got advantage Rs. 40 million per year. Does not the Minister of the Government of India look at the advantage to the Government of India and to the nation while taking decision? He took decision against the national interest and that to by telling blatant lie. Recently I came across a news item published in Economic Time of 1st October, 2006 which aptly confirms that politicians lie.

NETAS AND TRUTH BUG

"The political chaps in Europe have suddenly started speaking truth. Will the fad ever reach Indian shore?"

I was told this a number of times by friends and people that politicians lie but it was my first experience facing politician telling outright lie.

Urea Plant Technology (GNFC)

GSFC had received LOI for 1300 MT/day ammonia and 1600 MT/day urea plant during 1974. Ammonia plant was to be based on use of residual fuel from Gujarat Refinery as feed stock. GSFC after inviting tenders and negotiations with various parties selected M/s. Linde of Germany as contractor for ammonia plant and M/s Toyo Engineering Corporation of Japan as contractor for urea plant. This proposal was sent to the Government of India for the approval and for release of foreign exchange. The Government of India approved the contract for ammonia plant and released foreign exchange through KFW loans. However did not say anything regarding urea plant contract. We followed up with government of India. However no response was forthcoming and we were not able to find out where the proposal was stuck up.

One day the Secretary Fertilizers, Government of India telephoned Mr. M.D. Rajpal, who had retired as Additional Chief Secretary, Government of Gujarat and was at that time Managing Director of GSFC, that Mr. P.C Sethi, Minister for Fertilizers wants Mr. Rajpal to call on him. Mr. Rajpal asked me to accompany him. We first met Secretary fertilizer Mr. Ramnathan who told us that meeting would be in connection with the contract for the urea plant. He took us to the chamber of the Minister. After introduction by the Secretary, the Minister looked at Mr. Rajpal and asked him about the urea technology. Mr. Rajpal told him that Gami is technical person and he can reply to him. Minister then angrily told Mr. Rajpal I am asking you as Managing Director of GSFC and not Gami. You should reply. Mr. Rajpal was taken a back and kept mum.

After a minute minister said that you people do not know what Urea technology is. I tried to tell him that GSFC has two urea plants and are operating them satisfactorily since few years. He told again that he was not talking to me and he went on talking in impolite language implying that we were ignorant and do not have any idea about the urea technology and therefore how can we select a technology for urea plant. We kept mum while he was talking in this style. After 10-15 minutes, the Secretary Fertilizers, seeing that Minister was getting more and more angry, took leave of the Minister. After coming out of the Minister's chamber Secretary was very apologetic to Mr. Rajpal and told him that he never knew Minister was in such a mood, if he had known he would not have called us for the meeting. Afterwards he told us to inform our Board of Directors about what Minister had to say. He suggested that we may reconsider selection of technology for urea plant. Mr. Rajpal told that in his career of more than 35 years he was never insulted like this before.

After coming to Vadodara, we informed the Board of Directors at the next meeting (GSFC used to have Board Meeting every month) about what the Minister said and the advice given by the Secretary, Fertilizers. The Board discussed the matter and decided to stick to the same technology offered by M/s. Toyo Engineering Corporation and asked us to resubmit the application for approval of the Government of India. We then wrote to Secretary Fertilizers that our Board had reconsidered the matter and decided to stick to the same technology. After some days we received reply from the Secretary Fertilizers that no Yen credit was available for payment to M/s Toyo Engineering for urea plant. We may therefore select another contractor. In view of the reply of the Secretary, we referred the matter to the Board again and the Board of Directors selected Snamprogetti for the urea plant as it was second best. On applying to the Government of India, Government approved the same and also released free foreign exchange for the same. Again here while there was shortage of foreign exchange, Government released free foreign exchange for Snamprogetti urea contract, but not for the requirement of Japanese contract.

During those days it was talk of the town that Minister P.C Sethi was egocentric, perhaps due to personal reasons. He could have, without calling us, asked Secretary Fertilizers to write that Yen credit was not available in the first instance when we made application and the entire unpleasant episode could have been avoided.

Public criticism on Minor Matters

Plant Lighting

GSFC was the first fertilizer complex operating on 24 hours/day basis to be installed in Gujarat. At that time people and politicians had no experience of seeing hazardous complex operating on 24 hours basis. As in this plant most of the equipment were located out door, it was necessary to have proper lighting so that operators can see at night the operation of the equipment by taking round of the plants and take action in case of any problems. For this purpose the plant area had to have intensity of the light all most equal to the day light. As the plants were located on the highway, (unlike Gujarat Refinery which was not visible from the highway) passers by could see the light and therefore people in Ahmedabad started talking as if GSFC was enjoying Diwali everyday and some politicians and public figures would talk to chairman about the same. Chairman, being very sensitive to criticisms of politicians and public, therefore worried and asked us to cut down lights. When we explained to him that it was not possible to cut down the light for safety reasons he agreed, however he suggested that lighting on the road parallel to the high way and connecting township with the factory may be curtailed so that it is not visible from the highway. This pacified the Ahmedabad people.

Movement of Cars to Ahmedabad

During those days Vadodara was still an educational and cultural town with no availability of engineering goods and with no hotels of the category where foreigners could stay and with no heavy industry, as a result many times GSFC people had to go to Ahmedabad for various reasons such as purchases, attending seminars, discussions etc. As travel time from Vadodara to Ahmedabad was three hours, it will take whole day before returning to Baroda after completion of work. Naturally people have to take lunch in the city. Even though the GSFC cars were not marked by name plate, even then Ahmedabad people would find out that some one has come in GSFC car and would ring up chairman stating that officers of GSFC are enjoying themselves coming to Ahmedabad in the Company's car. Chairman therefore asked administrative manager to show him the registers of the movements of the cars, specially going to Ahmadabad, and asked him to minimize the car trips to Ahmedabad. In fact when he came for the Board meeting every month, he would invariably check car register to know who went to Ahmedabad and why.

Gift of Japanese Cars

When technicians and officers of the Japanese contractors started arriving in Vadodarsa in late 1965, the Japanese contractor had obtained approval of the Government of India to import 3 cars from Japan to India for use of their technicians and officers. After most of the technicians had left, Japanese contractor decided to gift these 3 cars to GSFC. Managing Director Mr.Srivatsa sent one car to Chairman's residence for his use. As soon as the car reached Ahmedabad the Chairman started receiving calls for congratulating him on acquiring Japanese car. This annoyed him very much and talked to Mr. Srivatsa, who informed him that M/s Toyo Engineering had gifted three cars to GSFC, He had sent one to the Chairman for his use. Where upon Chairman asked him to arrange to take back the car and see that all the 3 cars are returned to Japanese contractors. Chairman had not used Japanese car at all. All the cars were returned to Japanese contractor.

⌘ ⌘ ⌘

Chapter 12
Contribution to Social Development

GSFC had divided this activity in two parts (1) social activities and (2) Rural Development. All these activities were carried out 0lby the Company and by nearly 200 agronomists at Farm Information Centers (FIC), other employees and also through employees residing in the Fertilizer Nagar. Thus company had adopted "Corporate Social Responsibility" policy from the beginning without identifying it as CSR.

Social Activities

GSFC had started publication "Krushi Jeevan" This published information not only for the use of farmers but also for villagers. Almost 40,000 copies were distributed. It had organized training program for Secretaries of the Cooperative Societies so that they can provide better and more useful services to their members. Training center was also providing training to workers of various fertilizer factories such as

FACT Udyogmandal, Kerala; Shriram fertilizers ,Kota; IEL, Kanpur; State fertilizer Manufacturing Corporation, Ceylon; Workers from Tanzania etc) as well as to IPCL workers. Company was also organizing training program for marketing.

The Company had instituted a scholarship for three successive years at the Indian Institute of Management at Ahmedabad for awarding to a deserving student undergoing Institute's post graduate program in management. The company had endowed 4 chairs in Agriculture Science at different colleges of Agriculture Science in Gujarat, and a total of 25 Fellowships and scholarships at Universities and colleges of Agriculture and Veterinary science. Company had extended cooperation to M.S. University, Baroda for sandwich course for engineers and providing practical training in company's plants.

Prepared report on optimum utilization of water from Kadana Dam and other inputs to enable farmers to take maximum advantage when the dam is built up. Company also helped Government of Gujarat to establish Kadana Development Association to implement the findings of the report.

Company in association with LIC and Bank of Baroda had started crop insurance program in selected districts of Baroda and Surat under 4P program (Package of practices with plant protection). This was unique scheme adopted for the first time in the country. Government of India is now (in 2007) visualizing insurance scheme for farmers in 200 of the most backward Districts in the Country.

The Company provided loans at subsidized interest rate of 6% to employees to build their own homes for comfortable retirement. More than 1000 employees had taken advantage of this scheme.

M/S ICICI had undertaken studies on social impact of GSFC on villages. For this purpose they had deputed Mrs. Nita Mukherji to several villages around GSFC to make this study. Findings were very complimentary to GSFC.

Rural Development

Under this program the company had adopted two villages, Heranj in Kaira District and Ratanpura in Banaskantha District and six villages in Baroda District for overall agricultural development of villages. Leap Forward Project was designed to influence and increase the standard of living of Adivasi Rathwa farmers in some of the backward villages of Chhota Udaipur Taluka of Baroda District and Santrampur and Lunawada Talukas of Panchmahal District. Action program was established, on selective basis, aimed at improving skills and knowledge of farmers in back ward districts and semi-arid zones, in Mehsana, Banaskantha, and Gandhinagar Districts. Improvement in standards of living of people in these areas was achieved through establishment of libraries, dairy cooperatives, approach roads, tree plantation, clubs, etc.

Company participated in rural development by subsidizing construction of 20 houses around fertilizer Nagar in the rural housing project of Baroda district Panchayat. Company was also subsidizing by giving grants and providing technical inputs for establishment of Gobar gas plants on individual basis as well as cooperative basis for entire village or group of people. The company had taken further steps in this direction by creation of Rural Development Trust, planning novel projects of Bio-fertilizers and Biogas to emphasize use of organics, Bio-fertilizers as well as harvesting residual effect and efficient use of fertilizers. As a part of rural development program, company in association with Gujarat State seeds Corporation had undertaken production of high breed seeds.

From the above it may be seen that the company took up social responsibility many years ago and provided leadership before corporate started having policy on "Corporate Social Responsibility"(CSR). Today international organizations carry out study on this. Recent international survey carried out by "Society for Human Resources Management" (SHRM) found that more than four out of five organizations in India are practicing CSR ranging from donating to local charities to undertaking global fair labour standards. As can be seen from above GSFC was doing much more than this towards its CSR. Brazil reported highest participation rate at 95% with USA at 91% China reported lowest rate of participation.

The study titled "2007 Corporate Social Responsibility" revealed that with the exception of respondents from Brazil, the majority of organizations that currently do not have CSR policies have no plans to create them. In the United States, Brazil, Australia and Canada the main obstacles to CSR programs were reported to be cost, unproven benefits and lack of support from senior management. While some organizations consider cost to be obstacle to CSR practices, others point to improved image, competitive advantage and greater market share as clear benefits.

⌘ ⌘ ⌘

Chapter 13
Contribution to National & International Development

GSFC contributed to industrial development through (a) Joint Sector Concept, (b) its products and (c) Engineering technologies.

Concept of Joint Sector

The concept of the ownership of the GSFC itself was a har bringer of the new ways of promoting projects in the country and abroad. Dr. Jivaraj Mehta, on taking over as the first Chief Minister of Gujarat on first May 1960, decided on 15th. May 1960 to establish a fertilizer factory in Gujarat, with aim to make Gujarat self sufficient in food production. For this purpose he wanted Fertilizer Company to operate in business like manner with public interest. Therefore he did not want it to become a Government Company or a private company. During those days all the corporations were either government owned or privately owned. Dr. Jivaraj Mehta decided not to do this and have Government stake limited to only 49%. At the same time Government had sufficient control to ensure operation in the public interest. Later on this concept became known as Joint Sector". This may perhaps be the first"political Innovation" in the world.

Madras Government (Now Tamilnadu) approached GSFC, after it successfully completed the first project, in 1968 for advice on establishing such project. Later on in early 1969 Mr. M. A Chidambaram well known industrialist of south visited GSFC. Mr. Srivatsa asked me to take him around and explain to him about the company.

When I went to Tamilnadu in June 1969, Secretary, industry Department of the Government of Tamilnadu rang me up and asked me if I can meet him and spare about an hour for discussions on establishment of fertilizer complex. As a result of visits and discussions Government of Tamilnadu decided to establish southern petrochemical industries corporation limited in joint sector. This was the first similar joint sector as GSFC in fertilizer industry.

GSFC and the Government of Gujarat also co-promoted a joint sector company, Gujarat Narmada Valley fertilizer company Ltd. and which in turn has promoted other joint sector companies in the fields of petrochemicals, electronics etc.

The Gujarat Government established Gujarat Industrial Investment Corporation, Gujarat Industrial Development Corporation and Gujarat State Finance Corporation to promote small and minimum scale industry through joint sectors. The original concept was modified, with State corporations keeping 26% shares and private entrepreneur with 25% shares. There was further modification of the joint sector approach with 11% shares with State Corporation and called it associate sector. The number of other state governments including Tamilnadu followed similar pattern of establishment of Industrial Development Corporations. All these corporations developed thousands of small and medium scale industries in practically all fields in their respective states. These had given rise to large employment and also new category of entrepreneurs, large investment and fast industrial development.

Government of India, after liberalization, did sell during 1990s, a few corporations to private companies, but later on decided not to privatize but to dilute Government equity and offer the same to public, making each corporation a joint sector which is since then called Public Sector Enterprise.(PSE). Government offered 10% to 40% equity to public in different Government Corporations. Nine PSEs started making so much profit that Government gave special title to these corporations "Nav Ratna" meaning "Nine or New Jewels" and those doing reasonably well are given a title of "Mini Ratna". Today there are 34 PSES with mini ratna status.

Further modification of this concept, is, in the form of public private partnership (PPP), (which is partnership between Government and one or more private partners), This is nothing but a modified version of Joint Sector. PPP has led to tremendous development and huge investments in several countries. The concept got initiated in Australia and USA in 1990 and has spread to a number of developed and developing countries including India. This has made it possible for Governments of various countries to take up projects, with investment of billions of dollars, in social, infrastructure, service sectors and others in profitable manner through PPP. India has also carried out projects with investment of Rs. 250,000 million using PPP model and more are in pipe line.

Value of the contribution of the original concept of Joint sector and its modifications is very difficult to assess but suffice it to say that it is substantial not only on all India basis but also in the several countries of the world.

Contribution of GSFC Products

GSFC's motto was "basic to India's progress" with this concept GSFC established a number of products each was basic in nature as a result each product contributed to a number of industrial projects. We give below the contribution of GSFC products.

Fertilizers

When the GSFC was first established, every ton of fertilizer nutrient produced 15 Kg of food grains. This gave rise to agricultural development by not only providing food for which India was not self sufficient and was importing food grain till 1974-75 but making farmers more knowledgeable in agricultural practices and richer and giving rise to village developments in at least Gujarat. The fertilizers from GSFC alone contributed additional production of 1 million MT/ year food grain in Gujarat in 1970-71 over 1966-67. This increased agricultural income by Rs.3170million per year in Gujarat. Besides GSFC, other fertilizer companies also made additional contribution. As during those days GSFC was one of the largest fertilizer companies, its contribution is also one of the largest. The development of agriculture gave rise to the development of other industries such as production of tractors, farm equipments, pumps, diesel sets, equipment for fertilizer plants etc. Thus it gave fillip to the development of engineering industries in the country.

Caprolactam and Nylon chips

This is a basic product for Nylon Synthetic yarn and fabric. Nylon during those days was initially very popular among middle class and later on when it became cheap enough to be popular among the poor. The basic products are saris, nylon tire cord and nylon chips. The value contribution from caprolactam to sari is nearly 10 times the value of caprolactam and gave rise to a number of textile fabric units as well as processing units as saris are required in varying colors and for which nylon was an eminent material those days.

The second major use of caprolactam is for the production of Nylon Tire cord. The Nylon Tire cord is used in automobile industry. Not only it gave birth to six large Nylon Tire cord plants, as Nylon Tire cord has become indispensable part of tires which are essential for all cars and trucks.

The third major use of caprolactam is the production of engineering plastic which was practically unknown in the country at that time of conceptualization of caprolactam project. ADC developed, through Nylon Chips, new Nylon component industries in automobile, railway, defense, textile etc. The Nylon components not only provide strength and transparency but also colors and lubricity. Modern appliances used in home are very silent without noise thanks to nylon parts, such as bearings, gears etc.

It is difficult to estimate the total contribution the caprolactam and nylon chips(Engineering plastic) has made to the industrial development in the country as it covers various fields. It has also contributed to more comforts at home and in travels. We could not have visualized such beautiful cars and sophisticated equipment without nylon engineering plastics. There are 30 Nylon components used in automobiles made from various different grades of Nylon molding powder utilizing different molding as well as extrusion techniques. Similar is the case for textile industry, railways, defense, etc.

Melamine

Melamine is converted into melamine resins and melamine molding powder. Melamine Resins find application in decorative laminates. We are all familiar with this use as we see every day in our homes furniture, cupboards etc made from melamine. There are special grades of fire retardants laminates which are used in public building, buses, rail cars, ships, etc which require fire resistance. The second use is industrial laminates which are used as electrical insulating materials. The other use of Melamine are in paints, lacquers, adhesives, paper treating products, leather tanning products, super plasticizers, for cement industries etc. The melamine molding powders are used for dinner wares, buttons, electrical components, circuit breakers, rotary switches, contactor housing, gears for switch, power plug etc. The other use is in medium density fiber board which is finding large uses. There are more than 25 different grades of melamine resins and molding powders developed by application development centre for above uses. It will be seen that basic products are produced from melamine. These are useful for variety of industries and for all strata of population for their home use in various ways. In fact we find at least one melamine product in practically every home in every city, town and village. GSFC is the only melamine producer in the country since last 25 years.

Liquid Argon

Before GSFC started manufacturing Argon, it was in short supply as there were small manufacturers, who produced it by air liquefaction process in small plants. Further it had oxygen impurities up to 20 ppm which made it unsuitable for welding of sophisticated alloys. This was filled in small cylinders and sold as compressed argon gas. GSFC manufactured it in liquid state, from purge gases of ammonia plants, in very large quantities, more than 20 times the quantity available at that time, providing opportunities for further development of its use mainly for SS and alloy steel welding as it had no oxygen impurity. With best quality, large scale manufacture and bulk transportation in liquid form in cryogenic containers and reasonable price, it could develop a number of new uses for both argon gas and liquid Argon. The very large scale use, made possible through supply of liquid argon, is the manufacture of Stainless Steel (A.O.D process) and in metal refining and brazing. It is used in electronic lamps and valve manufacturing and number of high tech uses such as Geiger counting tubes, air craft, missile industry, nuclear application in the manufactures of metals, in cryogenics and refrigeration etc. The uses are very vast encompassing large areas of different industries. This has enabled the Indian companies to manufacture various high alloys and SS equipments with finish and workmanship comparable to international standard, whereby making it possible to export large quantum of such equipment.

Engineering Technologies

When GSFC was established practically every industrial project and equipment were imported. The country did not have any design facilities. Under these circumstances for establishing sophisticated and hazardous fertilizers and other petrochemical plants, it was necessary to import all components and major equipment. This meant large foreign exchange expenditure was required. The foreign suppliers were taking full advantage by jacking up prices of the components and equipments required for the replacement many times the normal price. To overcome this GSFC decided to establish import substitution cell (indigenous development). First task was to learn about the design and materials and method of fabrication of the components, which were required to be developed. It also associated a number of engineering and fabrication companies in this task of development and also with Technical Development Committee established by the Government of India with memberships from fertilizers and refineries. As a result not only GSFC itself developed new technologies but also a number of companies, more than 30, could simultaneously develop techniques of manufacture of sophisticated components and equipments. GSFC found that indigenously developed components not only were as good as imported ones but were one fourth to one twentieth in comparison to the corresponding price of the imported components.

In this manner GSFC developed components and equipment from special alloy steels, zirconium, titanium etc, which were not earlier manufactured in India. It developed its own workshop to manufacture equipment from these as well as passed on technologies to other fabricators. GSFC manufactured more than 30 heat exchangers and other equipment for caprolactam and oxosyngas plants, which otherwise would have to be imported. It imparted technologies to other manufacturers for fabrication of sophisticated equipment.

⌘　⌘　⌘

Chapter 14
Relevance of management practices at GSFC to the modern day management

GSFC had established a new concept that of ownership structure which, by itself and through its modifications, led to development of thousands of industries in India and has expanded not only in India but in several countries of the world. It has provided opportunities to do projects, in joint sector and/ or under Public Private Partnership (PPP) (in reality modification of joint sector concept), with better efficiency and large investment. These were hitherto undertaken by Governments. GSFC was ahead of its time in India in two other management practices. (1) Concepts of "customer is the king" and "Application Development Centre" in marketing management and (2) Introduction of "Corporate Social Responsibility" policy, Forty years later the first concept has become indispensable management tool and the second has become management reporting requirement..

Other management practices for project management, corporate organizations, strategy for expansion and growth, motivation of people, H.R. practices and marketing which management gurus advocated those days and followed by GSFC are still basically valid today except strategy of expansion and growth, as the present age of discontinuities does not permit accurate prediction of future growth.. Let us now examine these practices one by one and see relevance of each one. Relevance of these management practices are detailed bellow.

The new concept: The Joint Sector

Till GSFC came up, ownership structure of the companies was either as Government Corporation or as private company. GSFC company structure was neither, It was owned by Government and public jointly with Government having 49% shares and public plus financial institutions 51% shares. With GSFC success, State Government established, Industrial Development, Industrial Investment and Industrial finance corporations, which assisted entrepreneurs with technical assistance, infrastructure facilities, and financial assistance to encourage them to establish industrial projects in various fields. Joint sector concept was modified to the extent that Government corporations owned 26% shares, private party owned 25% shares and rest by public. In further modifications Government corporations reduced the share holding to 11% and called such company associate company. In this manner thousands of industrial projects got established with small and medium level of investments by entrepreneurs. This practice of Gujarat State was followed by practically all other States giving rise to tremendous industrial development in the Country.

When the country liberalized its economy in 1991 and dismantled a number of Government controls, there was tremendous internal as well as external pressure on Government to privatize (giving example- how Margret Thatcher, the then prime Minister of U.K. succeeded in such privatization), loss making as well as profit making Government Corporations. Government did sell a few corporations to private companies, but later on decided not to privatize but to dilute Government equity and offer the same to public, making each corporation a joint sector which is since then called Public Sector enterprise.(PSE). Government offered 10% to 40% equity to public in different Government Corporations and simultaneously started giving increasing level of freedom to such corporations who started improving results. Result was that loss making corporations started making profit. Nine PSEs started making so much profit that Government gave special title to these corporations "Nav Ratna" meaning "Nine or New Jewels" and those doing reasonably well are given a title of "Mini Ratna". Today there are 34 PSES with mini ratna status.

Between 1991 and 2007 Government of India realized Rs. 63000 million (about U.S. $1.5 billion) from sale of Government enterprises to private companies, on the other hand Government realized Rs. 490,000 million (U.S $12 billion) from disinvestment of equity of Government Corporations to the public, now called PSE . The market capitalization of these 43 PSES as on 31st. July 2007 was Rs. 7,760,000 million (or about U.S.$194 billion). Thus Public Sector enterprises grew tremendously under new joint sector concept.

In 1990 a new concept, called "Public Private Partnership" (PPP) was started in Australia and USA. PPP describes a Government service or private business venture which is funded and operated through a partnership of Government and one or more private sector companies. This again is a modified joint sector concept. National council for PPP is established in Washington D.C. This concept has spread to a large number of countries such as USA, Canada, U.K., India, Ireland, Australia and several other countries. Concept is used for investment in high ways, hospitals, Airport modernization, public schools, development of harbors, also for development of vaccine and immunization program to fight Aids, Tuberculosis, and Malaria, etc. Concept is also used for operation and maintenance of facilities and also for supply of services. Billions of dollars are economically and profitably invested in such projects. Rs.250, 000 million worth investments are done in India also under PPP concept and more are in pipe line. PPP concept is really an extension of the concept of Joint sector as first initiated by GSFC, as it involves Government and one or more private sector companies in partnership instead of Government and public as is the case of GSFC.

Thus GSFC concept of Joint Sector, albeit through modifications, has spread wide and beyond the shores of India and has become a profitable vehicle for investment in projects while ensuring interest of public service is maintained and yet investments are profitable.

Management concepts where GSFC was ahead of time:

"Customer is the King" (Fertilizers marketing)

When GSFC started there was no customer service concept in India. During those days if a person purchased anything (goods or services) and if the quality of the product/service was found to be inferior or the product was defective or did not work properly, manufacturer or his agent or service provider would not even listen to the customer's complaint or provide any remedial service. Before GSFC started production, farmers were using imported fertilizers and locally manufactured Super Phosphate. At that time GSFC started providing, as customer service, training to its customers (farmers) with a view to increase production, giving inputs free of cost, carried out demonstrations in farmer' fields to show how to increase their produce.

In this manner GSFC served thousands of farmers, at its own cost, for a period of five years before it started selling its fertilizers to the farmers. Thus concept of "Customer is the King" was born then in India. Even 40 years after GSFC started this service; the situation in the country has not come to a desirable level. After Government of India passed consumer protection act, the customers are going to consumer courts against manufacturers, suppliers and service providers to get redressed. Air lines, insurance companies, finance companies and some manufacturers of goods are the main culprits. Consumer forums are coming heavily with large penalties and Government is also making rules for finance and insurance companies to provide rights to the customers to receive compensation. It is now expected that customer service will improve.

Corporate Social Responsibility

Similarly concept of "Corporate Social Responsibility" was first initiated by GSFC in the country. This included (1) providing training to workers of several other fertilizer factories (2) publication and distribution of Gujarati magazine "Krushi Jeevan" to farmers and villagers (3) scholarships to students, creating chairs for agricultural sciences at different colleges and sandwich course at M.S. University, (4) Establishment of Kadana Development association, so that when dam is built, downstream villages and farmers can utilize the water in the most profitable manner (5) various programs to improve lifestyle of Adivasis in several backward districts (6) providing subsidies/grant for constructing houses and gobar gas plants in villages and adoption of villages in backward districts.

Today every corporation is required to have "CSR" policy and have to state in their annual reports their CSR policy and how they are implementing it. Recent survey indicated that only Tata group is properly implementing CSR policy. Since last five years, ITC, a large Indian corporation is providing, through its "E choupal" program, services to farmers in several thousand villages. They provide technical services to farmers, inputs at cost and buy back their produce. They are seeking Government help to provide such services in 100,000 out of 625,000 villages. Many large companies have now started CSR policy for providing services. Even in country such as USA, some corporations find it to be expensive as it does not provide commensurate return. All corporations of the world need to provide genuine "CSR" services to eliminate "Green House Gas emission", remove disparity in living standards of people and improving living standards of poor people of the world.

Marketing: Industrial Products-Application Development Center

We have seen above how innovation was introduced in marketing of fertilizers. Similarly for marketing of industrial products the Company introduced a new concept of "Application Development Center" (ADC) which showed the customers how to grow. This was done by ADC by developing new products and technologies for the same which customers can use to make new products from GSFC products, thus ensuring continuous growth of GSFC products as well as customers products. The company also helped customers by developing services, such as cryogenic containers so that GSFC can transport its products in bulk, which otherwise would not have been possible. This not only helped customers to reduce the cost of their products but develop new technology for their product. Production of some of the new products could not have been started but for this service. Production of new components from engineering plastic for automobile, railways, defence, textile etc started. Similarly, from GSFC melamine, production of house hold furniture, engineering materials, specialty paints and other products started and GSFC argon contributed to steel making process.

Management concepts which are also used to day.

Project management

This was carried out in GSFC (1) using the simplified pert system, which now a days, is completely computerized.(2) Pre qualifications and pre selection of vendors on the basis of their capacity and past performance including financial strength and categorizing them in three different categories on the basis of the assessment of their capacity for the purpose of issue of tenders,(3) Settling disputes in an objective manner (win-win strategy) and not allowing conflict to develop. The company completed 10 large projects in 20 years but did not have any arbitration, court cases or any major dispute with engineering companies, suppliers or contractors during the entire period.

(4) Negotiating with the lowest to reduce price further at the same time assuring that he gets reasonable profit, for this purpose company had always pre calculated the cost of work. (5) Slogan 'faith, discipline, hard work and success' was drilled in the minds of all to enthuse them to complete the project within time and budget. (6) Target setting technique to complete the work in time or ahead of schedule. (7) Stage wise completion schedule with bonus and penalty clause for civil works contracts. The company completed the first project, at that time the largest fertilizer project in the country, in record time and ahead of schedule and received bouquet from national press for this achievement. Indian Institute of Management, Ahmedabad (IIMA) made a case study of this project.

Corporate organization

GSFC organization had minimum hierarchy and communications were direct up to the lowest level. Target for annual, monthly and weekly production and safety record were prominently displayed in all plants. All problems were discussed in daily production meeting and problems which could not be solved immediately were given to multidisciplinary team for finding solution on priority basis. The suggested solution is discussed with concerned plant manager and safety officer and on their approval, solution is implemented. No one, who is concerned with the problem, is bypassed and everyone is kept in the loop. Finance was always made available for any productive purpose. As there are many products and profitability of any product do change from time to time and as plants were technically integrated, a techno economic model was made so that production of different products can be changed to optimize profitability. There was. IMC (Internal Management Committee) meeting every Monday at 11.M. where all heads of departments were members. The meeting was chaired by the Managing Director; The IMC discussed all aspects of company management. Nothing was kept secret and problems were discussed thread bare to find most appropriate solution. Decisions taken in the meeting are to be implemented immediately. Meeting must be completed by

1 P.M. This meeting completion time was important as it will direct discussions to relevant point.

Motivating people to work (Human Resource)

Fresh high school and college graduates and diploma holders were recruited from Gujarat and trained in company's training center for a period of two years including three months training in other fertilizer plants in the country. Bright trainees among these were sent abroad for training. After training they were absorbed as regular employees of the company. Few experienced managers and executives were recruited from outside. As this was the first plant of its type in India, engineer trainees, officers, managers and executives were also trained abroad in contractors' plants.

The company had built a township, about one KM away from the factory, with shopping center, school, hospital, sports complex, guest house, and temple. All employees could get house in the township with nominal rent and practically free electricity and water and free use of all facilities in the township. As factory was 12 KM away from the city, bus service was provided to employee's family to go to city. They were also provided loans at subsidized interest rate to build their own houses in the city or in their home towns

There was regular appraisal of all employees and promotion/increments were given on merit. Company had very good training system, including process simulator, and had good faith in their employees and did not recruit any experienced persons from outside for its new projects but managed with the same people. Additional requirements of persons for new plants were met through recruiting fresh high school and college diploma holders and graduates and training them in the company's training center. They were encouraged and deputed to seminars and workshops on the subject of their interest.. When I was managing director I had prepared a scheme which permitted them to go to Middle East for a job, to earn money and get new experience, for a period of two years, while maintaining their lien on the jobs in the company and allowing their families to stay in the Fertilizer Nagar.

Thus they were motivated to work better with higher efficiency as a result the company continued to grow, increase profit from year to year, paid good dividends and periodically issued bonus shares to share holders. Employees were encouraged to buy company's shares. There was hardly any turnover of employees and most of them retired after 30-35 years service in the company. Two retired as executive directors, a number of them as general managers, deputy general managers and hundreds as managers, officers and technicians. Thus employees got fully motivated to work for the betterment of the company. Practically each employee realized highest level of his potential as they worked till retirement.

Recently due to 9% growth of the Indian economy and manufacturing sector growing at 10-12%/yr and new investment coming up in new sectors such as telecom, highways, airports, ports, retail etc, there is a crunch in availability of manpower. Taking away employees from other competing companies does not help; as a result lots of companies have started their own training centers. Even Governments of India and Gujarat have started short term training courses for duration of three months- one year or so to train fresh school and college graduates for new sectors such as retail, construction and other infrastructure projects. Private enterprises have also started short term training courses for fresh graduates to make them ready for jobs in new sectors. Thus training facilities have become one of the biggest factors to motivate people to give their best. Establishment of training centers has now become a necessity for corporations to ensure availability of adequately trained and knowledgeable employees for successful management. This now has become one of the most important components for human relations department for retaining and motivating employees not only in India but in other countries also.

Strategy for growth

The most important criteria for this was the right selection of the products. It is necessary that selected product should have a long life, provide continuous growth opportunity and remain profitable over a period of at least 20 years. At the same time selected products should have some synergy with the company's operations. The company could have continuously grown with fertilizers, as demand of these is continuously growing even after 40 years. The company established 4 fertilizer projects, all working profitably. As prices and marketing of fertilizers were and are being controlled by the Government of India, it was not advisable to grow in fertilizers alone.

Synergy with existing operations was considered important criteria, besides opportunities for growth. Thus caprolactam, the first diversification project required only benzene from nearby refinery where as other six raw materials were available from the company, besides it also produces as co-product ammonium sulfate fertilizer which augmented the existing capacity of the company. Engineering plastic nylon was produced from caprolactam. It not only helped in the growth of caprolactam but also in the production of several new products like components for automobile, railways, defense, textile etc industries. Second project melamine required urea, which was produced by the company. Melamine also produced ammonia as by-product which is raw material for urea and other fertilizers. The third product was Liquid Argon, which was produced from purge gases from ammonia plants. Argon plant also recovered synthesis gas and methane, which reduced the cost of production of ammonia. Fourth product was MEK oxime which was produced from hydroxyl amine, an intermediate from caprolactam plant. 90% of this product is being exported and which earned valuable foreign exchange which was much needed by the country at that time. Fifth product was Liquid Argon which facilitated production of sophisticated equipment for fertilizers, petrochemicals and other plants. All these products have high growth rates and are still growing. Thus the strategy of the Company for selection of products keeping above criteria was successful.

Future Management

What will be the future management like? The book "Competing for the Future" (1994) by Gary Hamel and C.K. Prahalad has been seized on as the blue print for a new generation of strategic thinking. Gary Hammel says "To glimpse the future management, you must search the "positive deviants", organizations and social systems that defy the norms of conventional practice. The web has evolved faster than anything human beings ever created- largely, because it is not a hierarchy. The web is all peripheries and no centre. What is the chance that tomorrow's most successful organizations will be as different from today's corporate behemoths as the internet is different from plain old telephone service? The answer: "A lot higher than you think." Unlike your company, the internet already is adaptable, innovative and engaging. I believe we are on the verge of a "post managerial society," perhaps even a "post organizational society." Just as the coming of the knowledge economy didn't herald the death of heavy industry, a post managerial economy won't be entirely free of executives, supervisors, administrators and overseers. But it does imply future in which the "work of management" is less and less the responsibility of "managers". Activities will still need to be coordinated, individual efforts aligned, relationships nurtured, objectives decided upon and knowledge disseminated."

⌘   ⌘   ⌘

Chapter 15
Opportunities for investments in India

India was attaining growth rate at 9% per annum until 2007. However in view of the current global financial crisis and accompanied meltdown, growth in 2009 is expected to be of the order of 6-6.5%. To combat this unusual situation, Government of India is setting developmental policies to ensure future growth at 9% or higher. Very large investments are planned, both by Government and private sector in (1) service sector such as infrastructure (including highways, roads, power plants), power transmission and distribution, metro rails,. ports, air ports, university education, telecommunication, retail, real estate, internet, media, hotels, restaurants, health care, travel and tourism, and water supply, (2) manufacturing sector such as biotechnology pharmaceuticals, petrochemicals, plastics, oil exploration, food processing, seeds, fertilizers, pesticides, and environmental, control, (3) financial sector such as banking, non banking finance, asset reconstruction, microfinance, venture capital and investment in stock market.

Government of India has planned large number of Export Oriented Units (EOU). At present there are about 2500 companies working at 300 different locations of EOU throughout India. A large number of Special Economic Zones (SEZ) are also established. The companies located in both these areas/zones generally enjoy incentives in terms of duties and taxes. Generally 100% foreign equity is allowed. Government of India has also planned 1483 Km long Delhi-Mumbai Industriall Corridor (DMIC) at an investment of U.S.$ 90 billion. 563 Km of this corridor passes through Gujarat. To take advantage of this, State Government has planned to develop Special Industrial Regions (SIR) such as (1) Bharuch-Ankleshwar-Hansol, (2) Patan-Mehsana, (3) Banaskantha-Sabarkantha and (4) Vadodara-Halol-Kalol, falling within this corridor, at an investment of U.S.$ 30 billion. The planning process willl comprise land management plan, infrastructure development plan and setting up of an institutional mechanism to implement the plan in these pockets proposed to be developed as global manufacturing and commercial hubs.

The Government is planning to issue biometric identification cards to all citizens (1000 million). Major "IT/IS" firms have shown great interest in this potential big business. Government is also providing large sums of money for urban improvements and U.S.$ 25 billion flagship schemes such as building social infrastructure, providing education, health care service, and midday school meals; and providing special incentives for non conventional energy development such as from wind, solar, biomass and coal bed methane.

More than $ 150 billion investment is planned. Foreign Direct Investment in India is increasing every year and was $ 25 billion during 2008.In addition venture capital funds are coming at increasing rate. During the first quarter 2009 the Government of India approved applications of 129 foreign venture capital investors to invest (about $ 10 billion) in different sectors. Substantial increase compared to deals between private sector and foreign venture capital firms amounting to $ 5.7 billion in the first half of 2007.

Large numbers of foreign companies from U.S.A., Europe and Asia have established manufacturing and production facilities and also two hundred (200) R&D centers in India. General Electric, Microsoft, Pfizer, Novartis, Elli lily, Intel, A.C. Nielson, Microsoft and Boeing are the prominent ones establishing such R&D centers. According to the Survey made by London based Consumers International, India has been ranked top globally for enforcing intellectual property laws ahead of U.S,A. and U.K..

Regulations

In the present scenario, industrial license and Government approval are not required for manufacture of a large number of products. Import license for import of equipment is required. Investment in certain specific sectors such as electrical, electronic, aerospace, defence, nuclear power plants (will be opened shortly), and multi brand retail would require industrial license. Investment in supply chain and cash & carry store to cater to the needs of multi brand retail sector is allowed and a few foreign retailers have invested in these types of ventures.

Primary, secondary, university education and training are big business in India. There are 200 million students, one million schools and 5 million teachers but more are required. Annually 8,5 million degree holders including 500,000 engineers are produced. Student fees vary from U.S.$15/yr to U.S.$ 15,000/yr. . Private educational and training institutions are making good profit. A number of Universities from USA and U.K. have established, and more are planning, joint degree programs in India, subject to approval by appropriate authorities, whereby a student, while studying in India will get qualifying degree from the foreign university. Harvard Business School (USA) has established research and business centre. They are also organizing programs for Indian executives.

Regulations and licensing requirements are all current indications, but it would be advisable for interested companies to check with

Foreign Investment Promotion Board (FIPB) for details for specific products and/or services.

The percentage of equity participation by foreign companies in different sectors varies from 26% to 100% as briefly indicated in the following paragraphs:

100% equity: Development of new airports, highways, mining and coal exploration, non banking finance, trading of power and certain types of goods and services. Indian edition of foreign newspapers.

Up to 74% equity: Telecom, Modernization of existing airports, satellite communication, providing internet services, private sector banking

Up to 49% equity: Aviation, Direct to Home TV channel, Credit Information, Commodity Exchanges, Asset Reconstruction, Stock Exchanges, Domestic Air Lines, Infrastructure and Services, Personal Telecommunication Services, and Cable Television.

Up to 26% equity: defense industries, petroleum, natural gas, print media, insurance and F.M. radio.

The above is not a complete list. Trend is that the investment limits are generally liberalized. However check with Foreign Investment Promotion Board (FIPB).

Participation in the Growth Process

Foreign companies can participate in the growth process of India by 1. Establishing own Indian Company. 2. Investment in Indian companies (called Foreign Direct Investment, FDI), 3. Licensing of

Technology to Indian companies under royalty payment,4. Licensing brand names and/or trademarks for which royalty can be negotiated. 5. Offering products/services on franchising basis. 6. Establishing joint venture by investing with Indian partner or Indian company. 7. Exporting their products. 8. Establishing venture Capital firm to invest in start up or running Indian Company. 9. Establishing R&D center to develop technologies. 10. Microfinance: and 11 Establishing non banking fiancé company

The Companies, which are interested in manufacturing and exporting products from India, can establish units in Export Oriented Units (EOU) or Special Economic Zone (SEZ). These companies enjoy substantial concessions. in duties levies and taxes. These units can market their products in (India) domestic tariff areas by paying appropriate duty on such sale. . Generally 100% equity by foreign companies is permitted for units in EOU and SEZ.

Environmental Impact Assessment (EIA) report is required for all large projects (US $ 200 million or Rs. 1000 million investment or more) before commencing work at any selected site.

General Information on India

There are a number of books published by Indian and American authors on "Doing Business in India". These books provide general information on culture and customs, dealing with Indian partner, understanding the way Indian do business and developing business plan to create interest in doing business in India. However no book gives hands-on management practices that can be followed to make the enterprise successful in India. This book fills this gap, and it describes practical approaches and innovative management practices for successfully managing industries in India, and will facilitate corporations and entrepreneurs to take-part in the multibillion dollar investment opportunities unfolding within the infrastructure, manufacturing and service sectors.

Foreign Companies, while operating in India have to maintain flexibility in their management. Initially some companies such as Kellogg, Kraft, McDonald and some others did face problems while adhering to their original national plans. Flexible approach in marketing, product mix and packaging resolve initial hiccups. Fast moving consumer goods companies found that they can make more sales and profits if they market in small sachets, which are good enough, for only one use and cost 2 U.S. cents/packet, against very large packets in U.S.A. Indian consumer is very discerning and knows what he would like to pay for a given product or service.. He does not mind paying very high price for top luxury brands provided he sees "status" value in it.. Foreign companies operating in India are generally making more profits compared to their operations in their own countries.

Selecting Products/Services with high growth

As market is growing, investment can be done in a number of products and services. However competition is very stiff. There is a very large demand for power transmission and distribution equipment, power plants including nuclear power, supply chain for different sectors, logistics and transportation, and manufacturing sector It is prudent to select newer technologies which produce very good quality products or services and at the same time require lower investment and offer lower operating costs. India is the lowest cost producer of Aluminum, steel and Rayon/viscose. Its cost of manufacture of equipment for petrochemicals, fertilizers and power plants, and electrical equipment is equally low. Quality design engineering and detail engineering services are especially in demand by foreign companies;

Cost of some agricultural produce such as banana, potato, and tomato is low. Products from these can have good export market. India is the second largest low cost producer of vegetables and fruits in the world. It is the largest and perhaps the lowest cost producer of banana in the world and yet export potentials have not been explored. Contract farming by providing technologies and inputs and buying back the produce, which can be marketed domestically and/or further processing for domestic market or export, is already being explored by a few Foreign Companies.

Products based on new/newer technologies, such as coal to liquid to produce synthesis gas and subsequent petrochemicals/plastics products, biodegradable plastics, Nano technology based products: such as engineering plastics, textiles etc can be equally attractive. There is a phenomenal interest in biotechnology, pharmaceutical and healthcare industry.

Investment in solar panels and solar power plants, technical textiles, construction chemicals, energy and biofuels from biomass and non edible oilseeds, coal bed methane, manure from biomass, newer I.T. enabled services and products, .ethanol from sugar cane.

Manufacturing fertilizers in the country where cheap gas is available and exporting fertilizers to India under agreement with State Trading Corporation of India would be attractive. Manufacture of biofertilizers and micro nutrients to improve soil and crop productivity.

Participating with Government of India and/or State Governments is profitable for projects in infrastructures such as highways, roads, metro rails, ports, airports, power plants under Public Private Partnership (PPP) model. US$ 5 billion worth projects have been completed by the Government of India using PPP model and more are in the pipeline.

Microfinance: Now poor people in India are linking up with global capital market. Their loans are being handled with thousands of others and sold off as part of securitizing deal. Securitizing micro finance loans is the most effective way of getting market capital to the rural poor and pooling them out of poverty says chief economist of the top Indian rating agency Crisil.. India's pioneering program falls under the country's securitization Act of 2002, which has already approved deals worth U.S. $ 7.7 billion. The new legal structure and involvement of private banks lends India's model credibility that would help it spread throughout the developing world, says senior economist of the World Bank, New Delhi.

The loans are disbursed through self help groups, Non Government organizations or Government agencies, these groups also collect interest and repayment. Income stream from thousands of microloans is repackaged into an asset that mutual funds and insurance companies such as Life Insurance Corporation of India buy in the form of interest bearing notes.

Investors may invest few million $ to one billion dollars. This is profitable with minimum risk. Practically there is no default in paying interest and repayment of Micro loans. Loans may be around U.S. $ 100 (one hundred)/person. .

Interested Indian and Foreign Companies should undertake preliminary feasibility including market study to establish viability of the project before undertaking the same.

Financing Investment

There are various ways of financing the projects as indicated in the following paragraphs. It is best to take an example to show how this can be done, if one is interested in establishing an Indian Company. Let us assume techno economic and feasibility study showed total project cost at $ 100 million (Rs. 5,000 million). This includes cost of land, equipment and materials, construction, erection and commissioning and margin money, say $ 10 million, for working capital. Normally equity to debt ratio will be 1:2 that is in this case equity of $33million and debt of 67 million. The promoter can decide to have private limited company with one to maximum 25 share holders, or a public limited company in which promoter has to make public issue offering minimum 25% to maximum 74% shares to the public if listing of the company at stock exchange is desired.

Thus for a private limited company the promoter, together with other maximum 24 share holders has to bring $ 33 million whereas for public limited company he has to bring minimum of $ 8.5 million for his own equity of 26% to a maximum of $ 24.5 million for his own equity of 75%. 26% equity gives management control of the company, as articles of association and memorandum of association originally incorporated by the promoter can be changed or amended only by minimum 75% voting power. Thus with equity holding of 26% no changes can be made without the promoter's approval.

If project requires import of technology and/or equipment, the promoter must use foreign currency. If $ 40 million is required in foreign currency, then promoter must obtain loan of $ 13 million in foreign currency and balance $ 27 million to be arranged in Rupee loan.

For payment in foreign currency for import of equipment and/or technology, it would be necessary to obtain approval of the Government of India. Government may provide foreign currency from its own sources or from bilateral credit it may have negotiated with foreign countries. Alternatively it is possible for the promoter to obtain loans in foreign currency from International Finance Corporation, Asian Development Bank, U.S. Aid, German and other Countries' Banks, suppliers/buyers credits from foreign suppliers or buyers, some Indian and foreign banks and Indian financial institutions.

Though Government of India have no specific policy on countertrade, however it allows/encourages countertrade for purchase of defense, civil aviation, and high value capital equipment, bulk purchase of fertilizers, edible oils, etc to minimize foreign currency requirement.

All Indian Financial institutions, Indian banks and foreign banks provide required Rupee term loan.(in this case equivalent to $ 27 million) Thus entrepreneur, Foreign Company or Indian Company can do a $100 million (Rs. 5,000million) project with his own money of $ 8.5 to $24.5 million (Rs.425 to 1225 million) giving him 26% to 75% equity in the new Company. In addition, $ 40 million working capital loan from the Banks for the production and marketing of the products will be available, as the promoter has provided $ 10 million margin money in the project cost for this purpose.

Thus 26% equity is sufficient to exercise control over the Company. However, some promoters may prefer to have 51% equity for their own reasons.

⌘ ⌘ ⌘

Chapter 16
Author's Bio-Data

The Author, Mr. Dhirajlal C. Gami was the Ex-Chairman of the Fertilizer Association of India, Ex-CEO of Gujarat State Fertilizer Company, and has many accomplishments, some of the special Achievements of the Author include:

A. Projects planned, executed and operated for the first time in the world:

** Heavy Water project *based* on *distillation* of *hydrogen,* based on pilot plant operations in Germany by M/S Linde. Plant operated successfully for forty years.

** World's largest Ammonia plant based on high pressure Texaco gasification, pilot plant operations at Montebello, California, USA. Ammonia plant has been operating successfully since last 27 years.

** Melt crystallization as purification system for Caprolactam based on pilot plant operations by M/S Inventa at Chur, Switzerland. Plant has been working satisfactorily since last 25 years.

B. Projects conceived, planned, executed and operated for the first time in India:

** Ammonia plant, based on ICI naphtha steam reforming, which has been Operating successfully for 33 years.

** Caprolactam plant, based on Inventa process, expanded to 3.5 times original capacity, operating successfully since 35 years.

** Melamine plant, based on *Chemie Linz process*, expanded 3 times original capacity, operating successfully since 27 years.

** MEK oxime, based on GSFC Process, pilot plant and commercial plant, expanded 10 times, operating successfully since last 28 years.

** Planning and execution of the first nuclear reactor, Apsara Reactor in India.

Mr. Gami, a prominent hands-on manager involved in driving industrialization in India, was appointed by the Government of India, as a member of the advisory committee with the Department of Atomic Energy, Department of Chemicals and Petrochemicals, Economic and Social Council for Man-made Textiles and Fertilizer, and Sub-committee of the Department Council for Inorganic Chemicals.

Over the last 25 years, Mr. Gami has provided consultancy on investments, mergers and acquisitions, and expansions to many large and medium size companies, Banks and Financial Institution in the fields of fertilizers, petrochemicals, and power plants. He has travelled to 30 countries for plant visits, technology acquisitions, and contract negotiations. He has also been Chairman/Director of a large number of companies in the fields of fertilizers, petrochemicals, organic chemicals, synthetic textile, finance, and hospitality. Mr. Gami has chaired and addressed several seminars and contributed papers to several magazines.

His managerial expertise and approach will serve as a perfect guide for those who seek an understanding of how to "do business" within the corporate world of India.